Temperance
and Racism

Temperance
and Racism

John Bull, Johnny Reb,
and the Good Templars

David M. Fahey

The University Press of Kentucky

Editorial and Sales Offices: The University Press of Kentucky
663 South Limestone Street, Lexington, Kentucky 40508-4008

96 97 98 99 00   5 4 3 2 1

Library of Congress Cataloging-in-Publication Data

Fahey, David M.
    Temperance and racism : John Bull, Johnny Reb, and the
Good Templars / David M. Fahey.
        p.   cm.
    Includes bibliographical references and index.
    ISBN 0-8131-1984-7 (cloth : alk. paper)
    1. International Order of Good Templars—History.
    2. International Order of Good Tempars—Membership—History.
    3. Race discrimination   I. Title.
    HV5006.F33   1996
    363.4'1'09—dc20   96-12156

To my wife, Mary,
and our daughter, Juliana,
with love

Contents

Illustrations follow page 114

Acknowledgments

For my stories of Templar men and women, I am indebted to the libraries I have visited in Britain and the United States, as well as to institutions in these countries and in Australia and Canada that helped me by lending or copying materials.

The United Kingdom Temperance Alliance allowed me access to its private library, and the Grand Lodge of England permitted me to examine printed records at its office in Birmingham before they were deposited with the Alliance in London. I read extensively at the British Library, mostly at the Colindale newspaper library, and more briefly at the libraries of the University of London and the London School of Economics.

My most important research in the United States took place at the New York Public Library, whose massive James Black temperance collection is housed in the Annex; the State Historical Society of Wisconsin, Madison; the Department of Manuscripts and University Archives, Cornell University, where I consulted the Edward C. Sturges temperance collection; the Michigan Historical Collections, Bentley Historical Library, Ann Arbor; and the Ohio Historical Society, Columbus.

I also did research at the North Carolina collection, University of North Carolina; the Library of Congress; Wright State University (Martha McClellan Brown papers); the University of Washington (George F. Cotterill papers); the archives and library divisions of the Minnesota Historical Society; the Earl W. Hayter Regional Historical Center, Northern Illinois University; the Boston Public Library; the American Antiquarian Society; Florida State University; the University of Wisconsin; the Filson Club, Louisville; the State Historical Society of Wisconsin, Area Research Center, La Crosse; the Utica, New York, Public Library; the Chicago Historical Society; the Woman's Christian Temperance Union, Evanston, Illinois; the University of Illinois; Indiana University; Oberlin College; Earlham

College; the West Virginia state archives; Duke University; the Western Reserve Historical Society; and the Cleveland Public Library. Alas! I discovered that most of the non-Ohio material listed in the *National Union Catalog* for the last two institutions no longer exists.

I also obtained photocopied or microform materials from Canter Brown Jr., Tallahassee; the University of Georgia; the University of Kentucky (filmed for me by Stephen M. Savage); the State Historical Society of North Dakota; Martha M. Pickrell, Elkhart, Indiana; the South Caroliniana Library, the University of South Carolina; J. Edwin Hendricks, Wake Forest University; the Huntington Library; the Center for Research Libraries; Idaho Historical Society; Kansas State Historical Society; Depauw University (copied for me by John R. Riggs); the George Fox College archives (copied for me by Ralph Beebe); the California Historical Society, San Francisco; Monroe County May Hill Russell Library, Key West, Florida (copied for me by Tom Hambright); the Florida Collection, Jacksonville Public Libraries (copied for me by C.H. Harris); the Black Archives, Florida A&M University; the Germantown Historical Society, Philadelphia (courtesy of David R. Contosta, Chestnut Hill College); and, in Australia, the State Library Service of Western Australia, Perth; and the Mitchell Library, Sydney, New South Wales. My apologies for any oversights in this list.

Miami University photographed illustrations of G.W. Bain, S.B. Chase, John B. Finch, Jessie Forsyth, S.D. Hastings, J.J. Hickman, F.G. Keens, and Oronhyatekha, which appeared in Thomas F. Parker, *History of the Independent Order of Good Templars from the Origin of the Order to the Session of the Right Worthy Grand Lodge of 1887,* rev. ed. (1882; New York: Phillips & Hunt, 1887); of the Boston union conference in Frances E. Finch and Frank J. Sibley, *John B. Finch: His Life and Work* (New York: Funk & Wagnalls, 1888); of Eliza A. Gardner in Hallie Q. Brown, *Homespun Heroines and Other Women of Distinction* (Xenia, Ohio: Aldine, 1926; also reprinted, New York: Oxford Univ. Press, 1988); of Joseph Malins in Joseph Malins, *The Life of Joseph Malins, Patriarch Templar, Citizen, and Temperance Reformer* (Birmingham: Templar Press, 1932); of Morton Chapel and Frederic Richard Lees in Ernest Hurst Cherrington, ed., *Standard Encyclopedia of the Alcohol Problem* (Westerville, Ohio: American Issue, 1926-30); and, from the *International Good Templar,* of J.W. Hood (Aug.-Sept. 1878), John Pyper (Jan.-March 1879), S.C. Goosley (April-June 1879), Joseph E. Lee (July-Sept. 1879), Harriet N.K. Goff (Oct.-Dec. 1879), and J.G. Thrower (May 1895). The British Library photographed illustrations of W.M. Artrell, William Wells Brown, and

Catherine Impey in the *Good Templars' Watchword* (12 March, 11 July 1877, 30 April 1879). The shelfmarks are 89 (for Impey) and 151 (for Artrell and Brown). I thank Barbara Wheeler of Miami University's Applied Technologies and Claire E. Cumber of the British Library's Newspaper Library for making the arrangements, as well as the British Library for permission to publish illustrations from its collections.

Jenny Presnell, the interlibrary loan staff, and others at Miami University's King Library provided indispensable assistance. Computer access to other libraries enabled me to browse collections that I have never seen.

Jeri Schaner and Liz Smith printed countless drafts, created computer-readable texts of documents, and in general lightened my burdens. Pat Sterling, copyeditor, made innumerable improvements to my manuscript.

I am grateful to the Miami University history department and its chair, the dean of the College of Arts and Science, and the provost for a semester of sabbatical leave; to Miami's committee on faculty research for a summer research grant and a grant-in-aid; and to the National Endowment for the Humanities for a travel grant.

I am also grateful to the scholars who have read my manuscript in whole or in part, answered queries, or commented on a related paper that I presented in 1993 at an international congress on the social history of alcohol held at Huron College, London, Ontario. In thanking these people, I must begin with Frank J. Merli, Queens College, City University of New York, who read innumerable drafts. Perhaps vainly, he urged the merits of clarity and conciseness, transitions and topic sentences, and chapters that do not just stop but conclude. During times of discouragement my Miami colleague Ronald E. Shaw convinced me that the book was worth completing. Jack S. Blocker Jr., Huron College, Ontario, read the penultimate draft and persuaded me to reorganize the third chapter. Nancy G. Garner, Wright State University, also read this draft and insisted on a separate conclusion.

A number of people read drafts of the opening chapter: Mark C. Carnes, Barnard College; Lynn Dumenil, Occidental College; David W. Gutzke, Southwest Missouri State University; Beverly A. Smith, Illinois State University; and Ian R. Tyrrell, University of New South Wales. Thomas Appleton Jr., Kentucky Historical Society, read an early version of the section on Kentucky; Denise Herd, Alcohol Research Group, Berkeley, the section on the black Templars (in each case a draft about twice as long as the final version); and Margaret Barrow, University of Manchester Institute of Science and Technology, the section on England. The referees commissioned by the University Press of Kentucky (Richard F. Hamm, State University of New York at Albany, is the one whose name I know) rightly insisted on the need for more focus and less detail.

Most of all, I want to thank my wife, Mary Fuller, for her suggestions, support, and love.

Abbreviations

GL	Grand Lodge
GTW	*Good Templars' Watchword*
IGT	*International Good Templar*
GWCT	Grand Worthy Chief Templar
GWVT	Grand Worthy Vice Templar
IOGT	Independent Order of Good Templars (in twentieth century, International Order of Good Templars and, most recently, International Organization of Good Templars)
IOTT	Independent Order of True Templars
Proceedings	Report RWGL or GL meeting
RWGL	Right Worthy Grand Lodge
RWGL of the World	Right Worthy Grand Lodge of the World (British-dominated organization, 1876-87)
RWGT	Right Worthy Grand Templar
WCTU	Woman's Christian Temperance Union

Introduction

Readers may wonder why a historian who teaches courses on Victorian England would write a book that deals with the United States and its intractable problem of race relations. Many years ago, while I was studying the drink question in late nineteenth-century Britain, an international fraternal temperance society known as the Independent Order of Good Templars began to fascinate me.[1] The IOGT offered a fresh approach for the study of the temperance movement, the working and lower-middle classes, and gender relations. Gradually I realized that it also provided a new perspective for investigating racism in North America and transatlantic racial attitudes after the Civil War.

My quest for the Good Templars led me back to familiar places. My boyhood home in the Hudson River valley was not far from the west-central New York birthplace of the Templar Order. My home today is in an Ohio college town which, I have discovered, once boasted two Templar lodges. The airport that serves my locality is in Kentucky, the greatest bastion of the southern white Templars during the 1870s. My wife grew up in North Carolina, where black membership first became a practical question for the Order in the former slave states. Her sister lives near Boston, where in the late 1870s and the 1880s a few Templar lodges practiced a racial egalitarianism rarely matched in the United States even to this day.

Writing this book demanded rethinking what constitutes history. When I left graduate school more than three decades ago, I could not have imagined spending a substantial portion of my middle years studying a fraternal temperance society. In doing so, I have learned much that I never expected to need to know.

My book is a voyage of discovery that maps virtually unknown territory. To make my exploration manageable, I rarely venture beyond the North Atlantic, English-speaking community, although the Templars lived on every continent and spoke many languages.

As José Harris says of the Freemasons, the Templar Order "was a network that was simultaneously both more intimately parochial and more international than any nation-state."[2]

The book has multiple objectives. It contributes to the history of the temperance movement and the history of fraternal organizations, in part by combining them and in part by internationalizing them. It also reveals a new facet of African American history, the story of the black Templars. The controversy over black membership opens a new window on racial attitudes and behavior in the late nineteenth century on both sides of the Mason-Dixon Line and both sides of the Atlantic. It shows that a great many white Templars rejected the extreme versions of racism prevalent at the time; the Templar ideology of universalism helps explain why. Other moral reform organizations struggled with the contradiction between racism and quasi-religious assumptions of a common humanity, but they nearly always avoided dramatic confrontations by accommodating the views of their more racist members. In contrast, the Templar Order was rent by what I have termed the great schism from 1876 to 1887.[3]

Connecting the views and behavior of the Templars with those of the larger community is an important, difficult task that I barely start in this book. Sadly, I find no evidence that Templar universalism moderated racial prejudice in the United States or elsewhere in the English-speaking world. When I evoke grand-sounding themes such as a struggle between Britain and the American South, I refer only to the conflict between the small part of the populations that belonged to the IOGT.

Readers should be cautioned about two other things. It is not easy to generalize about a fluctuating membership, residing in varied geographical and sociocultural contexts at different times. Nevertheless, I argue that something distinctive can be found in the IOGT virtually everywhere and always. This distinctive feature is the ideology I have called universalism, which in theory welcomed into membership all teetotalers committed to prohibition. This ideology began to take shape shortly after the creation of the IOGT in the early 1850s, when male Templars accepted women as members with equal rights. In practice, however, the scope of that welcome varied. This book documents the ways that whites in the American South rejected black people as members of the Templar family. Yet the rhetoric of the Templar Order encouraged its universalist ideology to develop into literal universalism, differentiating the Order from most fraternal societies, which defined themselves by excluding women and blacks.

My other caution concerns moral judgments. Templars who claimed to be fighting for the rights of blacks often coupled selfish motives with an inconsistent and ambiguous record on black membership. Few were free from racism but then again, some Templars who supported the exclusion of blacks from the IOGT in the American South or the segregation of them in separate Templar organizations did provide African American temperance reformers with practical assistance. Templars seem to have been more open to compromise than other whites in the former slave states.

The controversy over black membership must take into account the frustrating truth that few blacks chose to join the Templar Order even when they could do so. The southern white justification for separate organizations was self-serving and bigoted but also recognized reality. Most blacks wanted their own churches and other institutions and did not find the lure of a slightly integrated fraternalism irresistible. It was only a small minority of African American men and women who found the Templar ideals of brotherhood and sisterhood attractive.

Finally, a few words about sources. Although scattered in location, Templar materials are abundant. Printed journals of the annual meetings of state, provincial, national and international organizations exist in large number. Newspapers published on behalf of Templar organizations and reports in the general temperance press are available for some places. Printed rituals and constitutions, didactic and controversial pamphlets, official histories, and semiofficial biographies are not hard to find. Yet almost no personal papers of Templar leaders exist for this period, which leaves the inner life of the IOGT mysterious. Bits and pieces of local lodge manuscripts such as minutes and membership lists survive to tantalize and hint at complexities now beyond recall.

For only a few places and times are many kinds of evidence available. An official in the relatively bureaucratic Grand Lodge of England had access to local lodge returns that permitted him to complain about the high proportion of tobacco smokers among the members who violated their teetotal obligation, yet most Grand Lodges failed to publish such important information as membership subtotals for men and women. With a couple of exceptions there are only broken sets of *Journals of Proceedings* for North American Grand Lodges, for some brief-lived Grand Lodges nothing. Quarrels within the Templar family enable us to know that such publications omitted embarrassing discussions, excluded important material for want of space, and published errors.[4]

Statistical evidence too is suspect. Secretaries exercised considerable discretion in deciding what figures to record and report. In 1875 Georgia's secretary announced that the membership was 14,746, but the subordinate lodges paid a per capita tax for only 5,079 dues payers. After investigating the records, a frustrated committee declared that it was "utterly unable to state, with any degree of certainty, the actual membership."[5] In 1886 an international officer apologized for the practices of his predecessor, who had published statistics for four Grand Lodges "not in existence" and for others from which "no reports had been received."[6] Membership returns always included guesses and outright errors.

Ill-educated, inexperienced, and irresponsible lodge secretaries made a mockery of the statistics that look so impressive in Templar publications. When a secretary failed to make reports on time, the Grand Lodge figures would either omit the lodge or retain its last reported membership. In turn, Grand Lodges often reported late or not at all to the international organization. Consequently, the statistics must be regarded with too much skepticism to risk using them in a quantitative methodology. I cite Templar numbers frequently but only as anecdotal evidence.

1

The Templars

A little over a hundred years after they attained their greatest fame, the Good Templars have disappeared from history books. Only an occasional mention in accounts of the temperance movement reminds us that they existed. Historians of race, gender, and international moral reform have forgotten them.

Rescuing the Templars from this neglect and obscurity will enhance understanding of the Anglo-American world in the middle and late nineteenth century.[1] In a remarkable amalgam the Templars brought together characteristics associated with other and now better-known organizations as diverse as the Woman's Christian Temperance Union, Alcoholics Anonymous, the Freemasons, the YMCA and YWCA, the Society of Friends, the Methodists, and that medieval crusading order of warrior monks called the Knights Templar, which inspired the Good Templars' name.

In the 1870s and 1880s, among groups hostile to alcoholic drink, the Templars were the world's most numerous and most militant. In addition to being a teetotal organization, the Independent Order of Good Templars was one of the world's largest fraternal societies. A mixture of lodge ritual, wholesome companionship, and denunciation of drink attracted a youthful membership in North America, Britain and its Empire, and other parts of the world. Millions of men and women joined the Templars after the Civil War, most of them white, a few of them black. Their motto was "Faith, Hope, and Charity."

Templars stood out in the world of nineteenth-century fraternal societies. Joining sisterhood with brotherhood, the Templars violated the gender basis of fraternalism by inviting women to join as full members. Among the innumerable quasi-Masonic ritual brotherhoods founded in North America, only the Templar Order developed into a genuinely international society with a sizable transoceanic membership and a powerful central organization. Most important for this book, in an age of white supremacist racism the IOGT tried to provide some kind of membership for African Americans. The controversy over the rights of blacks culminated in the great schism that divided the international organization from 1876 to 1887.

Such dramatic events could not have been foreseen in the early 1850s when a handful of young men and boys started the Templar Order in west-central New York state. Nobody could have predicted much of a future for the parochial new organization. Understanding the success of the IOGT must begin with the two social movements that can be styled its parents: temperance and fraternalism. They in turn owed a good deal to the Second Great Awakening, which transformed American society between the 1780s and the mid-1800s, and its optimism about moral reform through nondenominational voluntary associations.[2]

Connections with other topics, notably women's history, make temperance a respectable subject for research today, although in a secular age religiously motivated teetotalers and prohibitionists arouse a derision that diminishes the importance historians assign the temperance movement. To an even greater extent, intellectual snickers handicap the study of the fraternal movement as part of popular culture. Images of boisterous Shriner parades and smoky poker games at the Elks lodge make it easy to dismiss fraternal societies as ephemeral. The late twentieth century tends to find a previous generation's taste for lodge ritual unintelligible.

Until recently, historians have regarded fraternal societies as a curiosity, fraternal temperance societies as doubly quaint, and research that focused on them as antiquarianism leading nowhere. The only general study of the Sons of Temperance, the organization that pioneered fraternal temperance in North America, remains an unpublished dissertation completed in the mid-1960s.[3] In contrast, there is in print a shelf of books that focus on the WCTU, an antiliquor organization that historians study because of its female membership.

What was the temperance movement? After a brief period early in the nineteenth century when temperance meant refusing to drink spirits, it became identified with total abstinence from alcohol as a beverage. Many reformers also objected to medicinal alcohol and fermented wine in the eucharistic sacrament. They showed little patience with so-called moderate drinkers who lent respectability to drinking and the beverage alcohol trade. The arguments and rhetoric of the temperance movement drew heavily upon evangelical Protestantism. Borrowing from religious revivalism its emotionalism and demand for personal commitment, temperance reform became a mass movement in the United States.[4]

The temperance movement first called for a voluntary pledge against drinking and later for some kind of prohibition. When they became prohibitionists, temperance reformers entered politics to make the sale of alcohol illegal and so protect drinkers against temptation. In the United States many legislatures authorized local option against drink sellers. Maine pioneered a statewide prohibition statute. Some states incorporated prohibition in their constitution, a strategy culminating in the ratification of the Eighteenth Amendment to the United States Constitution.

Explaining the motives behind the American temperance movement and its timing is not easy. Why did so many people decide that the age-old problems associated with alcoholic drink required the remedies of teetotalism and prohibition? Did the temperance movement come into being to defend traditional values or to further modernization?

Explanation becomes even harder when one takes into account that the American temperance movement was not a unique phenomenon. A history of the Templars cannot ignore the fact that other countries developed powerful temperance movements in situations as diverse as Iceland and Ireland, Wales and New South Wales. Except for the rarity of wine drinking among the masses, the English-speaking and Nordic lands where the anti-drink agitation became a great public cause had little in common. Their development of commercialized agriculture, industry, and urbanization, their practice of domestic and international migration show no simple pattern. Interpretations that put to the fore social control by the respectable middle class or by wealthy capitalists do not explain the extensive involvement of men and women who worked with their hands.[5] Nor did the fortunes of the various national temperance movements show a uniform relationship with per capita consumption of beverage alcohol, the percentage of drinkers among adult males, or female activism that challenged male popular culture.

An interpretation that emphasizes evangelical Protestantism becomes a bit awkward in the light of the dramatic, if brief, success of Father Theobald Mathew in drying up Ireland; the less celebrated case of another Roman Catholic priest, Charles Chiniquy, who persuaded a majority of French-speakers in Quebec to take the pledge; and North America's forgotten Catholic temperance societies. Moreover, in the pre–Civil War period many evangelical Protestants in the United States opposed prohibition and even criticized societies that promoted voluntary abstinence.[6] In Britain the Wesleyan Methodists and most other Nonconformist denominations did not endorse the temperance movement until the 1870s.[7]

Despite these complications, it is impossible to dismiss evangelical Protestantism as an explanatory tool. Reform-minded evangelical women, asserting the hegemony of the home over the saloon, played a prominent role in the temperance movement in North America, as did evangelical clergy who argued for total abstinence and prohibition on both religious and secular grounds. Other Protestant countries with a strong evangelical movement embraced temperance with much more enthusiasm than those without such a religious environment, as the contrast between so-called sober Sweden and drunken Denmark illustrates.[8]

As a popular movement, teetotalism in the United States had an early triumph and disappointment in Washingtonianism.[9] In the early 1840s local pledge-taking groups collected tens of thousands of promises to abstain, many of them presented by drunkards and other drinkers. Although the Washingtonians adopted the patrician first president's name, they tended to be working class or lower-middle class. Female auxiliaries, the Martha Washington societies, enabled women to play an active part in the campaign to save men from drink. At a time when religiously oriented reformers emphasized sin and business leaders worried about economic impact, the Washingtonians focused their therapeutic message on a more immediate argument for abstinence: drinking worsened the lot of the drinker and the drinker's family. Critics of Washingtonianism deplored its rejection of the leadership of religious and economic elites, and they scoffed at the notion that the temperance movement need not enlist governmental power for the eradication of the drink problem. The Washingtonians themselves quarreled over the role of legislation and came to recognize that their societies lacked the organizational structure to help pledge-takers keep their pledges, a weakness that made many of them look for a remedy in fraternal temperance.

Fraternal temperance societies organized pledge-takers in a supportive community. In this way, the temperance movement combined with another important social movement, fraternalism, which employed a secret ritual to initiate members into a brotherhood. The phenomenon of the fraternal temperance society raises questions about both fraternal and temperance movements in the mid-nineteenth century. During the anti-Masonic furor of the late 1820s and early 1830s, fraternal societies had almost disappeared in the

United States, and the same reform-minded evangelical women and clergy who supported temperance often opposed fraternal societies. Yet ironically, temperance organizations led the midcentury revival of secret fraternal societies. The Sons of Temperance, originating in the early 1840s, had attracted a larger membership by 1849 than much older secret organizations such as the Freemasons and the Odd Fellows. Although a few prominent divines vehemently denounced fraternal temperance societies, for half a century the dry lodges attracted young abstainers in large numbers.

In the 1890s, at the height of the fraternal movement, the *North American Review* estimated that in the United States more than five million men belonged to lodges.[10] Most societies claimed to welcome all men, or at least all white Protestant males, regardless of class, but virtually none admitted women except into sex-segregated auxiliaries. The Elks did not admit women until 1995. In the late nineteenth century many societies required members to buy various kinds of fraternal insurance, in effect excluding the poor, those in ill health, and the very old. Further, despite elections and democratic rhetoric, oligarchy characterized the central organization of most fraternal societies.[11] A sense of the equality of all members, regardless of their status outside the lodge, coexisted with a hierarchy of degrees—rungs in a status ladder within the organization—and a small army of officers set apart by exalted titles and regalia different from that worn by the rank and file.

Fraternal societies enjoyed their greatest popularity in North America, though they were also popular in Britain and, to a lesser extent, elsewhere in Europe and its overseas empires. Those who try to explain their popularity in the United States during the middle and late nineteenth century emphasize the failure of a feminized evangelical Protestantism to satisfy the emotional needs of men, the practical appeal of fraternal insurance after the Civil War, and the painful social and economic modernization that the United States was undergoing. Bewildered and angry artisans, shopkeepers, and others dislocated by the growth of a market economy and the beginnings of industrialization sought solace in the lodge room. Many immigrants in the late nineteenth and early twentieth centuries huddled together in their own fraternal societies, as did blacks and religious minorities.

Students of fraternalism stress different features. A sociologist, Mary Ann Clawson, presents fraternalism as a cross-class, gender-and race-defined movement, nostalgic about a half-lost artisan culture and its spirit of masculine autonomy and comradeship, whose adherents felt themselves under attack by new techniques of industrial production and amoral business ethics. A historian of masculinity, Mark C. Carnes, represents fraternalism as a sort of youth counterculture, the reaction of young men to homes and churches dominated by women. Supposedly, fraternal initiation provided an ideology that supported middle-class male values and provided youth in their teens and twenties with self-respect as men. Two historians of Freemasonry, the archetypical fraternal society, point in other directions. Anthony D. Fels depicts the development of a substitute religion with its own world view, ethical principles, and ritual. In her pioneering book Lynn Dumenil argues that Freemasonry "mirrored middle-class culture": the nineteenth-century lodge emphasized morality and respectability; the twentieth-century organization provided public service and private recreation.[12]

Although scholars seldom focus on the twentieth-century decline of the fraternal movement, they hint at several explanations: a new generation's acceptance of the changing social and economic order, a growing secularism uncomfortable with quasi-religious ritual, alternatives to fraternal insurance and sociability, more years of schooling as a substitute for the growing-up experience that youthful membership in a fraternal lodge had provided, the competition with service organizations, and the partially successful effort to defeminize middle-class Protestantism.[13]

Recent monographs have weighed the symbolic and the material attractions of fraternalism. Were members fictive brothers joined together through ritual, or were they business associates brought together by material advantage such as insurance? New interpretations have emphasized the ideological content of ritual symbolism, not practical benefits for the rank and file.

The Templars did not offer mutual insurance, and temperance reformers often joined the IOGT despite discomfort with secret ritual and regalia. Since by the 1870s people hungry for ritual had innumerable alternatives to the Templars, I do not describe their ritual or attempt to reconstruct its meaning to participants. The widespread fondness for some kind of ritual cannot explain why somebody chose to be a Templar instead of a Maccabee or a Woodman. Members of the IOGT wanted temperance reform as well as fraternalism. They also wanted something that rival fraternal temperance societies could not give them.

A decade after the Sons of Temperance had pioneered teetotal lodges and nearly a generation before the high tide of North American fraternalism, an organization called the Cadets of Temperance tried to interest young people in the campaign against drink. In the "burned-over district" of west-central New York state, the home of many religious and social reforms, Cadets in their teens and early twenties resented being lumped together with young children. These disaffected Cadets first set up the semiautonomous Encampment, next the Knights of Jericho, and then in 1851 the Order of Good Templars. A year later a discontented faction seceded to form the Independent Order of Good Templars.

The crucial figure in the early IOGT joined a few days after it was organized. Nathaniel Curtis was not a youth but a middle-aged baker and hotel keeper.[14] An ex-drunkard, he had been active in the Washingtonian movement and the Sons of Temperance. Nat Curtis helped establish two IOGT principles: the rejection of insurance, and the recruitment of women members on a basis of nominal equality. By avoiding the cost of fraternal insurance, the Templars could attract teetotalers who had little money, many of them young people. The more radical departure, the welcome to women, brought sisters, wives, daughters, and mothers into the Templar family. By the end of the IOGT's first year, women occupied several minor offices in its central organization. This occurred even though the innovative Templar rhetoric of domesticity clashed with the more traditionally masculine, warlike rhetoric that described the IOGT as "the drillmaster of the trained battalions of the Great Army of Reform." Templar analysis of the drink problem, taking for granted that men did the drinking, called for manliness. Alcohol "robbed [the drunkard] of his manhood," and in reclaiming him the IOGT endeavored "to make of him a MAN!"[15]

The Templars quickly spread beyond upstate New York, replaced their original crude ritual with a more religious one, and devised a complex institutional culture. Lodges sprang up in Ontario to the north, Pennsylvania to the south, New England to the east, and the Great Lakes, Ohio Valley, and upper Mississippi states to the west. The Templars developed an elaborate code of laws, with written constitutions supplemented by case law established through quasi-judicial interpretations. In addition, the IOGT created innumerable and frequently revised ceremonies, an "unwritten work" of secret handshakes, signs, and passwords, and special clothing or regalia for different degrees and offices, as well as seals, emblems, banners, pageantry, and spectacle. The Templars saw themselves as a separate community withdrawn from a corrupt world and a missionary organization to redeem that world. In 1855 a convention held in Cleveland, Ohio, set up a new central organization called the

Right Worthy Grand Lodge (RWGL). A minister from Kentucky was elected to the highest office, Right Worthy Grand Templar (RWGT).

In the next few years the RWGL struggled to survive. Ineffectual leaders could not resolve controversy over an uninspiring ritual. A Canadian faction, outraged by a proposal for an insufficiently Christian ritual, seceded to form the British-American Templar Order. The temperance cause had to compete for attention with abolitionism and the sectional conflict that led to the American Civil War. When tens of thousands of Templars and prospective Templars left home to fight, IOGT membership fell drastically, by more than a third between 1860 and 1863.[16]

Nevertheless, the Templars rebounded to enjoy their North American golden age. The IOGT benefited from the radicalizing of temperance reform as a prohibition movement. Men and women who wanted to battle drink rallied to the most militant organization available. Two able leaders, Simeon B. Chase of Pennsylvania and Samuel D. Hastings of Wisconsin, settled the controversy over ritual, improved the Templar organizational machinery, and made the endorsement of prohibition a commitment that helped define the Templars. At a time when voters in general were showing hostility to laws banning drink, the IOGT made support for prohibition a condition of membership. For many years Templar Grand Lodges and local lodges constituted the backbone of the temperance agitation for prohibition, both the enactment of legislation and its implementation through local option referendums.

During the last years of the Civil War and the first years of peace, the IOGT's membership grew explosively. At the end of 1868 the Templars reached their peak membership for the United States and Canada, more than half a million men and women.[17] In 1863, when Hastings had replaced Chase, it had been no more than 57,000. This remarkable growth occurred in the face of an ever more severe interpretation of the Templar "obligation," as the IOGT styled its pledge. For instance, the drinking of sweet cider was banned; moreover, unlike other pledged teetotalers, Templars could not serve alcoholic beverages to guests and customers.

Why, then, did the number of Templars decline in North America after 1868, despite the advantage of recruiting members from a growing population and the continued popularity of fraternal societies? And, even more curious, why did the fortunes of the IOGT separate from those of the temperance cause in the United States and Canada?

The Templars spent the late nineteenth century doggedly fighting what the IOGT called "leakage." Membership fluctuated, occasionally rising but more often declining. Large numbers of new recruits were offset by large numbers of suspensions. Although cadres of loyal members continued, most Templars were always new members. According to the returns for the reporting year that ended 31 January 1866, the IOGT had initiated 84,970, a figure that nearly doubled to 169,021 in 1867, and rose to 207,387 in 1868—its greatest number of new members in North America. This tumbled in 1869 to 184,538—still impressive, but fewer than the number of men and women who had departed.[18]

Leaders seldom blamed drink for the losses. Supposedly, those who left had stopped paying dues but remained total abstainers. For most members, the Templar Order constituted only a fleeting, youthful involvement. It was not so much that they turned against the IOGT as that they had joined it without a real commitment and became busy with other things. Although indifference probably explains the defection of most of those who drifted out of the Order, another reason was the semimigratory life of many youthful Templars in the nineteenth century. In 1883 the Grand Worthy Secretary of Wisconsin experimented with a postcard survey to query local lodges on the reasons for declining membership. Mostly located in "small rural communities," the responding lodges reported that nearly all the ex-members had moved away.[19]

Other problems complicate the picture, however. New organizations devoid of fraternal ritual provided temperance reformers with an alternative. Templars made up a majority of the founders of the National Prohibition Party, organized in 1869, which absorbed the time and energy of many prominent IOGT members. Yet even though the number of Templars in the United States was declining, until the end of the nineteenth century the IOGT was still the largest body of voters assembled in any temperance organization. The Prohibition Party appears to have regarded itself as the temperance general staff devising strategy, and the IOGT as the infantry fighting the battles. As the IOGT, previously nonpartisan, became closely identified with the new third party, it alienated many committed Republicans in the old Templar heartland.[20] Nor did this identification with party prohibitionists help the Templars in the South, where most whites were dedicated Democrats and where during the 1870s and 1880s the National Prohibition Party offended white sensibilities by courting black voters. Moreover, the emphasis on legislation made the Templars seem irrelevant where local or state prohibition eliminated the saloon.

Further, fraternalism became less of an asset. Men who abstained from drink crowded into aggressively masculine but respectable fraternal societies such as the Knights of Pythias, the Redmen, and the United Workmen. In the late 1860s evangelical women and ministers, two groups prominent in the temperance movement, founded the anti–secret society National Christian Association. Women who earlier worked for temperance through the IOGT organized themselves in single-sex movements and societies: the Women's Temperance Crusade of 1873-74 and the Woman's Christian Temperance Union, founded in 1874. Women who had developed leadership skills in the IOGT applied them for the benefit of the WCTU. For instance, years before she headed the WCTU in Ontario, Letitia Youmans had helped edit a Templar magazine, run a Templar auxiliary for children, and acquired confidence as a public speaker in Templar lodges.[21]

Although membership in North America never again matched 1868's impressive total, the IOGT leaped the oceans to recruit members in Europe and elsewhere who more than offset losses in the Order's home continent. In that same year, 1868, a young artisan returning from Philadelphia to his native land organized the first Templar lodge in England. Five years later the Grand Lodge of England counted more than 200,000 members, the most numerous adult membership for a Grand Lodge in Templar history.

In the mid-1870s the IOGT occupied every inhabited continent. Lodges sprouted throughout the British Empire and among expatriate British merchants, mariners, and missionaries elsewhere.[22] In 1874-75 a retired international chief officer toured the new Templar lodges in Australia, New Zealand, and Hawaii. By 1876 the IOGT had initiated nearly three million men and women.[23] In addition, the Templar Order encouraged children to join a juvenile auxiliary, guarded by a fourfold pledge against alcoholic drink, tobacco, gambling, and bad language. The Templars flourished not only among English speakers but also among other peoples of Protestant Europe. Soon after the IOGT reached its shores in 1879, Sweden became a Templar stronghold, supporting a membership larger and much more durable than that in bigger, Anglophone countries; in fact, the Templars were an integral part of the populist folk movements that challenged the Swedish elites. Fifteen years after the end of the great schism the IOGT took a new name that fit the old initials, the International Order of Good Templars. A Templar song proclaimed: "The world's our field—our battlefield."[24]

Yet however far-flung their movement, paradox characterized the Templars, as they themselves sometimes recognized. A prominent English member marveled that while "professing to illustrate a perfectly democratic government, [the IOGT] yet invests its chief with unassailable prerogatives of no trivial kind," and although "it seems to assert the equality of all men, yet [it] has instituted degrees or gradations of rank, the steps to which are guarded with jealous care." He went on to point out that the Templar Order "like all secret societies, [is] under the ban of the Romish Church, and is pre-eminently a 'Nonconformist' Order, yet [the IOGT] has its ritual, the use of which at every meeting is imperative." Furthermore, although "largely the refuge of the poor, it yet rejoices in [grand] sounding titles, and glitters in imposing regalia." Finally, "it affects the most stringent, not to say, ascetic pledge, yet is to its own members the centre of sociability."[25]

Although discerning, these observations missed still more important paradoxes: that the trumpeting of the IOGT's almost military discipline contrasted with the chronic factiousness that prevailed in practice, as well as with the apathy and carelessness shown by many local lodge officers toward directives from their Grand Lodge; that the notoriously high turnover, with ex-Templars far outnumbering dues-paying members, contrasted with the IOGT's objectives of adding stability to the teetotal pledge and organizing the temperance army.[26] Little could be more routine than complaints about halfheartedness on the part of what purported to be the elite troops in a desperate battle for an alcohol-free society.

Still, although old Templar bastions have crumbled—first in North America, then in the British Isles, and finally in Scandinavia—and the attraction of secret ritual and colorful regalia faded long ago, after nearly a century and a half the IOGT continues. Now called the International Organization of Good Templars, it has shed its fraternal trappings, operates as a loosely knit confederation, and works for world peace and cooperation almost as vigorously as it fights drink and drugs. Few outsiders know that the IOGT survives, but when it held an international convention in Sri Lanka in 1992, it claimed, together with its youth organization, a membership of over three and a half million in more than fifty countries.[27]

Today people counted in such statistics need never have participated in a lodge ritual, but in the nineteenth century the only way to belong to the IOGT was to belong to a local lodge which held weekly ritual meetings. If a lodge collapsed, those who had belonged to it lost their membership in the IOGT unless they could find another lodge to join.

A sketch of Templar organizational structure must begin with the local lodge or, as it was officially called, the subordinate lodge.

For most of the IOGT's members in the nineteenth century Good Templary meant the local lodge. A lodge needed ten members to get a charter; most had several dozen on the rolls, and a hundred was not uncommon. Although the original minimum age for membership was twelve, the growth of juvenile auxiliaries encouraged Grand Lodges, semi-autonomous in their geographical region, to raise it to fourteen or sixteen. Candidates for membership could be blackballed, but this rarely happened. Lodges issued clearance cards to members who left to join another lodge or who moved away.

Lodge meetings are difficult to reconstruct. They evidently involved quasi-theatrical ritual, face-to-face relationships, and a variety of oral discourse. Recitations, popular songs and religious hymns, speeches, and debates took place under the heading "the good of the Order." The subject matter of these activities wandered far afield. A lodge in Nova Scotia found diversion in arguing whether clam-digging should be classified as fishing or farming.[28] Members also enjoyed a recess for socializing and politicking. Lodges kept loyal members occupied between the weekly ritual meetings as well. Public meetings promoted the temperance cause; social occasions such as teas, strawberry festivals, and band concerts provided recreation and raised money. Some lodges offered members access to modest libraries and sponsored choirs, manuscript magazines, and other opportunities for enjoyment and personal growth.

The Templar Order was as strong or as weak as its local lodges. Some were hardworking lodges toughened by temperance zealots who found new energy in the wholesome recreation and fellowship afforded by the Templar family, the egalitarian atmosphere in which members of varied economic circumstances greeted one another as sister and brother, and the sense of being a useful cog in the world-wide Templar machine. Others functioned only as comfortable teetotal clubs, showing little missionary zeal and often wasting energy on tiffs and hurt feelings. Indeed, parochial disputes among quarrelsome personalities drove out more members than did remote battles, grandiose ambitions, and insistence on ideological purity. Backbiting and wearisome squabbles contrasted sadly with the initiation obligation in which new Templars promised "not knowingly [to] wrong a member of this Order, or see one wronged" and to offer "cheerful obedience." Keir Hardie, a founder of the Labour Party, quit his Scottish lodge in disgust at its petty rivalries.[29]

Other than the payment of dues, what could the IOGT expect from the brothers in Indiana who, when criticized for eating mince pie laced with brandy, defiantly said that they "would do so again"?

The lodge polled the entire membership about "whether he or she had eaten mince pie with any of the forbidden liquors in them." Demonstrating how plentiful was human weakness, five brothers and twelve sisters, including the woman who headed the lodge, confessed their guilt.[30]

Lodges seldom thrived in isolation. Every three months the international secretary issued a new password to the Grand Lodge secretaries, who forwarded it to local lodge officials, who issued it to their members. With the permission of the host lodge, Templars from other lodges who knew the password could attend the secret ritual meetings, and visitors were common in areas saturated with Templar organizations. In addition, representatives of local lodges sometimes held joint meetings as county or district lodges.

The Templars offered many opportunities for office-holding. Every three months each local lodge filled a large number of elective and appointive posts. The Worthy Chief Templar led the lodge, seconded by the Worthy Counsellor. A woman generally occupied the third office, Worthy Vice Templar. In practice, the fourth-ranking officer, the Worthy Secretary, mattered more than either the counsellor or the vice Templar, who had no administrative duties. At every level, disputes over obtaining office left as many discontented as satisfied. Unfriendly critics sneered that the Order had been created "to put little men into big places, and as there are so many little men, they cannot all be provided for, and hence the scramble."[31]

The head of the Grand Lodge appointed a local member as lodge deputy for liaison with the parent organization. In turn, lodges elected representatives to the Grand Lodge annual meeting—except in England, where, because of the great number of subordinate lodges, local lodges sent representatives to district lodges, and they in turn sent delegates to the Grand Lodge meeting.

Grand Lodges enjoyed enormous authority in their jurisdictions, whether the geographical area was a state or a province or a historic nation such as England or an independent country. By 1876 there was a Grand Lodge for every state in the United States and several of its territories. Although the names of Grand Lodges in the United States referred to an entire state or territory, often the membership was concentrated in a limited region, complicating any attempt to calculate a ratio between Templar membership and the general population.

The representatives of the subordinate lodges ordinarily convened once a year in what was called the Grand Lodge annual session. Ceremonies and elections and ratifying decisions in judicial appeals dominated these brief meetings. In the first few decades of the IOGT there existed special lodges called degree temples for those who had advanced to the higher degrees within Templar membership. This old system of advanced degrees was later reworked so that attending a Grand Lodge session as an official representative automatically meant initiation into a degree higher than those the subordinate lodge could confer.

An executive committee of elected officers carried out the business of the Grand Lodge between annual sessions, and to a large extent the success of the Grand Lodge depended on its officers. Heroic personal efforts did not guarantee success, however. In 1874 the GWCT of Connecticut boasted that despite holding another job he had "filled *seven hundred and ninety-two* official appointments and traveled nearly *forty thousand miles!*" Yet he glumly added that "as I contemplate this amount of work done, I feel sorry that so little apparent good has been the result."[32] Although the Grand Worthy Chief Templar and the Grand Worthy Secretary sometimes received substantial salaries, most Grand Lodges operated with little money, and only occasionally could they hire organizers. Grand Lodges got their income from a quarterly tax paid by subordinate lodges for each member in good standing and the sale of official supplies such as membership forms. In turn, each Grand Lodge paid tax to the Right Worthy Grand Lodge, the supreme Templar body. At all levels, however, the IOGT depended heavily on volunteers who contributed their services in their spare time. In North America it was rare for a Grand Lodge to publish its own newspaper, a financially risky proposition, and more common to designate as its official organ an existing temperance or religious newspaper that provided a column or two for official announcements.

During most of the period looked at in this book the Right Worthy Grand Lodge met annually, but during the 1880s the expense of travel forced a change to biennial sessions, first for the RWGL of the World (the British-dominated faction in the great schism) and then for the reunited RWGL. Just as being a representative to the Grand Lodge had come to signify admission to a higher Templar degree, serving as a representative to the RWGL conferred admission to the IOGT's highest degree. Since many delegates traveled great distances, even overseas, elaborate entertainments and sightseeing excursions were organized to justify the trouble. Although delegates' trips were subsidized by mileage allotments from the RWGL treasury, Grand Lodges paid most of the travel expenses, so at RWGL sessions there were always some Grand Lodges unrepresented because of poverty and others that could not afford to send as many representatives as the size of their memberships authorized. The RWGL of the World allowed proxy representatives.

In recognition of its judicial role the RWGL was sometimes called the Supreme Court. In the case of proposals for constitutional change, a two-thirds majority of those present was needed. RWGL rules required substantive motions to be submitted a year in advance, but amendments offered at the session could change the content of the original proposals.

What kind of men and women inhabited the organizational structure just sketched? The most obvious generalization is that they were diverse, a fact that reinforced the Templar universalist ideology which made the great schism possible. Groups lacking social prestige—such as young people, ex-drunks, manual workers, and women—made up most of the membership.

The IOGT has been a chameleon that adapted to different circumstances. It appealed to black ex-slaves and white racists, to pacifists and professional soldiers, to business entrepreneurs and trade unionists. During the nineteenth century most Templars were evangelical Protestants. An English leader described the Order as "a mild kind of freemasonry tempered by Methodism."[33] In contrast, Sweden elected agnostics to high office, while India provided a few Hindu members who lobbied for permission to replace the Bible with the Vedas in their rituals.[34] In the twentieth century a Templar was elected to the British Parliament as a candidate of the Communist Party.[35]

In short, saying that somebody was a Templar does not tell much, other than that the person had promised to abstain from beverage alcohol and not to supply it to others. Those initiated into the IOGT varied in their motives for membership, and not all aspects of the Order's work interested all of them equally. There is little evidence about those outside the activist cadres, but ordinary Templars probably focused their involvement only on sobriety and fellowship, belonged simultaneously or successively to other fraternal and temperance organizations, and ignored the great schism and the other controversies that dominate official Templar history.

Beyond a few revered elders, the Templars overwhelmingly consisted of young people, which helps explain the volatility of the membership. Over 40 percent of the delegates to state Templar meetings in Wisconsin during 1856-60 were under age thirty at the 1860 census.[36] Although the age of delegates came to resemble that of the general adult population of Wisconsin in subsequent decades, the members left behind at the lodges were probably even younger than the delegates. Writing his autobiography, a Georgian remembered joining a lodge near Lost Mountain in 1879 when he was twelve.[37] The Grand Lodge of Minnesota obituary lists for 1890-1901 record the age at death for 130 members; the mean age at death was a little over twenty-two.

Did youthful members join to fight drink or to have a good time? One Englishwoman admitted in her memoirs that in 1872, when she joined a lodge near her north London home, she did so out of boredom and in search of wholesome recreation. She was not even a teetotaler.[38] Yet though initially enticed by the prospect of fun and friendship, Jessie Forsyth became a committed temperance reformer, remained in the IOGT for sixty-five years, and, after emigrating, served as a Grand Lodge officer in Massachusetts and Western Australia and as an international officer. More typical recruits in their teens or early twenties came for a look and then drifted away for a dozen different reasons, which implied that the lodge did not much matter. Not every Templar was a teetotal spartan, eager to sacrifice for the cause. But a sizable minority were, and they grumbled about how the business of amusing casual members distracted lodges from reformatory and political work and embarrassed a quasi-religious cause.

During its heyday many recovering alcoholics joined the IOGT. Most other temperance fraternities rejected this rough crowd in order to keep rowdy songs and uncouth talk out of their lodge rooms and because they lacked patience with frequent lapses from sobriety. Early Templars eagerly accepted people that the general public looked down upon, but ex-drinkers eventually dwindled in number to become exotic trophies in most jurisdictions. By the 1880s in the Anglo-American world the IOGT was depending for its membership on the recruitment of young teetotalers.[39] Enacting prohibitory legislation to protect uncontaminated abstainers had come to matter more than the messy work of rescuing individual drunkards. One Templar leader declared with disdain that he preferred "to check the growth of evil [rather] than to 'mop up the slops.'"[40]

Still, in 1885 a former head of the international organization estimated that the more than five million people who had belonged to the Order at one time or another included 400,000 hard drinkers, at least half of whom "kept their pledge."[41] England maintained the best records on ex-drinkers. The North-West Yorkshire district lodge provided detailed, if ill-defined, statistics for 23 April 1873. Describing drinking practices prior to Templar membership, the district deputy identified 1,719 men and 795 women as having already been abstainers before joining, 842 men and 496 women as moderate drinkers, 138 men and 2 women as occasionally intemperate, and 238 men and 1 woman as confirmed drunkards.[42]

A few lodges and Grand Lodges kept statistics on backsliders. Illinois published figures for violations, beginning with the November 1855 session and continuing to the end of the 1860s. Considering the high risk incurred when admitting problem drinkers, these statistics indicate that surprisingly few members stumbled, typically around 5 percent each year.[43] In the years 1872-75 the English Templars published figures for their Grand Lodge. The first report showed that about 5 percent of the membership had violated the obligation, but the number of male violaters grew alarmingly during the year May 1874-May 1875 to over 27,000 despite the decline of male membership in the English organization to fewer than 107,000.[44] These figures in fact understate the amount of boozing by pledged teetotalers. The much larger figures for those suspended for nonpayment of dues conceal members who consumed alcohol. Offsetting this to a minor extent is the fact that "violations" included faults other than drinking, such as divulging lodge secrets.

What was the class composition of the Templar Order? How did it differ from that of other temperance societies and fraternal organizations? Answers to these questions are elusive because the categories are debatable (should income, status, or life-style define class?), evidence is scarce, and typicality impossible to prove. One can only report impressions: most Templars came from the working class and lower-middle class and their rural counterparts, certainly in Britain and probably in North America, but the leadership at all levels was drawn disproportionately from solidly middle-class people; the middle classes provided most of the members for temperance organizations in general in the English-speaking world; all kinds of people belonged to fraternal societies, although not necessarily to the same lodges or the same orders, with the typical member belonging to the middle or lower-middle class.

Joanne Judd Brownsword argues that the Templars became middle class within a few decades of the IOGT's formation. Her study of delegates to Wisconsin state conventions between 1854 and 1880 shows a decline in artisans such as carpenters, blacksmiths, and printers (but of teachers as well) and a rise in the number of ministers and "fairly successful farmers." Her argument assumes, unconvincingly, that the rank and file were comparable to the delegates in money and status.[45] A great deal of contrary evidence suggests that most Templars in Britain and Scandinavia and probably in North America could be classified as working class or lower-middle class or the rural equivalents. A large number of Templars worked with their hands and lived modestly. The membership rolls of Bangor Lodge in LaCrosse, Wisconsin, for 27 August 1881 to 6 October 1883 list the occupations of proposed members, most of them Welsh immigrants: twenty-seven laborers (presumably farm hands); twenty-two farmers (an ambiguous term); twenty-one women and seven men specifying no occupation; two each of masons, millers, "operators," and housekeepers or housewives; and single instances of a dressmaker and a dishwasher (both women), and a carpenter, a butcher, a painter, a railroader, an "agent," a "scholar," a teacher, and a landlord (all men). Over 88 percent of the members of Swedish-language lodges in Worcester, Massachusetts, "held blue-collar jobs" in 1909.[46]

Anecdotal evidence is endless, so a few samples must suffice. When Samuel C. Robinson, formerly secretary of the Grand Lodge of Georgia, was killed in a railroad accident, a memorial tribute identified him as a flagman. "Most of the male members" of Lake lodge at Black River, Ohio, were sailors who worked on the Great Lakes during the summer months. John K. Fogle, an officer in a New Albany, Indiana, lodge during the 1870s, was an ironworker prominent in the puddlers' union and the Workingmen's Reform Association. Among the lodges organized in England during nine days in June 1871 were the Working Man, the Hopeful Labourers, and the British Workman, names reflecting the class identity of the membership. An English pamphlet described the Templar lodge as "a fraternal circle where the sturdy workman enjoys club comforts," together with "his honest wife" and their children. Of course, members might shift status, as did Stephen Humphries Kearsey: an army sergeant when he helped organize the Templars in India during the 1870s, he later became a minister.[47]

Despite the humble livelihoods of most of its members, the IOGT rejected a class identity that might offend its few well-off members. "This was not a working class Order, and as Templars we should endeavour to kill all these distinctions in society." The plea came from England, where leaders feared that the perception of the Templars as working class would alienate middle-class prohibitionists.[48]

The Templar Order took most of its leaders from its small middle class. Daniel Wilkins, who headed the Grand Lodge of Illinois during 1867-70, was an Oberlin College graduate who taught Latin and mathematics at Illinois Wesleyan University. The author of an early Templar history published in England, S.P. Thompson, was an electrical engineer best known for writing biographies of British scientists. Prosperous Templars often were self-made men and women who had escaped childhood poverty. When Jonathan H. Orne was elected to head the international Order in 1868, he owned a shoe factory in Massachusetts. In contrast, his childhood home had consisted of "one finished room and an unfinished attic," his mother was a fisherman's daughter and his father a shoemaker, and for years he himself had earned his bread at the shoemaker's bench.[49]

The Templars promoted an ideology that middle-class reformers could support, so it is tempting to depict lower-class Templars as deferentially emulating middle-class mores, but the IOGT's discipline also appealed to advocates of working-class autonomy and self-respect. As another shoemaker remembered, "I was about eighteen [in 1879] when I began to think I was entirely on the wrong track in wasting so much money [on drink], and I made up my mind to be a Good Templar."[50]

In religion the typical Templar belonged to a Protestant denomination whose worship service featured simple rites, a plainly dressed minister, and a communion table, yet at lodge meetings the Templar took part in elaborate rituals led by officers wearing regalia and in the presence of what the Order called an altar.[51] Although real and intriguing, the contrast was partly terminological. Templar "altars" were regarded as everyday furniture. At Suffolk lodge in Cutchogue, Long Island, copies of a Templar newspaper "were on file in the altar."[52] Although few ministers joined the IOGT, this handful of clerical Templars achieved disproportionate prominence in the Order's leadership, especially in North America, Scotland, and Ireland. For instance, of 293 Grand Lodge of Scotland officers in the period 1870-1929, there were only twenty-nine ministers, but divines were elected to the highest office, GWCT, during 1876-83, 1893-97, and 1903-16.[53]

From nearly the beginning women were an important part of the IOGT. A month after the Independent Order of Good Templars came into existence, Forest City lodge in Ithaca, New York—Nathaniel Curtis's home lodge—initiated the first women Templars. When he was elected to head the IOGT central organization, Curtis complained that no lodge had sent women as delegates to the convention. He argued that female membership provided great benefits. Entire families could join the fight against drink at the Templar lodge room: "Here, our sisters, our wives and our daughters, could unite with us in this great work."[54] The earliest Templar women, however, had not yet attained equality even in theory. One remembered that "we were to be seen, not heard"; another described the rights of women members as "paying dues and taking the [teetotal] obligation."[55]

It was Curtis who presided at the Grand Lodge meeting in November 1852 which voted to invest women members with equal rights, something almost unthinkable outside the IOGT. Four of the five women who attended this session as delegates became minor Grand Lodge officers. Recognizing that women had little money of their own, the Order set their dues at a lower rate. Otherwise the new Templar regulations treated women the same as men. They could speak, vote, hold office, and participate in secret rituals. By June 1853 the Order claimed 1,316 female members, together with 2,424 males.[56]

Throughout the nineteenth century, women made up at least a third of Templar membership in the United States and Canada. Unfortunately, only scattered statistics are available, for after the first few years the annual returns of the central organization did not include statistics on the sex of members; nor did those for important Grand Lodges. As an exception, the Grand Lodge of Ohio did report the number of male and female members. Surviving *Journals of Proceedings* from the 1850s, 1860s, and 1870s show that women constituted a large minority, both when the membership was growing in Ohio and when it was declining.[57]

Fraternal temperance societies as a group had a better record in welcoming women than other fraternal organizations, probably because temperance societies had a practical purpose to pursue: fighting drink. Another fraternal temperance society, the Good Samaritans, founded in 1847, admitted women shortly before the Templars did. The Samaritan women technically belonged to a separate society, the Sisters of Samaria, but met jointly with the male society, each with its own set of officers. The pioneer North American fraternal temperance order, the Sons of Temperance, acknowledged the Daughters of Temperance as an affiliated organization and sometimes allowed women to attend meetings as silent visitors. Yet in 1852, when representatives of the Daughters of Temperance joined a meeting of the Sons of Temperance at Albany, New York, and tried to speak, the presiding officer refused to recognize them. In 1856 an officer of the Sons' National Division reported that in Michigan the whole membership "went over in [a] *solid body*" to the IOGT in protest over the exclusion of women.[58] In a compromise after the Civil War the society provided its state and provincial Grand Divisions discretionary authority to admit women, but the name remained the Sons of Temperance.

Reform circles in the 1850s seldom acknowledged sisterhood. The World's Temperance Convention, meeting in New York City in 1853, outraged Amelia Bloomer and other early advocates of women's rights by refusing to permit women delegates to participate; subsequently, they organized a rival Whole World's Temperance Convention.[59] Bloomer had joined the Templars earlier in that year, and her home lodge unanimously condemned the sexism of New York City "as an act of gross injustice and intolerant bigotry." Bloomer rejoiced to see women at a meeting of the Grand Lodge "on a perfect and entire equality with their brothers."[60]

She may have exaggerated the absence of sexism, but the Templars did surpass other organizations in recognizing the rights and potential contributions of women. In North America many were serious about the IOGT's invitation to women. In 1857 the Grand Lodge of Wisconsin resolved to change its constitution to add female pronouns to male ones. Soon after the establishment of a Grand Lodge for Ontario, its chief officer ruled that no lodge should be "without a fair proportion of female applicants." In 1870 the Committee on the State of the Order for the Grand Lodge of Massachusetts urged that Templar sisters "should be asked oftener to fill official positions not only in Subordinate Lodges but in the Grand Lodge." In 1876 the Grand Lodge of North Carolina adopted a sister's suggestion "that women be put upon committees whenever it is practicable to do so."[61]

Nobody has suggested that people quit the IOGT out of dislike of the integration of the sexes. Some non-Templars complained that letting women into a secret society of men fostered immorality, but this seems to have been a passing attitude when the IOGT was new and unfamiliar. In 1854, when the IOGT reached Hamilton, Ontario, one of the attractions that encouraged youthful Cadets of Temperance to change organizations was that young women belonged to Templar lodges. A California lodge reported five marriages among members.[62]

A key to the Templar understanding of gender can be found in the terms "brothers" and "sisters" used for male and female members. In the ordinary fraternal society, brotherhood signified a relationship among men, as if brothers had only male siblings. In late twentieth-century feminist discourse, sisterhood signifies a relationship among women, as if sisters had only female siblings. For the Templars, the terms brothers and sisters implied family relationships with fictive siblings of both sexes. To offer an analogy from my own life, I am a brother because of my two sisters. I have followed convention in calling the Templar Order a fraternal society, even though a fraternal group, construed literally, could not include women. A better descriptive term would be a "family organization." Templar ideology represented the IOGT as a family. In some lodges this was a practical reality, such as the English lodge that in 1874 enrolled from one family the mother, the father, two daughters, three sons, two daughters-in-law, two sons-in-law, one daughter-in-law-to-be, one sister-in-law, one niece, and two nephews, supplemented by nine grandchildren and two nieces in a juvenile temple, the auxiliary for children.[63]

The family in the nineteenth century was a patriarchal unit. What that meant in practice varied enormously. Normally, it precluded women's taking a formal position of leadership over adult males. Since the seventeenth-century Quakers, English-speaking women had had a history of participation in moral reform that both liberated them from conventional domestic roles and confirmed female stereotypes of purity and self-sacrifice, the basis for their moral authority. This did not challenge the patriarchy; rather, the emphasis on the difference between the sexes in female moral authority confirmed male dominance, the power to decide and to act. Female influence often mattered, but it was not a power to command. Women could only implore.

Templar women, by contrast, occasionally exercised the power to command. After a vacancy let a woman assume the office of Ohio GWCT, Queen City lodge in Cincinnati acknowledged that "in you we cheerfully recognize the head of Our Order in the State." This acceptance of female leadership had limits, however. According to her husband, "an organized conspiracy . . . of both men and women" unsuccessfully tried to block Mattie Brown's election to a term in her own right in 1873. The conspirators objected to what they regarded as a scandal: she had "assumed her right to travel alone by public conveyance without an escort."[64]

Templar sisters seldom, if ever, enjoyed a status of true equality with their brothers in the Templar Order, but they were part of the family, not outsiders. Joining together at weekly lodge meetings, including secret initiation ceremonies and other rituals, and voting in the same lodge elections, Templar brothers and sisters refuted the presumption of a crippling female disability, the presumption on which a defensive wall was erected against women by the typical fraternal organization. It is difficult to calculate the practical impact of the integration of women in the Templar Order, but any attempt must take into account that most members remained only briefly, so the combined numbers of men and women who at some time belonged far exceeded the figure for any particular date.

Templar leaders knew that the Order needed women. During the Civil War, when many male Templars and prospective members had entered the army, the IOGT owed its survival to female Templars. A lodge in Iowa elected only women officers, apparently because of an absence of officer-material men. In 1862 the chief of the IOGT in Illinois combined condescension with respect when he asked the sisters to "take the helm": "No matter if the rough tarred rope besmear those beautiful hands—no matter if the exposure browns that beautiful face."[65]

No woman ever headed the international organization, but several women served as GWCT. The two most important were Amanda M. Way in Indiana in the late 1860s, and Martha McClellan Brown in neighboring Ohio in the mid-1870s; Way later headed Grand Lodges in Kansas and Idaho as well.[66] The other American women who led nineteenth-century Grand Lodges were minor figures: Ada Van Pelt and Anna M. Saunders of Nebraska and Allie E. Parker of Rhode Island. At the end of the great schism a woman known only as Mrs. William Wilkinson headed one of the rival Irish Grand Lodges.[67]

Way and Brown deserve a more detailed analysis because of what they had in common and how they differed. One never married; the other was a wife and mother of a large family. In the great schism one supported John J. Hickman of Kentucky, the other Joseph Malins of England. Both were devout Christians: one was licensed as a Methodist preacher and later became a Quaker minister; the other was the wife of a Methodist minister. Both were Prohibition Party activists and advocates of woman suffrage. Both were outstanding platform speakers. Both moved frequently: Indiana, Missouri, Kansas, Idaho, and California in one case; Maryland, Ohio, Pennsylvania, and New York in the other. Both played important roles in the WCTU in its early days but never held WCTU elective office or chose to be active in the single-sex temperance organization. One became GWCT when her predecessor died, the other when the incumbent was expelled from his lodge.

Way was a fighter. According to fragments from her unpublished and lost autobiography, drunkenness in the Way family intensified her hatred of liquor: "Her youngest brother, a mere baby boy, was laid at her door as apparently dead, drugged with alcohol."[68]

In revenge for her temperance work in Indiana, whiskey drinkers set fire to her house. She insisted on the IOGT's relevance even where the sale of alcohol was illegal: "There are drunkards still to reform in Kansas, notwithstanding we have prohibition. Where can it be done better than in our fraternal home that holds him up, while it leads him into the church and up to a loving Saviour." Hostility toward activist women sometimes confronted "Old Mandy." A Kansas newspaper announced her lecture appearance with the jibe "Tonight a hen will try to crow." Once when a heckler addressed her as lady, she retorted: "Don't call ME a lady": "I want you to understand that fashion made me a lady but God made me a woman."[69]

Mattie Brown saw herself as a champion of women in public life. In her final report as GWCT she thanked her fellow Templars for electing her to high office, an honor conferred upon women "whose pathway to higher usefulness has been generously paved by this order." Brown regarded the insistence upon the equality of women within the Order as its most important innovation. She praised the order for "uniting the whole home circle, with equal privileges and opportunity for women as for men."[70]

Many women held lesser Templar offices. In local lodges they were often the wives or relations of a male officer. In the English-speaking world women almost always occupied the number-three office of vice Templar. In North America women frequently served in the even more important office of secretary. For instance, L. Ellen Wright, elected Pennsylvania's secretary in 1856, served seventeen consecutive terms, and with one brief interval Sarah A. Leonard held the same office in Massachusetts from 1877 until her death in 1904.

Supervising children was often women's work. In North America women headed the juvenile auxiliaries because male Templars dismissed organizing children and youth as unimportant, and nearly all male Templars used tobacco, something prohibited to the adults who led the juvenile societies. In Britain, where many male Templars considered tobacco almost as hateful as alcohol and the IOGT made work among children a high priority, men often directed the juvenile societies. Women occupied the international office responsible for children, from 1874 until 1908.

Women served the Templars further as editors and speakers. When her brother died in 1866, Emma Brown succeeded him as editor of the *Wisconsin Chief* and continued until her own death in 1889. In fact, she had managed the paper since its founding in New York state in the 1850s as the *Cayuga Chief*. She even set type.[71] In the mid-1880s Jessie Forsyth edited *Temperance Brother-*

hood and from 1901 to 1908 did the work without the title at the *International Good Templar.* Other Templar women earned a living as itinerant temperance lecturers, among them Emma Barrett Molloy of Indiana.[72]

Still, equality for Templar women, nominal in North America, remained even more of a fiction in other parts of the world. In 1874, after England's Lincoln Excelsior lodge elected Sister Blinkhorn as its chief, seven members in a sexist huff asked for clearance cards to form a new lodge.[73] In 1885 the Scottish representatives to a session of the RWGL of the World opposed placing a woman on the executive committee.[74] A caucus of women revolted at the Grand Lodge of England annual meeting in 1893 and, after a half dozen ballots, got one of their number elected to the minor office of Grand Marshal, ordinarily held by a man. This was not repeated, and a few years later an American visitor expressed surprise that the nine-member Executive Committee of the Grand Lodge of England included only one woman.[75] Outside the English-speaking countries women were even worse off. At an RWGL of the World meeting in Stockholm the local organizers relegated female international officers to the back row of seats on the speakers' platform.[76] From 1911 to 1930, when Scandinavians dominated the Order, women held no international executive office.

As a mixed-sex organization, however imperfect, the Templars were nevertheless remarkable for what they promised and what they delivered to women. Women were grateful for what the Templars offered: community, recreation, and a chance to develop their talents and to do good (although when the WCTU provided an alternative, many women showed that they preferred to run their own organization). Female membership was Templar universalism's most dramatic success. Templar universalist ideology transcended gender at a time when for most men's organizations difference in gender justified a rigid exclusion of women.

Female membership also prepared the way for the controversy over black membership. The need to justify and celebrate membership for women strengthened the Templar ideology of universalism, but the ambivalence between sexism and protestations of gender equality found a parallel ambivalence between racism and protestations of racial equality.

This parallel had its limits. The men of the IOGT at all times and in all places took for granted the presence of large numbers of women. Except for military lodges, virtually all Templar subordinate lodges had a substantial female membership, and none had the right to reject women—whereas in its early years the IOGT provided blacks no such protection. Many white Templars refused to have blacks in their own lodges as members or as visitors, only grudgingly accepted the fact of black members in other lodges, and never personally encountered a black Templar. Nearly all black Templars belonged to segregated lodges in the American South; most of the rest lived in northern seaports and often belonged to de facto segregated lodges.

Yet it was their evolving universalist ideology that made the Templars different from other late nineteenth-century organizations. "Convinced of the 'infinite worthiness' of all persons," adherents of evangelical perfectionism reinforced the postmillennialist hope widespread in North America that by building a moral community people could prepare the way for Christ's return.[77] Arguably, Templar universalism grew out of such religious ideas, but the evidence is far from clear. The same religious environment did not affect everybody the same way. What seems beyond dispute is that the fact of a diverse membership encouraged Templars to prize it.

In 1871 at a meeting in a provincial English town, the GWCT shared with his largely female audience of nearly two hundred the glory of Templar universalism. Although he acknowledged that in the United States there had been "a terrible struggle about the admission of coloured people," he added, naively, that it had been won: "Good Templarism admitted not only both sexes, but also people of every shade and colour—white, black, red, and all other colours that people happened to grow." He quoted an Indian in Canada who had argued that "if Good Templarism could make a Red Indian sober, and a white man honest, it could do anything." He linked racial inclusiveness with other aspects of universalism. He pointed out that temperance benefit societies such as the Rechabites, the Sons of the Phoenix, and the Sons of Temperance "were not adapted to receive the whole human family." Unlike these insurance organizations, the Templars opened their ranks to the aged and the infirm and, he could have added, the very poor. With regret he admitted that most Templar lodges in England kept women off their executive committees but pointed out, as a happy exception, that "the largest lodge in the midland counties was presided over by a lady, and it was found that the ladies went through their business like a man." To show the potential role for women in the Order, he told his audience about Amanda M. Way, who had served as the GWCT of Indiana. The Templars welcomed people of all religions. Roman

Catholics, Unitarians, and trinitarian Protestants had succeeded one another as lodge officers in his hometown of Birmingham. The Grand Lodge of England counted men and women "of every rank and grade, and almost of every colour."[78]

This kind of self-congratulatory universalist rhetoric and Templar expansion to parts of the world unaccustomed to rigid racial segregation challenged members of the IOGT to open lodges to non-whites everywhere. White members in the former slave states came under pressure to modify their exclusion of black people. Southern whites made concessions to mollify Templars from outside their region, concessions that had few parallels in other fraternal organizations but were insufficient to prevent the great schism. Templar universalism is the key to understanding the controversy over blacks joining the IOGT in the American South, where the white Templars did not want them.

2

The Adversaries

A struggle between Templars in the American South and in Britain strained the unity of the IOGT and eventually shattered it. Controversy over black membership grew explosive in the 1870s, when large numbers of white southern and British recruits swamped the Templar Order. The unexpected new geographical and cultural diversity unsettled the balance of power and made Templar decision-making about African American membership divisive.

Contemporaries personalized the dispute as a duel between a Kentuckian and an Englishman. The charismatic John J. Hickman, a farmer turned insurance agent, headed the Grand Lodge of Kentucky and later the international Order. The tenacious Joseph Malins, a former furniture painter who for a couple of years had lived in Philadelphia, dominated the Grand Lodge of England. During the great schism of 1876-87 the rival parties were nicknamed the Hickmanites and the Malinites (or Malinsites).

The controversy can also be dramatized as a clash between leading Grand Lodges, those of Kentucky and England, whose roles in the conflict went beyond Hickman's and Malins's leadership. Kentucky, the oldest and the largest of the southern Grand Lodges, claimed to speak for the American South. The much younger Grand Lodge of England was the biggest in the world. Excited by the IOGT's universalist ideology, the English Templars helped organize lodges in British colonies and northern Europe and among overseas British merchants from Argentina to Japan.

In retrospect, the competition between the Templar organization of a medium-sized state and that of a country with many times its population seems unequal. In late 1873 and early 1874 England had over 200,000 adult members. With a much smaller population its neighbor and ally Scotland boasted 62,000 in 1875 and 1876, while Wales and Ireland created lesser Grand Lodges that looked to England for leadership.[1] The RWGL acknowledged the importance of

England and in 1873 held its annual session there, the first time that the convention had taken place outside North America. The RWGL also rewarded English delegates with international offices. In 1874 and 1875 Malins was elected to the second highest office, Right Worthy Grand Counsellor.

Yet during the period when people who lived in the United States and Canada controlled the IOGT organization, the giant Grand Lodge of England appeared to many Templars remote and peripheral, whereas the flourishing Grand Lodge of Kentucky constituted the gateway to a promising mission territory in the American South. By the mid-1870s at least a third of the Templar membership in the United States lived in the former slave states, and many Templars expected the proportion of the membership living there to increase.[2] Since membership was volatile, large numbers of southerners belonged to the IOGT briefly. For instance, over 194,000 white Georgians joined the Templars from the time that the state's first lodge was organized in 1867 until the end of the great schism twenty years later.[3] Meanwhile, during the late 1860s and early 1870s the IOGT faded in its old northeastern and Great Lakes strongholds, so Templar successes in the southeastern states during the mid-1870s were all the more gratifying. According to RWGL statistics, Tennessee had some 10,000 members in 1875, as did Georgia in the following year. In 1876 Alabama counted nearly 11,000. In 1877 Missouri had over 14,000. Virginia, atypically, reached its peak of nearly 14,000 around the time of reunion that ended the schism. Although every former slave state had a Grand Lodge at one time or another, North Carolina and South Carolina were the only other southern states whose Grand Lodges reached a significant size; their largest memberships were over 7,000 and 3,000 respectively.[4]

An alliance with the large "Grand Temple" of Canada strengthened southern influence.[5] From 1873 until he was defeated for reelection in 1880, a Napanee, Ontario, journalist and mayor, Walter Scott Williams, served as the international organization's secretary, while Kentucky's Hickman was elected the RWGL's counsellor in 1871 and 1872 and RWGT in 1874, 1875, 1876, 1879, and 1880. In 1881, as a kind of consolation for the South, when Hickman was defeated for reelection, Kentucky's current GWCT was elected Counsellor. A Virginian was elected in 1882. As further evidence of southern influence, the RWGL met at Louisville, Kentucky, in 1876, the fateful session at which the unity of the Order was disrupted.[6] During the schism years it met at Charleston, South Carolina, in 1882 and at Richmond, Virginia, in 1886.

Transatlantic differences should not be exaggerated. A strong temperance movement had sprung up in both Kentucky and England amid a popular culture of alcohol consumption: Kentucky's excise-paying bourbon distilleries, illegal moonshine stills, and whiskey-drinking churchgoers; England's ubiquitous public houses and beer-drinking workingmen.[7] In both the American South and the United Kingdom the Templars were teetotalers committed to some form of prohibition of beverage alcohol and attracted to the fraternal community that lodge life offered. Typically, members in both Kentucky and England were young evangelical Protestants of modest circumstances, mostly male but with a large female minority.

In both jurisdictions too, turnover was rapid. Kentucky's secretary sadly observed that of the sixty delegates to the annual session in 1867, only one or two attended four years later.[8] In both Kentucky and England, keeping old members and old lodges proved more difficult than getting new ones. Often it seemed that expansion into new geographic areas was easier than retaining existing lodges. For instance, in 1866, the Grand Lodge of Kentucky drew most of its support from the western part of the state; by 1871 it was predominantly a north-central organization with major urban strongholds such as the river towns of Louisville and Covington. The glory days of expansion were brief. Initiations struggled to keep ahead of losses and often failed to do so. In the RWGL statistics for 1875 Kentucky is credited with initiating nearly 11,000 new members and instituting 180 new lodges. At the same time the state lost nearly 6,500 members who had belonged to 185 defunct lodges, as well as nearly 3,800 suspended for nonpayment of dues, over 1,000 expelled for persistent drinking or other violations, and 100 who died.[9] Between the mid-1870s and mid-1880s English membership declined from over 200,000 to below 80,000.

In both jurisdictions the status of Templar women failed to equal that attained in the northeastern and midwestern American states during the IOGT's formative years. Until membership had declined drastically, neither jurisdiction elected a woman to a Grand Lodge office other than the traditionally female post of vice Templar, and women almost never headed subordinate lodges. The Women's Temperance Crusade of 1873-74 did not cross the Ohio River southward in force, but after the decline of the Templars the more genteel WCTU became the most important temperance organization in Kentucky, with the wife of a former GWCT as the head of the state society.[10] Templar women in the South rarely joined their sisters in the North in working for woman suffrage. A Kentucky woman declared in 1874 that "the ladies in Kentucky don't want to vote in elections," as they were honored with a more important influence "at the fireside."[11] Although the Grand Lodge of Kentucky did not report membership subtotals by gender, some individual lodges did. Nearly half the membership of Capital lodge in Frankfort was female in February 1872, when there were 124 sisters and 154 brothers.[12] Although Templar women helped establish the British Women's Temperance Association in 1876, single-sex women's temperance organizations in the British Isles failed to match the influence of the WCTU in North America. The women's societies in England and Scotland had many members but little money, a minor presence in temperance journalism, and no leader with the charisma of Frances Willard.[13]

On both sides of the Atlantic the period of Templar strife took place amid economic discouragement. After the panic of 1873, depressed agricultural prices blighted the lives of Kentucky farmers and those who depended on farmers as customers. The price of tobacco "fell from ten cents a pound in 1872 to six cents in 1878."[14] In England the great depression of 1873-96 did not bring about large-scale unemployment or reduce real wages but struck a heavy blow at the profits and confidence of entrepreneurs and investors.

There were also marked differences. Although the United Kingdom was a single polity with one monarch, cabinet, and parliament, it contained several historic nations, and each had its own Grand Lodge: England, Scotland, Wales (eventually with separate organizations for Welsh- and English-speakers), and Ireland. By North American standards the Grand Lodge of Scotland was very large, and the Grand Lodge of England dwarfed all others. In the United States each separate state had its own legislature and Grand Lodge. But despite a strong regional identity in the American South, a still stronger sense of states' rights or autonomy hindered the kind of close alliance displayed in Britain by the Grand Lodges of England and Scotland, whose single Parliament met at Westminster without the competition of English and Scottish legislatures. The unity of the South existed more in rhetoric than in practice, although white southerners did sporadically attempt to work together. At the RWGL's annual session in 1878, for instance, the southern delegates "retired to ante-rooms and consulted."[15]

At their peak the Templar membership in Kentucky and England attracted a much higher proportion of the general population than did most Grand Lodges in other jurisdictions. England had over 210,000 adult members in 1874, while Kentucky counted slightly

over 24,000 members in 1874 and nearly 25,000 in 1878, membership zeniths followed by sharp declines. In April 1871 England's
population was 21,299,683.[16] The white population of Kentucky was
1,098,692 at the 1870 census and 1,377,179 in 1880. This means that
fewer than one of a hundred in England belonged to the IOGT at the
height of its membership, whereas about one in forty-four and one
in fifty-six whites in Kentucky belonged at comparable moments.
Taking into account that the Grand Lodge of Kentucky did not
admit blacks, the density of membership was about twice that
in England's Grand Lodge. Comparisons are not that simple, however. Most white people in Kentucky were evangelical Protestants,
whereas a large proportion in England were Anglicans, only some
of them evangelicals, and a good many Irish Catholics. The Grand
Lodge of England recruited its members mostly from the Nonconformist minority.

The critical difference between Templars in England and the
rest of the United Kingdom and in Kentucky and the rest of the
American South was the attitude toward race. Blacks made up a
smaller part of the population in Kentucky than in the Deep South
and declined from under 20 percent of the population in the mid-
1860s to about 15 percent in the mid-1880s. Despite this decided
minority of blacks, race was a central question for white Kentuckians
who insisted upon white supremacy and racial segregation.[17] Debate
over the racial question dominated the meetings of the Grand Lodge
of Kentucky in the late 1860s and the early 1870s. Since Kentucky
never seceded from the Union, slavery continued there until the ratification of the Thirteenth Amendment after the conclusion of
the Civil War. The RWGL, under a Uniform Constitution adopted in
1867, prohibited the constitution of new Grand Lodges from excluding anybody on the basis of race. But the Grand Lodge of Kentucky,
although it had collapsed in the 1850s, was reestablished in 1864, so
its constitution's prohibition of black membership was unaffected.

In 1866, a year before Hickman joined the IOGT, Kentucky
protested the RWGL's organization of segregated black lodges: "This
Order was gotten up by white men, to be carried on by the white element of our population." The Kentuckians believed that "God created
the white man superior to the negro, Socially, Morally, and Intellectually." Nothing could make a black person "a fit associate for our
Mothers, Wives, Daughters and Sisters, in either the parlor, Lodge-
room, or the common walks of life." "Being unused to associating
with the negro as our equal or superior, believing that the negro is
not capable of self-government, and that we make an entire surren-

der of all we hold dear in our beloved Order when we admit him," the Grand Lodge of Kentucky threatened to secede from the RWGL.[18]

In 1867 Kentucky emphasized that the policy of the RWGL would destroy the Templar Order in Kentucky and throughout the South: "We cannot under *any circumstances,* accept such a doctrine [of racial equality] *as true in any sense,* having always considered, and still considering the Negro our inferior in *every* respect, as much unsuited and unfitted for membership in our Lodge Room, as around our firesides."[19]

In 1868 representatives of Kentucky and Tennessee challenged the RWGL to appoint a committee "to take the sense of this R.W.G.L. on the subject of admitting to membership in our Order, on terms of perfect equality, the negroes of the South." The border state delegates were dissatisfied with the eventual committee compromise, which affirmed racial equality in principle but also acknowledged the complete autonomy of Grand Lodges in determining the membership in their own jurisdictions. Recognizing that an exclusively negative position would attract little support, Tennessee and Kentucky urged the creation of a separate organization for blacks, to be called the Colored Templars of North America.[20]

Kentucky took the lead in establishing such a society for African Americans. In 1871 Hickman said that he could not grant IOGT charters to the black Kentuckians who asked him for them, for three reasons: "1st. Their limited education would not permit them to work successfully the somewhat complicated machinery of our Order. 2nd. While we are compelled to acknowledge their political rights as citizens, and should be, and are willing to aid them to become upright and moral citizens, we are not prepared to acknowledge the social relationship which would necessarily exist in the Order." He added that "the establishment of colored Lodges in Kentucky, upon the same footing with the white Lodges, with the same ceremonies, passwords, &c., would be the death-knell to the cause in our State." Yet he wanted to help the blacks of Kentucky "throw off the shackles of intemperance" and recognized that if blacks stopped patronizing barrooms "very many of the *immoral* institutions will die out for the want of support."

Hickman invested his prestige in the project of a black fraternal temperance society. He suggested that his Grand Lodge draw up for black teetotalers "a plain and comprehensive ritual, with plans of organization, &c., suited to their capacities." He asked his Grand Lodge to pay the expenses of starting a black fraternal temperance society and to provide white organizers; then, "when properly inaugurated, let the entire management be given into their own hands."[21] Rev. H.A.M. Henderson, a onetime Confederate army officer, wrote the ritual for what became the United Order of True Reformers. Hickman had been asked by the RWGL to draft a ritual for a segregated black organization. He did not do so. Instead, at his suggestion the RWGL executive committee adopted Henderson's ritual and paid $150 to Kentucky for 265 copies of rituals and 1,400 of constitutions.[22] The True Reformers became an organization for blacks throughout the former slave states.

In contrast to the white racists in Kentucky, few British people had had any personal contact with blacks. Except for a handful of black Templars in Britain, mostly at seaports, virtually all the British members of the IOGT were white, and probably few of them had ever met a black person. A combination of Templar universalism, a Nonconformist distaste for racist practices derived from the era of slavery, and the sparseness of blacks in the British Isles disposed Templars there to take up the cause of equality in the American South. The Templars in Britain were determined that blacks should be able to join the Templar Order everywhere.

Two historical motives may have contributed to the British response to post–Civil War racism. The first was Britain's preeminence in the nineteenth century's crusade against the slave trade. Most Britons hated slavery and could be persuaded to condemn any leftover racial discrimination. The second is more ambiguous and problematic. One hesitates to ascribe to so amorphous a concept as war guilt the British response to the resurrection of racism in the former slave states, but surely it does not go too far to suggest that, after the settlement of the *Alabama* claims, many in Britain decried the role their country had played in aiding and abetting the South's struggle to perpetuate human bondage.[23]

It is not that the British were free from racism. During the middle of the nineteenth century their reaction to the Indian Mutiny and black rebellion in Jamaica showed a hardening racism that the popular understanding of Darwinian evolution intensified. The British, however, vehemently condemned slavery as a crime against humanity, civilization, and Christianity and in their home islands did not impose racial segregation on non-whites through the force of law. Few people in the British Isles shared the southern white obsession with racial contamination.

Although race relations constituted the most contentious difference, a larger difference between Britain and the American South was economic and social. The Templars in the former slave states belonged to an agricultural economy and society, as a standard description of nineteenth-century Kentucky emphasizes: "For many Kentuckians their universe centered on a small hamlet where they received mail and purchased supplies. Hundreds of these small places, hardly villages . . . had a general store, a mill of some sort, perhaps a blacksmith, and often a preacher, doctor or lawyer."[24] Lodges situated in such communities sent representatives to the Grand Lodge session in 1871: for instance, Antioch lodge, Earle's Post Office, Muhlenberg County; and Logan lodge, McLeod's Station, Logan County.

Only a minority of the Kentucky membership appears to have been this rural, though; most Templars lived in some kind of town or village. Some larger towns and cities were represented by multiple lodges in 1871. Louisville—a manufacturing, commercial, and transportation center—boasted seven; Covington, five; Frankfort and Winchester, four; Owensboro, three; and Henderson, Hopkinsville, Lexington, and Richmond, two. Other lodges were located in fairly substantial towns such as Bardsville and Bowling Green, smaller ones such as Augusta and West Point, and villages such as Rochester and Woodburn.[25] The contrast between Kentucky and England was great but should not be exaggerated into a great divide between isolated Kentucky farms and busy London streets.

Still, even if they did not themselves farm, most Kentucky Templars had been farm-reared and had lives and work intertwined with that of the countryside. George W. Bain left the hard life of a farmer years before he was elected GWCT, but he remembered getting ready for a humble country supper as a newly married man just turned twenty: he first fed the horses and chickens and then washed his face "in a tin pan on the kitchen steps."[26]

Unlike the Kentucky Templars, the membership in England and in other parts of the United Kingdom lived in a decidedly industrial environment, either in cities and large towns or in mining districts, extensions of the industrial revolution into the countryside. The bulk of the English membership was working class and nearly all the rest lower-middle class. Before he became the perpetual Grand Worthy Chief Templar, Joseph Malins had been a decorative painter, not an industrial occupation but definitely a working-class one. The geographical concentration of working-class and lower-middle-class Templars in English cities, towns, and mining districts permitted the growth of a durable lodge subculture rarely matched in Kentucky because of its more thinly distributed population and membership.[27]

A critical mass of friendly Nonconformists also helped sustain the Templars in England. At the end of April 1873 the membership of the Grand Lodge included 205 Primitive Methodist ministers, representing a comparatively small denomination that pioneered in its commitment to teetotalism. There were also 135 Independent or Congregational ministers, 125 Wesleyans, 95 Baptists, 79 from the Methodist Free Church, 49 from the very small Bible Christian or Plymouth Brethren denomination, only 30 from the numerically dominant and politically privileged Church of England, 22 Presbyterians, 21 from the Methodist New Connexion, 14 Calvinistic Methodists, 95 miscellaneous ministers, 25 home missionaries, and no Roman Catholic priests.[28] Probably the rank and file membership was also overwhelmingly Nonconformist, although a great many Templar lodges lay in metropolitan London, where Nonconformists made up a smaller proportion of the population than in the industrial north-central districts. Similar statistics are neither available nor relevant for Kentucky, where the American equivalent of the Nonconformist denominations included nearly the entire population.

Although in both jurisdictions the leadership tended to belong to a higher socioeconomic group than did the rank and file, England claimed few lawyers, whereas Kentucky had a great many of them, such as Tim Needham, briefly GWCT and for many years Grand Worthy Secretary. G.W. Bain's column in the 7 January 1875 number of the (Louisville) *Temperance Advocate* credited "the influence of the young lawyers, all but two of whom are Templars," for the success of the Madisonville lodge in implementing new local option legislation.

Despite its abundance of lawyers, late nineteenth-century Kentucky suffered violence, lawlessness, and political corruption unknown in England. On one occasion "twelve armed men" had to protect Bain from an anti-teetotal mob; on another occasion he reported that his "wife placed herself between my body and a desperate mountaineer."[29] Hickman mentioned an encounter with a drunken desperado, later transformed by the teetotal pledge into a preacher and a Templar.[30]

For England the 1870s were part of the period of alternation in power of the two major political parties, Conservatives and Liberals. Politics in Kentucky were dominated by Democrats, often former Confederate soldiers; no Republican was elected governor or United States senator until the mid-1890s. Templar leaders, however, included men active in both the Republican and Democratic Parties, and both former Union and former Confederate soldiers. In Kentucky during the late 1860s and the early 1870s Templar leaders opposed any commitment to the National Prohibition Party. In his final report as head of the Grand Lodge, Hickman claimed that in rejecting a divisive endorsement of the Prohibition Party, "I utter the sentiment of nine-tenths of our entire membership."[31] But the people who succeeded Hickman after 1871 championed this third party. In England only a few eccentrics considered a separate prohibition party.[32] Instead, the Templars supported the Liberals as the party most likely to put prohibition by local option on British statute books. In 1886 Malins repudiated William Gladstone's endorsement of Irish Home Rule—like a more famous Birmingham Liberal, Joseph Chamberlain—yet as the paramount question for Malins was temperance, Ireland did not destroy the Templar alliance with the Liberal Party.[33]

There is no similarity between the kind and quantity of sources available for the Templars of the two Grand Lodges. Even though historians have virtually ignored the English Templars, abundant sources survive: a continuous series of annual *Proceedings,* two weekly newspapers, a small mountain of pamphlets, a competent family biography of its founder, and reports of several controversies that brought into print a good deal of its inner history.[34] For Kentucky, in contrast, sources are amazingly meager, considering its importance for ten or fifteen years. All that survives are Grand Lodge reports for three years (the 1866 semiannual and annual sessions, the 1867 and 1871 annual sessions), supplemented by a few numbers of a not very informative official organ published under various names at Lexington and Louisville, plus short biographical sketches of several Grand Worthy Chief Templars, the minutes of two subordinate lodges, and bits and pieces in Templar writings published outside Kentucky, such as the *Proceedings* of the RWGL. This scarcity of documentation reflects the breakdown of the IOGT in Kentucky in the early and middle 1880s and the departure of many Templar leaders from the Order or the state.

For Malins and Hickman the contrast in the availability of sources is extreme. Malins's teacher son wrote a full-scale biography, based in part on his father's autobiographical memoirs that had appeared serially in a newspaper. For Hickman the best account available is a short sketch that appeared in the (New York) *Good Templar Gem* in July 1880. That newspaper does not survive, but the few pages of biography were reprinted in T.F. Parker's official history of the IOGT, first published in 1882 and republished in 1887.[35]

Hickman left Kentucky to reside in Missouri for the last decades of his life, so the standard biographical reference works for Kentucky ignore him.

Comparison is difficult, therefore, but one can see at least superficial similarities between the best-known leaders of the rival Grand Lodges. Hickman and Malins both joined the Order in 1867 and were elected Grand Worthy Chief Templar while still in their twenties at the first Grand Lodge session that they attended. Both rejected tobacco as well as alcohol and experimented with food reform: Hickman never drank tea or coffee; Malins in middle age became a vegetarian.[36] Both Hickman and Malins lost their fathers while young and had mothers who encouraged them to embrace tee-totalism. Malins's father was an alcoholic, and the period in which Hickman's father lived makes it unlikely that he was a teetotaler. The rivals were both evangelical Protestants: Hickman a Baptist, Malins a Methodist. Both remained active in the Templar Order until they died in the twentieth century.

The other biographical facts available for Hickman can be stated briefly. John James Hickman was born on 26 May 1839, apparently at Lexington, Kentucky, where he spent his early childhood. His uncle Thomas Metcalfe had been governor in 1828-32 and a Whig member of the United States Senate in 1848-49. When his father died, Hickman's mother moved with her children to the southern part of the state. He married at age nineteen and, after early attempts at farming, studied law and medicine. In later years he suffered from ill health, which may explain why he appears not to have served in the military during the Civil War—though he styled himself Col. J.J. Hickman, an honorary title awarded in 1873 by a Kentucky governor. What Hickman's sympathies were in the War between the States are unknown. After the war he became a sales agent for a St. Louis company that sold life insurance to total abstainers, and he sometimes promoted his business when traveling for the IOGT. His biographer, a fellow officer in the Grand Lodge, described Hickman as impulsive, generous, and warmhearted, a man of integrity, made powerful by "his burning eloquence, deep earnestness, and impassioned zeal."

Hickman joined the IOGT at the South Carrollton lodge in Muhlenberg County in western Kentucky on 15 May 1867. He was soon appointed a state deputy and moved to Louisville. At the first Grand Lodge session he attended, in October 1868, he was elected GWCT. Unlike his predecessors he engaged in Templar work full time. Inheriting a Grand Lodge with fewer than 3,000 members and

60 working lodges, he left office three years later with nearly 25,000 members and more than 500 working lodges. At that time he was being paid the substantial annual salary of $3,000; thereafter he was appointed state lecturer with a generous salary of $2,500 and complete discretion about what duties he might choose to perform.

Hickman affected a mixture of humility and pride. In his final year he instituted 100 new lodges with 5,200 members and claimed to have been responsible for adding nearly 7,000 new members in old and new lodges: "It is certainly gratifying to me to know the fact, that since my official connection with the Order, I have initiated more than half its membership, and it is very pleasant to know, that I have never taken one dollar from its treasury without, by the result of my labors, adding two in its place."[37] He gave 400 lectures, made 200 visits to lodges, and wrote 1,000 letters. Over the previous twelve months the membership had grown by 85 percent.

Hickman's ideology, like that of many in the Order, combined religion with warlike and patriotic rhetoric and sentimental appeals to the sanctity of the family. In 1871 he spoke about "the old battle-flag." At least twenty-five of the lodges that he organized that year incorporated "star" in their names, analogous to the stars representing states in the national flag. In luxuriant oratory Hickman spoke of Templars "rescuing thousands of victims from [the] captivity [of drink] and restoring them to loved ones who have long mourned them as lost," after driving the enemy with "truth steeled bayonets, over the rugged hills as well as through the fertile valleys of our own beautiful State."[38] Seventeen new lodges whose names embraced a female reference, such as Ladies' Victory, suggest Hickman's ideology of hearth and home. Although women exercised little power in Kentucky, the Templars honored them with an abundance of gallant language. Hickman spoke of the joy of the daughter, sister, mother, and wife of the reclaimed drunkard: "The fires of pure love are once again rekindled about the desecrated altars of the family circle."[39]

As a major figure in the Templar Order, Hickman built a position as liaison between the RWGL and the South. In 1869, at the first RWGL session he attended, he was named marshal. In 1871 and 1872 he was elected to the second highest office, counsellor. Skipping the RWGL session in England, he was out of office for a year but was then elected RWGT in 1874 and reelected in 1875 and 1876—unanimously in the latter crisis year. He declined renomination in 1877, probably because a virtually bankrupt RWGL could not pay a salary, but was elected RWGT again in 1879 and 1880. In 1881 he was defeated in a straw vote which the *Journal of Proceedings* did not record.[40] Until his death in 1902 he served frequently as a paid organizer for the IOGT, particularly in the South. Renowned as an orator, he delivered more than 10,000 speeches during his lifetime.

In few places during the schism was the decline of the Templar Order more rapid than in Kentucky. On the one hand, the availability of prohibition under the permissive local option legislation of 1874 may have made a fraternal temperance society appear irrelevant. On the other hand, whatever the complications of illegal moonshiners and the varying size of distilleries and breweries, Kentucky still appeared to produce plenty of intoxicating alcohol, which suggests that the IOGT continued to have work to do. In 1872 there were 237 distilleries and 46 breweries in the state; in 1880, 570 distilleries and 42 breweries; in 1889, 581 distilleries and 37 breweries.[41]

Identification with the National Prohibition Party and the northern women's rights movement and the absence of continuity in leadership probably hurt the Templars in Kentucky as much as the controversy over black membership.[42] In spite of the racial question the IOGT staged a modest revival in some other southern states during the mid-1880s.[43] Yet according to RWGL statistics, Kentucky reported 24,393 members in 1878 but only 15,549 in the following year and 10,187 in 1882; thereafter, the Grand Lodge never again claimed a five-figure membership. In 1884 Kentucky had 2,521 members; in 1885, only 1,943.

The Grand Lodge of Kentucky had sunk into insignificance before the reunion of the Order in 1887. In that year Kentucky claimed slightly more than 2,000 members. A delegate representing Kentucky at the Saratoga session of the RWGL voted for the nominal equality afforded black Templars.[44] The Grand Lodge rallied the next year, with a membership of nearly 4,000, but that revival lacked staying power. By 1892 the Grand Lodge counted its membership in the hundreds, and soon after the beginning of the new century it ceased to exist. The disintegration of the Templar Order in Kentucky was so rapid and so complete and the turnover in membership so devastating that few ex-members bothered to preserve its memory or its records. It is almost as if the Grand Lodge of Kentucky had never enjoyed its few sweet years of triumph in the Bluegrass State and its position of leadership in the Templar Order.

Unlike other Kentucky leaders who drifted out of the Templars, Hickman left the state but not the IOGT. By the late 1870s he had moved to Columbia, Missouri, where his two sons studied at the state university, and he continued to make Missouri his home for the rest of his life. Hickman was head of the Grand Lodge of Missouri in the reunion year of 1887.[45] He died, apparently in Missouri, on 29 April 1902.[46]

There is much more information about Malins (pronounced MAY-lins) than Hickman. Beginning with minimal skills as a speaker and organizer, Malins developed into a successful leader of a large, predominantly working-class temperance society. He established the English Templar commitment to overseas missions and symbolized its American connection. Despite a skimpy education, he became a prolific polemical writer in prose and verse. On the eve of the First World War an American woman praised England for producing the two greatest men of the nineteenth century: the Liberal prime minister William Gladstone, and the Templar leader Joseph Malins. Over forty years earlier the same American had described him as "a modern John Wesley for Good Templarism, taking the world for his field."[47]

His father, John Malins, was a builder in the north Oxfordshire town of Chipping Norton. Shortly after marrying Jane Allen, a cheese factor's daughter, he relocated at Worcester, where Joseph Malins was born on 21 October 1844.[48] He had two older brothers and a younger sister, in addition to four siblings who died in early childhood.

Drink and bad times reduced the elder Malins to the status of a journeyman. When he decided to make a fresh start at Birmingham as a cabinetmaker, his wife insisted that he take a total abstinence pledge before she would follow him there with their children. ("She and her infant children . . . travelled all night in a carrier's cart.") At Birmingham the Malinses prospered for a time, so at age eight Joseph Malins entered King Edward VI's School in the company of his brother Clement.[49]

Unfortunately, John Malins took to drink again, and after a year or two of schooling young Joseph began a lifetime of work, earning eighteen pence a week for filing watchkeys ten hours a day, every day but the Sabbath. At twelve he was employed at bookbinding and subsequently found work at a stationery and printing shop. At fourteen he entered an apprenticeship as a decorative painter or, according to an alternative account, as a furnituremaker, presumably painting furniture. When nearing seventy he recalled these years of poverty and hard work: "I have been 'chivied' [chased away] from the railway stations for saying 'Carry your bag, sir?'"[50]

A month after his father died, Joseph Malins, then aged sixteen, took the total abstinence pledge.[51] Although a Wesleyan Methodist, he chose two years later to join an Anglican temperance

organization, the St. Thomas's, Bow Street, Total Abstinence Society, and also took part in Bible lessons on Sunday afternoons at
St. Thomas's. In its two years of existence the Bow Street society
persuaded over 1,600 persons to sign the pledge. Young Malins occupied a seat on its executive committee and served as its book agent.
When a new rector showed himself hostile to the society, it broke up,
and many of its adherents migrated to the Hope Street Temperance
Society. During the two years that Malins belonged to the Hope
Street organization, it recruited eight hundred members.[52]

In his teens and early twenties Malins improved himself by
attending evening classes. Like other mid-Victorian autodidact workingmen who "grafted on to the Protestant stock . . . the English
literary tradition," he "acquired a library of improving books" and
read widely, with special fondness for theology, ancient history, and
Shakespeare.[53] He attended lectures by the famous temperance advocate Dr. F.R. Lees, nearly thirty years his senior, who many years
later took part in the institution of the Grand Lodge of England and
still later became Malins's adversary in the great schism. In 1865 he
began to contribute poems and stories to the *Alliance News,* the
weekly newspaper of the United Kingdom Alliance, a prohibition
society: In his own words, "he was an Alliance man before he was
a man."[54]

About this time his apprenticeship ended, and at age twenty-
two he took over his master's furniture-painting business. He entered into an arrangement over minimum pricing with other small
masters in a Birmingham trade society of decorative painters. His
discovery that some of those who had signed the agreement under-
cut the others by working for lower rates contributed to his decision
to emigrate to the United States after attending a lecture on America at the local temperance hall. After Malins informed the Hope
Street Society of his decision, his friends gave him a farewell supper
and a purse. On 8 November 1866 Malins delivered his final lecture
for the society, at which time its leaders provided him with a testimonial to present to temperance organizations in the New World.[55]

Before he left, Malins became a family man. He was engaged to
the daughter of a commercial traveler, Lucy Ellen Jones, four years
his senior, whom he had met when they both worked at bookbinding.
At first he intended to send for her after he got a job in the United
States, but his mother persuaded him that they should marry at
once and emigrate together. Joseph and Lucy married on 11 November 1866 (their marriage certificate describes him as a furniture
painter), and three days later the young couple sailed to Portland,

Maine.[56] They traveled from there to Philadelphia, where he became a grainer, decorating the woodwork of railroad coaches for the Pennsylvania Railroad. Their only daughter, Frances Alice, was born on 16 September 1867. He planned to set up as a furniture dealer, and some accounts say that in fact he did so on Market Street in West Philadelphia, but the illness of his wife and perhaps homesickness made them decide in May 1868 to change their plans and return to England.[57]

At work in Philadelphia, Malins met an Englishman from his native county of Worcestershire, an ex-drunkard who belonged to the Templar Order. Drink had reduced this man from a position of responsibility to one of sweeping and keeping fires. Having recovered his sobriety with the aid of the lodge, he became the missionary who recruited Malins.[58] Malins joined the IOGT shortly after the birth of his daughter, probably on 13 October 1867, at Ketchum (or Ketcham) lodge, West Philadelphia. His initial experience there was chilly: "No one greeted him during the recess . . . and it was a wonder he ever went to the Lodge again."[59] Yet despite this unfortunate beginning he quickly grew enthusiastic about Good Templary.

When he decided to return home, Malins wanted to take the Templar Order to England—a seemingly naive ambition for a new member who had never held office or been initiated into more than the first degree. But a Templar who was about to depart for Detroit to represent Pennsylvania at an RWGL session advised the head of Malins's lodge that he could meet the young Englishman at the West Philadelphia railroad depot at ten in the evening: "I could then talk the matter over more fully, besides making his acquaintance, which is important, as I must be able to give some sort of a voucher for him."[60] When Malins met the delegate, he handed over the Hope Street testimonial that he had brought from England to establish his credibility. A few days later the delegate returned with authorization for Malins to organize the IOGT in England. The midsummer night before he sailed, a sleepy Malins was initiated into the second and third degrees, though his official commission arrived only after he had returned to England to resume his career as a furniture painter. Malins retained little direct contact with the RWGL, but Isaac Newton Peirce, the Quaker historian of the IOGT, who had met him in Philadelphia, sent him letters of encouragement.

Young Malins was by no means so self-assured as the patriarch who stares out from the frontispiece of his biography. When he retired, he acknowledged that he had started with no grand ambitions but simply did the task at hand. He broke down in his first attempt at making a speech,[61] and some critics sneered that he affected a slight Yankee accent.[62] A contemporary commented that his features were "not very expressive, except the small but sharp eyes." One of his most enthusiastic supporters, when he visited her lodge five years after his return to England, described him as "a short, slight young man with a smooth face, . . . so boyish that I could scarcely believe he was indeed the veritable Joseph Malins." Malins later described himself as "a young stripling with no presence, means, influence, or speaking power" who "grew with the work."[63]

Organizing the Templars in England went slowly at first. Malins had returned home only a year after most urban working-men had been enfranchised and two years before Parliament created a system of state elementary schools. Denominations such as the Wesleyan Methodists had not yet formed their own temperance organizations, and few women were active temperance workers. Although a handful of Liberal MPs supported prohibition by local referendum, most scoffed at the idea. The principal prohibition-ist organization, the United Kingdom Alliance, had only a few thousand members, most of them middle class. The future backbone of the Templar Order, working-class and lower-middle-class Noncon-formists, showed no enthusiasm for Malins's message. The medical profession and the ministers had not been persuaded that total abstinence benefited physical and moral health.[64]

A longtime teetotaler who joined the IOGT in the early 1870s recalled that "many looked upon [Good Templary] as an absurd American notion."[65] For instance, English abstainers regarded Templar constitutions and rules as excessively complex. Unlike the existing fraternal temperance societies in England, such as the Rech-abites, the Templars offered no mutual insurance scheme.[66] Many reformers were suspicious about women attending the meetings of a secret society and the assertion of the equality of the sexes within the Order. Malins was accused of being a republican and a freethinker.[67] A fad of temperance "Life-Boat crews" had swept Birmingham and then collapsed, so embarrassed reformers were reluctant to support a fresh novelty.[68] Once, when Malins offered to pay another temper-ance society in cash for a few minutes of speaking time at the end of its public meeting, he was refused. Another time, when he was al-lowed to speak, he was interrupted in reading his paper on behalf of the Templars so that another speaker could make his own remarks in time to have them reported in the morning newspapers.[69]

Probably the situation for the early Templars in England was similar to that in Scotland, for which some vivid testimony survives.

Scotland got its first Templar lodge seven months after England did but counted ninety affiliated lodges when England had instituted only a dozen. The RWGL sent a teacher turned bookstore keeper, "a quiet-looking little Scotchman [Thomas Roberts, who had emigrated to the United States in 1846] to plant the banner of Good Templarism in his native land," but "not one of the existing [temperance] associations would receive him." Consequently, "he began among *the people,* and in a little shop, situated in a back street in Glasgow, a few were initiated; there were only baskets for seats and bales of goods for tables." Yet in ten months the IOGT had over a thousand Scottish members. The self-reliant Scots avoided dependence on wealthy benefactors: "We support ourselves, and we can say what we like, for we don't care for [the opinions of] anybody."[70]

Roberts had among his first initiates two important converts, Thomas Mackie, president of the Glasgow United Working Men's Total Abstinence Society, and the pugnacious Jabez Walker, an English-born agent of the Scottish Permissive Bill and Temperance Association and earlier of the Ayrshire Temperance Union. Contrary to the claim that the IOGT received no help from established organizations, the Templars were supported by many workers in the Permissive Bill Association and the City of Glasgow Temperance Electoral Association. The weekly newspaper of the Evangelical Union, the *Christian News,* also promoted the Templar cause, and its printers soon published in addition the monthly *Good Templar.*[71] The Templars quickly became popular as well in western Scotland, where they allied themselves with Thomas Corbett's Great Western Cooking Depot, which sold "penny lunches" to workingmen to "lure them from public houses." The Grand Lodge held its organizational meeting at the Cooking Depot's hall. The Templars were also helped by the strong connections that reformers in Glasgow had established with the United States. Despite its comparatively small population, Scotland initiated over a million Templars in the nineteenth century.[72]

In England success came more slowly. Malins arranged a tea and conference with leaders of Birmingham's Band of Hope Union, but "it was not a case of love at first sight." Uncomfortable about making a speech, he instead asked for questions: "Only one of the invited guests was induced then to join."[73] Despite this inauspicious start, Columbia lodge, named in honor of the United States, initiated eleven members when it was instituted at Morton Chapel on 8 September 1868. Within a week eighteen had joined, and they are counted as Columbia's charter members. Malins recruited fifteen of them from the then defunct Hope Street Temperance Society, which he had belonged to prior to emigrating to America. Among the little band of charter members were family: Malins's mother and wife and his brother Clement, who was elected secretary.

Even in so small a group, there were quarrels and intrigues. According to Clement Malins, "a cloud arose" when a couple of members tried to oust Joseph Malins. Their pretext was that he had a traveling card, not the clearance card necessary for transfer from his old Philadelphia lodge to the one in Birmingham. The RWGL officers in North America backed Malins against the rebels.

Unable to afford travel, Malins focused on Birmingham. The second lodge was organized on 12 December 1868 at Clement Malins's business premises, Oriental Ink Works, and Clement became its Worthy Chief Templar. When the Templars invited thirty guests for a Christmas soiree, only two showed up. Trying to make the IOGT attractive, the Templars sponsored a singing class. After nine months there were still only three lodges, all in Birmingham. They "had suffered by emigration; but the new recruits more than made up the deficiency; and the total membership was 47." In May 1869 Joseph Malins reported that his diary recorded that he had made 202 visits in the previous three months. For instance, he had courted a rag dealer who attended infrequently; Malins gave up on him when he admitted that after a year of abstinence he had gone back to drinking: "Last Saturday my Missus give me a dish of mushrooms and I felt it would go good with a pot o' porter and I had one." Malins irked officers by knocking on their doors at six in the morning to instruct them in their kitchens. By the end of the first year two more lodges had been organized, a fourth in Birmingham (named after George Washington) and, late in November, one in London.[74]

The early meetings were humble happenings. Columbia lodge began at a chapel next to a washhouse. On meeting nights "often as many cockroaches as members [were] present." Bothered by the noise of tub-thumping, the lodge moved to "the rear of a penny pie shop." The heat drove the lodge to move a second time, to premises over a stable. The stench was terrible. The lodge moved to more respectable quarters at the Unitarian mission room and later to the St. Martin's church school.[75]

What was Malins's message? From early days he emphasized the universalism of the Templar Order. During a public meeting at Birmingham on 14 November 1869 Malins said that the Templars welcomed people of all creeds and colors. He pointed out that women headed three lodges in England at a time when there were only seven. He defended the role of the Templars as a secret society that employed rituals by minimizing their secrecy and emphasizing their respectability. He explained that the Order's "ceremonies were only kept private to make them more impressive" and that "the initiation consisted of good advice, reading of scripture, and prayer and praise to God."[76]

The Grand Lodge of England was organized on 25 July 1870 in Birmingham with only twelve lodges, eight of them located there. Ten subordinate lodges was the minimum number for a Grand Lodge and ten members the minimum number for a lodge. According to one account, Malins had to split a few of his lodges to create enough of them to qualify England for a Grand Lodge.[77] Malins was elected Grand Worthy Chief Templar. He relied heavily on old friends. A lay reader from St. Thomas's Church, Birmingham, who had organized the first temperance society Malins joined, briefly served as Grand Worthy Secretary, and when he resigned, Malins's Sunday School teacher at St. Thomas's took over this important office. Clement Malins was assistant Grand Worthy Secretary. The new Grand Lodge held a public meeting presided over by the United States consul, a lifelong abstainer.[78] Among the early organizers for the Grand Lodge of England were Templars from Ontario and Ohio, S.T. Hammond and David H. Throope.

Instituting the Grand Lodge did not mark any dramatic turning-point. Malins continued to work with almost no money other than the charter fees paid to him when he organized a subordinate lodge. At the end of 1869 the RWGL sent him a $60 grant but did not renew it in 1870. Neglecting his painting business to work for the IOGT, Malins came near the end of his resources. At Christmas 1870 he sold his overcoat for twelve shillings to pay for Templar handbills. His clothes looked so wretched that he declined to attend a Band of Hope meeting held during daylight. Unable to afford even potatoes, his family made do with the bread and pickles provided by a friendly bakery. He pawned his most prized book for four shillings; appropriately, it was *Don Quixote*. It was not until the Grand Lodge session in March 1871 that the English Templars could pay Malins a salary of 150 pounds. Later that year he laid down his paint brush to work full time for the Order. During these early years Malins developed as a speaker, writer, organizer, and administrator. "As the Order grew he grew in organising power, ability, usefulness," wrote his son later, "a splendid example of the self-made man."[79]

In May 1871 the Right Worthy Grand Lodge dropped "of North America" from its title in recognition of the expansion of the IOGT to

England and Scotland whose new Grand Lodges quickly surpassed in size those in the United States and Canada and challenged the North American hegemony. By late 1871 the growth of the Grand Lodge of England seemed inexorable, as the accompanying table shows.[80] In fact, Malins's Grand Lodge became larger than any previous Grand Lodge. Its membership peaked at over 210,000 in May 1874. Only the enthusiasm for "blue ribbon" gospel temperance, proclaiming the power of prayer and introduced from the United States in the late 1870s, offers any English parallel to this explosive growth.

Arguably, the Grand Lodge of England reached the zenith of its vitality in July 1873 when the RWGL met in London as the guest of its rapidly maturing daughter.[81] Earlier in the same month the Grand Lodge, not yet three years old, had met for its annual session in Bristol, where more than 1,200 delegates from over 2,000 lodges were in attendance and 10,000 persons joined a street procession. The Grand Lodge at that time claimed nearly 184,000 members. Malins impressed the delegates with a mountain of self-congratulatory statistics: during the preceding twelve months he had dispatched over 20,000 letters and circulars, and the Order had held more than 11,000 public meetings. In addition to publicity in temperance newspapers, the Order had attracted the interest of the general press. Lodge deputies and district deputies reported nearly 8,700 stories in local newspapers.[82]

The last day of the Bristol session marred his triumph; exhausted from overwork, Malins was unable to preside (subsequently, he suffered a number of such breakdowns). Otherwise, both July meetings were a time of glory for him, as he had overcome a host of internal enemies, and the slackening of Templar growth in England did not begin until the winter of 1873-74. This slowdown foreshadowed the sharp drop in membership that would devastate the Grand Lodge during 1874-75, preceding the great schism.

As a result of his Templar career Malins entered the middle class. As GWCT he received a salary of 500 pounds for his duties in the Grand Lodge, a magnificent income for an almost unschooled former furniture painter in his twenties. Shortly afterward, when membership plummeted, his salary was reduced to a still substantial 400 pounds. Malins headed the Grand Lodge of England until 1914. In the RWGL he was counsellor for 1874-76 and 1893-97, and RWGT in 1897-1905. In the breakaway RWGL of the World during the schism he served as secretary in 1876-80, RWGT in 1880-85, and counsellor in 1885-87. When they grew up, his four sons earned middle-class livings, the eldest as pharmacist, dentist and dental

Date	Lodges	Members
Sept. 1868	1	18
Nov. 1868	1	21
Feb. 1869	2	39
May 1869	3	47
Aug. 1869	5	97
Nov. 1869	7	159
Feb. 1870	9	200
May 1870	12	257
Aug. 1870	13	840
Nov. 1870	25	1,000
Feb. 1871	65	2,212
May 1871	125	5,200
Aug. 1871	235	11,750
Nov. 1871	390	19,500
Feb. 1872	580	29,000
May 1872	910	45,550
Aug. 1872	1,256	87,920
Nov. 1872 (estimated)	1,625	113,750

supply managing director, the others as foreign language teacher and headmaster, Methodist minister and artist, and sanitary inspector. Malins named his eldest son Templar and his third son Wilfrid Lawson, after the longtime leader of the United Kingdom Alliance. Malins's children all joined the Templar auxiliary at age five and grew up to be lifelong teetotalers.[83]

The elder Malins eventually held many temperance and local government offices. From 1884, when he helped establish it, until 1909 he served as honorary secretary of the National Temperance Federation, an umbrella organization for the advanced temperance party, and was elected presiding officer in 1913. He also became a vice-president of the venerable United Kingdom Alliance, as well as of the British, Midland, and Western Temperance Leagues. In 1913 he was elected president of the National Association of Temperance Officials, an insurance society. In 1889 he enjoyed the support of all the political parties in his election to the Worcester county council. In 1907 he became a justice of the peace and in 1911-20 served as alderman, strongly promoting technical education. When Malins died in 1926 he left a modest estate of 1,748 pounds two pence, one-fifth of which went to the Grand Lodge.[84]

In 1926, the year Malins died, he appeared to have been the inevitable leader of the English Templars, but from the perspective of
the early 1870s it is surprising that the inexperienced young man
managed to retain control of the Grand Lodge after it grew beyond
its humble Birmingham origins to become the largest temperance
organization in England. Numerous potential rivals, established
figures in the temperance movement, joined the Templar Order—
successful businessmen, respected Nonconformist ministers, experienced temperance agents and lecturers—encouraged by their
perception that the Templars might succeed in consolidating the
mass of working-class and lower-middle-class teetotalers as a temperance voting bloc. For instance, John Kempster joined the IOGT to
provide the United Kingdom Alliance with mass support, although he
disliked regalia (thinking himself too old, he said, to wear a baby's
bib).[85] The support of such veteran reformers helped turn the struggling Templar lodges into a national giant, but the self-assured
new recruits did not necessarily feel any loyalty to Malins. The fact
that he had introduced the IOGT to England guaranteed him nothing; in Scotland the Grand Lodge never elected Thomas Roberts to
any office, and he quietly returned to the United States. In fact, few
Grand Lodges anywhere remained loyal to the same Grand Worthy
Chief Templar for more than four or five years, and no other for
the forty-odd consecutive years that Malins achieved. Repeatedly
overcoming critics in the tumultuous 1870s and 1880s who had more
experience, more status, and more money, Malins almost never faced
an opponent at re-election. His enemies knew he was too popular to
lose in a vote.[86]

His critics attacked Malins as vain and insecure, quick to crush
anyone who appeared independent-minded, a kind of spider at
the center of a web of power and patronage. Many of his enemies
disliked ritual and regalia and wanted smaller, provincial Grand
Lodges. The campaigns against Malins combined differences in principle with a struggle for power. Many Templar pioneers left the IOGT
after a quarrel with him. For instance, the celebrated Methodist
minister Charles Garrett, once an enthusiastic supporter, became
a bitter opponent. Yet there is always a case to be made for Malins
in what might look like ceaseless purges of the people who had
helped him when he was in need. Adversaries who tried to set up
rival Templar organizations turned out to be leaders without follow-
ers. Even factions which, defeated by Malins in early battles, enjoyed
his discomfort in later conflicts rarely joined subsequent anti-Malins
factions, a fact that facilitated his success in the piecemeal struggles.

Despite all his problems Malins strengthened his position in England during the great schism. Those leaders who did not join the Hickmanites became bound to Malins by their partnership in the fight for equal rights. He faced another challenge when he ended the split in 1886-87 on terms that in the opinion of close allies sacrificed the ideal of racial equality. Many well-known Templars, including much of what remained of its small upper-middle class, opposed him over the terms of reunion, but most accepted defeat and remained in the IOGT. A much diminished Grand Lodge of England, with fewer than 45,000 adult members, was alive and well and very much under Malins's control when he retired as its chief on the eve of the First World War.

The English Templars had created a vibrant organization. The membership was unevenly scattered; a sketch map published in 1885 shows the IOGT strong in regions as diverse as metropolitan London and South Lancashire and Durham, while weak in agricultural districts such as East Anglia. "Some Lodges consist of poor folk doing good work among the poor; most of the Lodges have workmen, clerks and tradesmen fraternally mingled."[87] In any case, during its first twenty-six years in England the IOGT administered the teetotal pledge to more than 1,300,000 persons over age fifteen.[88] The Grand Lodge operated a complex and sophisticated machinery; for instance, in the mid-1880s the Templar press in England comprised eleven different periodicals.

In large part Malins owed his success to a willingness to work and work and work still more. During the great schism he traveled to Sweden at two hours' notice when he learned of an opportunity to organize Templars loyal to his faction.[89] In the early 1880s he said that when at his office he put in a twelve-hour day. Out of exhaustion he often slept on the speakers' platform before his time to speak.[90] When on the road, he traveled by night in order to keep the day for work, rarely stayed anywhere a day more than his itinerary required, and often had departed before his hosts rose for breakfast. He took virtually no holidays other than sea travel. Malins made thirty-seven transatlantic round trips and once traveled around the world on Templar business. He never watched an entire cricket or football match and seldom permitted himself diversions. After his retirement he said that he still rose when he heard "the tramcars at 4:45 A.M."[91]

In addition to maintaining an enormous correspondence and making frequent speeches, he was a prolific editor and writer for temperance publications. Committed to public readings, recitations, singing, and all sorts of competitions, he put out the popular *Prize Reciter and Reader* for a decade and wrote large quantities of verse such as "Factory Chimney" and "The Fence and the Ambulance." He also published as a separate book a more ambitious propaganda poem, *Professor Alcoholico,* about the evil magician intoxicating drink.[92]

Malins had little use for moderation and compromise. His commitment to the Templar cause was absolute and unshakable, his temper suspicious.[93] He was a worker and a fighter, a master of the inner workings of Templar politics, a highly effective presiding officer, and enormously popular with the English rank and file. In his hatred of the drink trade he drew little distinction between the sin and sinner. In 1872, at the first RWGL session that he attended he heard with unhappiness an Alabama representative urge the Templars to "use the soft words of persuasion, not abuse the rum seller, but pity him." The young Malins rejected the notion of pity for publicans. In a brutal play on words, he said that instead of being afforded pity, "in his opinion, they ought to be pitted with the small pox."[94]

Throughout his life Malins was fiercely protective of the principles of the advanced temperance movement, the IOGT, and the Grand Lodge of England, and identified himself completely and proudly with the organizations he served. At the end of his many years as head of the Grand Lodge, Malins described himself as "not a very humble man."[95] When he died, the *Manchester Guardian* (7 January 1926) characterized the history of the Templars in England as "largely the life story of Malins."

Although the adult membership in England had fallen to below 66,000 by the end of the great schism and the numerical decline continued, the Grand Lodge endured and remained an important part of the temperance movement for many decades. In contrast, most of the Grand Lodges in the large and lightly populated American South disappeared before the end of the nineteenth century or lingered as ghosts before surrendering their charters in the early 1900s. It was not that the people of the South repudiated teetotalism and prohibition. Local option legislation made more and more of the region dry, particularly in the rural districts. The Woman's Christian Temperance Union flourished, as later did the Anti-Saloon League. By contrast, prohibition was nearly dead in English politics by 1895, while the IOGT remained relatively strong. By the end of the nineteenth century the strength of prohibition-temperance had become disconnected from the IOGT in the Anglo-American world.

Although the Grand Lodge of England now is very small, its historical record is secure. Hickman has been forgotten, while Malins remains revered in the worldwide IOGT.[96]

3

The Road to Louisville

After the Civil War several paths and tracks crisscrossed on the way to Louisville in 1876. In justifying their behavior, Templar factions quarreled over the relative importance of the resulting controversies in bringing the IOGT to the great schism, each faction assigning blame for the fratricidal disruption to people other than themselves.

On these intersecting disputes the central collision, affecting all the others, was the struggle over African American membership— especially in the former slave states. White southerners quarreled about how to protect white supremacist policies, by secession or compromise. To mollify critics from outside their region, they created an African American fraternal temperance society, the True Reformers, which the British and many blacks dismissed as a demeaning kitchen order. Along another road to Louisville the British resisted proposals for multiple or duplicate Grand Lodges in the same geographical jurisdiction. North Americans saw such a constitutional change as opening a new segregated route through which blacks could enter the IOGT, while the British feared it as a stratagem preparing for the breakup of the large Grand Lodges of England and Scotland.

The emergence of powerful Grand Lodges in Britain and in the American South aggravated the strife over black membership. Without these Grand Lodges separated by thousands of miles and divergent racial attitudes the great schism would not have occurred, for in 1876 Templars in the northern states who identified with the abolitionist heritage played a marginal role, and most of them ended up on the side of the white southerners.

The larger racist culture affected the IOGT, but the turmoil over race among the Templars demonstrated that a universalist ideology softened or at least complicated racism. Virtually all other fraternal orders in North America simply rejected blacks. There is little evidence to suggest that the northern and Canadian lodges in such societies objected to the racial views of their southern brethren.

Decades before the Civil War, white Freemasonry's Grand
Lodges admitted a handful of blacks to white lodges. In the first
few years after the Civil War the reaction against slavery made a few
white Masons eager to show that they repudiated extreme racism,
so they admitted another half-handful. For instance, in December
1867 the *New England Freemason* mentioned a Boston-area caterer,
Joshua Bowen Smith, whose skin color—"a shade darker than the
Caucasian"—and facial features were not decidedly African. Also in
1867 the Grand Master of New Jersey urged his fellow Masons to
honor the "universal brotherhood of man" by admitting persons of all
races and religions. Five years later the newly organized Alpha lodge
in Newark, New Jersey, admitted black members. But after it elected
a black man as Worshipful Master in 1878, the white members
drifted away. Into the mid-twentieth century Alpha lodge stood out as
the only black lodge affiliated with a white Grand Lodge, and in 1950
only one person who admitted to being black was a member of an
otherwise white Masonic lodge in the United States. The racism that
afflicted Freemasonry had grown rigid. The white Grand Lodges did
not even acknowledge the legitimacy of the numerous independent
black Masonic organizations, often called Prince Hall lodges.[1]

Other fraternal temperance societies sometimes admitted
blacks. The Good Samaritans did so a few months after the organization was established in 1847. As a result of white defections, the
Good Samaritans became virtually an all-black organization during
the Reconstruction era when African Americans could join in large
numbers.[2]

After the end of slavery the Sons of Temperance opened their
doors to blacks a little. In 1866 the National Division delegated discretionary authority over black membership to the Grand Divisions.
Four years later the National Division authorized the Most Worthy
Patriarch to organize segregated Grand Divisions for blacks wherever the white Grand Division approved. In the following year the
National Division, meeting at Boston, seated "without discussion"
William Wells Brown, a black representative of the virtually all-
white host Grand Division of Massachusetts, and "after considerable
discussion" a delegate from a new all-black Grand Division of Maryland. In a shift from its policy of organizing black Grand Divisions,
the National Division then declared its dislike of segregation and distinctions based on "race, color, or former condition."[3]

Despite the fact that this affirmation of racial inclusion was
never enforced, the Sons of Temperance lost many white southerners. A member of a rival fraternal organization sneered: "If the

negroes desire Temperance Lodges in Georgia, let *'em take massa's old coat,'"* the Sons of Temperance.[4] The editor of the *National Temperance Advocate,* John N. Stearns, helped orchestrate a northern revolt against the "most unfortunate" initiative of 1871. In 1872 only five votes were cast against a committee report advocating repeal of the controversial Boston resolutions. The convention returned discretionary authority over black members to the Grand Divisions, with a toothless reservation: "subject to the review and control of the National Division at its annual sessions."[5]

The attempt of the Sons of Temperance to be racially inclusive resulted in segregated organizations for a few blacks and a place in predominantly white societies for even fewer, but though it altered the official rhetoric, it did not much increase the appeal to African American people. William Wells Brown, who had been a fugitive slave, became disillusioned with the halfheartedness of the National Division. In 1875 he failed in his final effort to persuade the Sons to champion equal rights and thereafter pinned his hopes upon another fraternal temperance order—the Good Templars.[6]

The Templars began without making race an explicit criterion for membership. Unlike the Sons of Temperance, the IOGT initiated a few black people during the age of slavery, and in 1853 a lodge located in a small town in upstate New York placed a black man on its delegation to the second meeting of the Grand Lodge. A Quaker abolitionist who wrote an early history of the Templars emphasized that James R. Jones was dark-skinned, of pure African descent.[7]

In the absence of any general policy about black membership, however, the decision to admit or exclude could be inconsistent. In 1854 a Cleveland, Ohio, lodge by a narrow majority admitted a black man, William Howard Day, later editor of the *Aliened American,* but by another narrow majority it rejected his wife, Lucie, an Oberlin graduate, "simply for her color." An angry minority withdrew to organize Freedom lodge, which gladly accepted both husband and wife.[8]

Often Grand Lodges set racial policies. In 1855 the Grand Lodge of Indiana placed a moratorium on the organization of black lodges while a committee considered creating a special ritual for them—in effect, a separate order. A unanimous vote at the Grand Lodge of Missouri expelled a black slave admitted by Sonora lodge and declared the charter of the offending lodge forfeit. The Grand Lodge of Ohio, seeking to encourage black lodges, made them separate and unequal; the RWGL had drafted a new ritual, so the Grand Lodge donated all the obsolete rituals to whatever impecunious black lodges might be instituted. In 1859 the Grand Lodge of Wisconsin recognized "*no* exclusive distinctions in our Order on account of nationality, creed or color," but seven years later its GWCT ruled that a member might blackball a prospective initiate on the basis of race if the member believed it would be for the good of the Order.[9]

For blacks the Templar Order posed some of the same contradictions that it did for women, but without the minimal acceptance that women could take for granted. No one challenged the right of women to be members or to hold token executive offices. The only consensus about blacks appeared to be that they could be members where whites let them, and some white supremacists wanted to close even this half-open door. Only a small minority of Templars appeared to have been committed to local or subordinate lodge integration. Nearly all white Templars looked upon blacks through racist spectacles, but the racism varied considerably, so, to continue the figure of speech, not everyone could wear the same eyeglasses with comfort.[10]

After the Civil War, blacks in the northeastern and midwestern United States and in the Canadian provinces of Nova Scotia and Ontario began to join the Templar Order in conspicuous numbers, though mostly forming segregated lodges. The nature of their welcome often revealed northern racism. In 1865 an antiblack faction at Milton lodge, Janesville, Wisconsin, tried to trick a black member, Andrew Pratt, into resigning by telling him that his membership might destroy the lodge and that if he refused he would be expelled anyway. In this case, fifty defenders threatened to withdraw from the lodge unless Pratt remained.[11] Illinois's GWCT uneasily granted charters to black lodges: whether blacks were "man or monkey, human or brute," he said, "one fact is patent—mean whiskey will make them drunk—and when drunk they act about as bad as white men."[12] Anna Raymond asked Raymond lodge (named in her honor) to establish fellowship with a black lodge in Jersey City. Her resolution carried, but the thirty-one to thirteen vote showed substantial opposition.[13] In 1873 the Grand Lodge of Nova Scotia organized four lodges for blacks with over three hundred members. Condemning proposals for a separate black fraternal society, the GWCT declared that the province's black population "embrace our principles with avidity."[14]

Following the enactment of the Thirteenth Amendment abolishing slavery, northern leaders promoted black membership, something that seemed a practicable goal since many blacks supported the temperance movement and were joining fraternal lodges. In 1866 the RWGT, Samuel D. Hastings of Wisconsin, ruled: "I do not understand that our Order takes in account the color of a man's skin any more than it does the color of his hair or eyes," so a Grand Lodge should "proceed in all cases as though they were white." Answering another question, he added: "There is no law of our Order that would interfere with the granting of Charters for Lodges composed of persons of African descent, and my own opinion is that it would be expedient to encourage them in every way in our power to protect themselves from the evils of intemperance, and to aid in our efforts to drive intemperance from the land." He emphasized his "most earnest desire that in meeting questions of this kind the Order of Good Templars may always take the high ground of *Christian principle,* and trust in God that all will be well in the end."[15]

The questions that Hastings answered show the assumption of white Templars that if blacks were to join the Templar Order, most of them would belong to segregated local lodges. In the subordinate lodge, members were fictive brothers and sisters, and the weekly meeting was a kind of family gathering. Some of the whites who took local segregation for granted, however, believed that black members had a right to representation at Grand Lodge and RWGL sessions where the social aspect of the IOGT was less prominent.

Hastings made his celebrated rulings when the Civil War was barely over and virtually no one was prepared to dispute his defense of black membership. In 1866 the IOGT had only a few white southern members, mostly in border states that had not seceded. The situation was much the same in the following year when the RWGL met in Detroit. The representative from Kentucky, Dr. W.J. Berry, went home with the resolution that his Grand Lodge had adopted denouncing black membership still in his pocket, having realized that Kentucky would get no support.[16]

During the early Reconstruction years the Templars sent organizers into the former Confederacy. In 1867 the Committee on the State of the Order recommended that Grand Lodges with large memberships help support lecturers who would go there to organize "without distinction of race or color."[17] That fall the RWGT commissioned several deputies: one instituted a Grand Lodge of Tennessee; another organized several lodges in Virginia; still another visited Georgia for a few weeks with no success. All these organizing efforts took place among whites.

Hastings sent a Congregational minister, Thomas H.L. Tallcott of Connecticut, to organize lodges in the Carolinas, where he worked from October 1867 until April 1868. Although he instituted a couple of lodges in Charleston, South Carolina, most of his modest success took place in North Carolina. The official record listed nine lodges. According to William Wells Brown's account, Tallcott did better than that, though he had no success during his first two weeks. Then, while getting a Saturday afternoon shave, he told his barber about the Templar mission. When the barber, a black man who also was a preacher, learned that Tallcott had tried only among the whites, he invited him to preach at his church, extravagantly promising Tallcott 200 members. According to Brown, by the time Tallcott left North Carolina in 1868 he had organized eleven lodges, one of them white, three mostly black, and the others entirely black in membership. Since the state had no Grand Lodge, they received the quarterly password directly from the Right Worthy Grand Secretary, J.A. Spencer, a critic of racism who in 1854 had helped organize Freedom lodge.[18]

The formerly slaveholding border states of Maryland, Missouri, and West Virginia and the District of Columbia acknowledged a few black members in the years following the Civil War. In 1867 the Grand Worthy Secretary of the District of Columbia refused to provide General Oliver O. Howard, commissioner of the Freedmen's Bureau, and his brother General Charles H. Howard a set of ritual books and a charter to institute a lodge "because [the secretary] believed that this new Lodge intended to admit some colored persons!" Supporting the two generals, the GWCT instituted Purity lodge, but the executive committee withdrew the charter. The dispute was appealed to the RWGT. On the technical ground that the lodge had not been given two weeks' notice and a hearing, he ordered the restoration of the charter. Purity lodge admitted two black men "of eminent intelligence and moral worth." Opponents of black membership seceded to organize the Legion or Cohorts of Temperance.[19]

Maryland had the most black Templars. In 1868 the GWCT recommended organizing black lodges and five years later Maryland claimed over 800 black members, about a third of the state's membership. Supposedly, the blacks did "not desire a mixed membership in the Subordinate Lodges."[20] They got Grand Lodge representation only on the eve of the great schism. Resenting the blacks, most of the white Templars in Maryland withdrew to form a separate Grand Lodge once the RWGL authorized multiple Grand Lodges in the same geographical jurisdiction.

The other border states had only a handful of black members. For Missouri there is a report from 1867 of Fletcher lodge, Jefferson City, consisting of thirty women and twenty men, mostly black. Only five of the black members could read well enough to serve as officers, so the lodge had "to depend on the assistance of white Brothers and Sisters." In 1868 the Grand Lodge of West Virginia chartered a black lodge at Clarksburg. Six years later the question of a newly chartered black lodge at Charleston inflamed a meeting of the Grand Lodge, which refused to seat the black delegates and voted not to charter any more black lodges. According to a local historian, "This matter caused a great deal of warm discussion, bitter feelings and unbrotherly conduct."[21]

By the time of the RWGL meeting in Richmond, Indiana, in 1868, the white South could no longer be ignored. Since the previous year the subordinate lodges in Kentucky had increased from 74 to 121, while those in neighboring Tennessee had grown from a single lodge to 26. Representatives of the two states challenged the Templar Order with a resolution that sought "to take the sense of this R.W. Grand Lodge on the subject of admitting to membership in our Order, on terms of perfect equality, the negroes of the South."[22] Blacks rubbed elbows with southern whites at this meeting of the RWGL. When, in an oratorical flourish a Kentuckian pointed to a door and said "Just so sure as you allow colored persons to enter that door . . ." several black Templars entered. The southerner whose speech had been interrupted was the genial Tim Needham, who joined in the laughter.[23]

In response to the white southerners, the RWGL created a committee made up mostly of northerners. The majority report spoke mildly on behalf of equal rights for all races but conceded that the RWGL had no jurisdiction where a Grand Lodge existed—and in the former slave states the Grand Lodge refused to charter black lodges. This was the case for the Grand Lodge of Kentucky, organized in 1854 and reorganized in 1864. Since the RWGL mandate that Grand Lodge and subordinate lodge constitutions contain no racial restrictions came later, and was not retroactive, Kentucky's continued unaffected, as even champions of racial equality conceded. Hence, the committee's northern majority defended the right of Kentucky to do as it chose, although lamenting that it chose to do what it did: "We hope that soon, in the providence of God, Kentucky will receive that higher light of a most ennobling, political and christian faith, that all men are 'equal' before the law, and that God hath made of one blood all men that dwell on the face of the earth."[24] In practice the RWGL averted its eyes when newer southern Grand Lodges violated the legislation meant to protect blacks.

In a minority report a Tennessee delegate urged creation of a segregated order for blacks to be entitled the Colored Templars of

North America, with its own ritual, passwords, and signs. He wanted supplies to be furnished without charge to existing black Templar lodges, which would be compulsorily transferred to the new organization. For a decade white southerners would pursue this segregationist strategy of entirely separate organizations for the two races. But northerners sympathetic to the black cause still dominated the RWGL in 1868. General O.O. Howard successfully amended the majority report to demand that "that a colored membership should not exclude a regularly organized Lodge from the Grand Lodge, to which it would otherwise be entitled to admission."[25] Only a handful of votes were cast against the amended majority report, including three from Ontario, a Canadian province that struck an enduring alliance with the American South.[26] In any event, no Grand Lodge in the old Confederacy would charter a black lodge, so the amendment was of only symbolic importance.

Templar lodges for blacks remained an anomaly in the former slave states. For instance, in 1871 a white man who had moved from Philadelphia to Port Gibson, Mississippi, asked a Pennsylvania friend to describe the various temperance societies so that he could choose one for the local freedmen. The result of this inquiry was the chartering directly by the RWGL, in September 1872, of Olive Branch lodge, with over 250 members. The lodge died when the RWGL, at the insistence of local whites who had subsequently organized their own Templar lodge, refused to renew the quarterly password.[27]

Frustrated by northern interference, some southern Templars met with other southern temperance reformers at Chattanooga late in 1871. Members of the Sons of Temperance, the Friends of Temperance, the Templars of Honor and Temperance, and the Knights of Jericho participated as well as Good Templars. A variety of grievances motivated the southerners: the decision earlier that year by the National Division of the Sons of Temperance in favor of racial integration, the presence of blacks at RWGL sessions, and the inflexibility that national governance structures imposed on state and local organizations. Hickman was elected a vice-president of the new Council of Temperance for the Southern States, a federation that claimed it did not seek to displace any existing temperance organization. Soon, however, a new defeat for the white southern Templars inspired the Council of Temperance to seek a more ambitious role.

The question of a separate organization for blacks was taken up in 1872 at the RWGL session in Madison, Wisconsin, with delegates from the Deep South participating for the first time. Georgia's secretary, W.E.H. Searcy, drafted a memorial in favor of a separate temperance society for blacks. With the support of Alonzo S. Elliott, Alabama's secretary, he suggested an Order of Colored Templars, which would use the ritual and supplies of the Good Templars but replace the word "good" with the word "colored" and make changes in the unwritten symbols such as signs and grips. All black Good Templars wherever they were located would be transferred to the new organization, and no blacks could join the IOGT in the future. Later, Searcy explained that Elliott and he wanted not to make the IOGT "the father and patron" of the African American society but rather to "clean our hands of the work of fraternal recognition."[28]

At this point the young Grand Lodge of England intervened.[29] Joseph Malins, attending his first RWGL session, proposed that the Grand Lodges create a society for blacks with its own distinct name and ritual. There was much controversy about his motives. His critics said that the effect of his proposal was to block a concession to blacks for something close to Templar membership; years later, Malins explained it as a parliamentary stratagem to keep the blacks in the IOGT, not evidence that he was a racist. In retrospect, he acknowledged that he had operated with "very limited information" about the facts of racial discrimination in the South: "Had we known all earlier, the Disruption [as many Templars euphemistically designated the great schism] might have taken place sooner." He never wanted to separate the races; indeed, at the Madison meeting he had warned Hastings that if the RWGL purged African Americans from the IOGT, his Grand Lodge "would probably sever."[30] White southern racism had provided a rude awakening for the representatives of England and Scotland: "The first Southerners we Britishers had ever spoken to" berated them for arranging that a black Templar whom they had met at Madison give a speech to the RWGL.[31]

The RWGL referred Malins's substitute proposal to a committee. It reported in favor of creating a separate organization for blacks under the supervision of the existing Grand Lodges on the model of the organizations already established for children. Templars from the South were appointed to prepare a ritual, subject to executive committee approval.[32] The southerners at Madison wanted the power to revoke the charters of the existing black Templar lodges, but they got only the right to revoke them "as provided by the Constitution," such as for nonpayment of dues.

The conspicuous presence of black Templars at Madison added to the anger of the disappointed Searcy. When a local black lodge helped Capitol lodge, a white organization, host a reception for delegates. Searcy exploded in racist rant: "The gentleman who welcomed our Southern Delegates to the R.W.G. Lodge, was a *big black buck nigger.*" The Georgian added that "among the party was a lovely lady, one of the noblest specimens of our Southern sisterhood," and as a result of the insulting presence of the black man, "our noble Sister shed tears at the humiliation."[33] Searcy also complained when a southern white woman was appointed to serve on a committee that included a black man. His *Temperance Watchman* quarreled with the *Keystone Good Templar* over the admission of blacks to the Templar Order. The *Watchman* declared that "we have too much respect for our sisters, mothers and wives to drag them into the company of an inferior and degraded race." The Pennsylvania newspaper urged Templars to "treat the black man as you treat the Irishman or the German,—having more respect for their *merit* than for their nationality."[34]

A few weeks after the RWGL spurned the Searcy-Elliott proposal for a segregated black society and the elimination of blacks from the IOGT, Searcy was elected secretary and Hickman president of the Council of Temperance of the Southern States at a second Chattanooga conference. The conference unanimously endorsed "consolidation upon a WHITE basis" of the various fraternal temperance societies and applauded the news of the preparation of "an organization for colored people exclusively."[35] Hickman was commissioned to meet with the various state fraternal societies to persuade them to join the new organization. Malins speculated that at an executive committee meeting held shortly afterward, John Russell of Michigan, the RWGT, conceded authority over blacks in the former slave states to the white southerners and that Russell's concession caused Hickman to change his mind over a break with the IOGT. It is a fact that despite his earlier role Hickman did not participate when the third Chattanooga conference, in November 1872, organized the United Friends of Temperance.[36]

In contrast with Hickman, other southern Templars remained dissatisfied with Templar policy. Searcy called on Georgia to withdraw from the IOGT. He claimed that an Augusta lodge, "a mess of Radicals," had admitted blacks (an improbable assertion), and he asked white temperance reformers to join the United Friends of Temperance. His *Temperance Watchman* said that only the assurances of Hickman, who presided at Georgia's annual session in 1872, kept the Grand Lodge from seceding. Loyalists in Georgia supported symbolic defiance, illegally adding a whites-only amendment to its constitution in 1872 and urging a separate temperance society for blacks as

gestures short of secession that might appease the white membership. The leaders of the Grand Lodge resented the sneer of the
United Friends that the Templar platform included "dark planks";
the GWCT, John W.H. Underwood, "born, raised, and educated" in
Georgia, refused to dignify with a reply this attack on his commitment to white supremacy and racial segregation.[37]

The white southern Templars insisted that they were reliably
racist and outspokenly rejected blacks as unfit for Templar membership. Together with North Carolina's illegal Article Ten that only
whites could belong, the (Raleigh) *Spirit of the Age* published the
promise of Rev. T.H. Pritchard, the state's GWCT: "I hereby pledge
myself to sever my connection with the Order at once if this article of
the constitution cannot be maintained." Georgia called the prospect
of black membership "an incubus" that had almost destroyed the
state's first lodge in Atlanta. An officer in Donaldsville lodge, South
Carolina, exploded when a local newspaper alleged that his lodge
had admitted blacks: "We don't take negroes in our Lodge" and if the
paper meant to advocate integration, "dont send me any nother
number." Louisiana had a lodge named Caucasian.[38]

The United Friends stood for states' rights and with exaggeration claimed to be the only "White Man's Temperance Order."[39]
The United Friends also objected to the involvement of temperance
societies with political parties, such as the close connection between
the Templars and the National Prohibition Party. In contrast with
its militant stand on racial separation, however, the United Friends
society was cautious in its interpretation of total abstinence; unlike
the Templars, it did not ban sweet cider. But like many organizations
called "united," the new society was crippled by disunity. Members
could not agree whether the teetotal pledge should be for life or
only for as long as the person was a member. This question could not
even be discussed at Chattanooga "for the simple reason that it
would have blown the body into fragments." The United Friends of
Temperance allowed the pledge to mean whatever the pledge-taker
chose.[40]

The Grand Lodge of Kentucky, the self-appointed champion of
the former slave states within the IOGT, worried that the RWGL
might charter black lodges in jurisdictions that lacked a white Grand
Lodge. As early as 1868, the Grand Lodge session voted "that we will
do all in our power to aid and assist the citizens of our sister Southern States who have no Grand Lodges, to prevent the organization of
negro Lodges of our Order in said States."[41] Accordingly, invited by a
state temperance convention, Kentucky's Hickman organized several

white lodges in North Carolina during 1872 and instituted a Grand Lodge there. Later he was criticized for not inviting the existing black lodges to the meeting that formed the Grand Lodge. In response he said that he had not known there were any black lodges in North Carolina and speculated that Tallcott's black lodges had become dormant until his own organizing efforts had "aroused" them.[42] After the establishment of the white Grand Lodge, the RWGL could no longer charter new subordinate lodges directly, and since the Grand Lodge refused to provide them with charters, black Templars in North Carolina could organize only outside Templar law.

Whatever their legal status, these black teetotalers regarded themselves as Templars. None of Tallcott's black lodges paid dues to the RWGL after May 1872, but blacks continued to use the IOGT name. During a revival of interest in 1873, thirteen blacks formed Queen of the South lodge at a meeting held over the Freedmen's Bank in Raleigh. As their chief they elected Charles N. Hunter, aged about twenty-one, who was employed at the bank.[43] Within a year the black Templars claimed 650 members throughout North Carolina. A statewide black Templar convention met in the eastern part of the state at New Bern early in June 1873 and proclaimed itself the Colored Grand Lodge.

Hunter's brother described the youthful delegates as "the bone and sinew of [black] North Carolina." Several were prominent in the African Methodist Episcopal Zion Church. Pennsylvania-born James W. Hood, a man in his early forties, had been consecrated a bishop the previous year. J.C. Price, who was in his late twenties, became a college president and the best-known black temperance advocate in the United States. Sixteen-year-old John C. Dancy worked as an apprentice typesetter. He later edited A.M.E. Zion periodicals and was appointed to lucrative federal posts.[44]

In his call for temperance Charles Hunter emphasized the poverty of black people and the need for moral emancipation. He attacked alcohol as a "fateful destroyer, initiating misery, want, degradation, and death" and argued that sobriety would be "one of the grandest arguments that blacks are yet to exert a powerful influence as a Nation." The convention elected him secretary of the newly organized black Grand Lodge; Edward R. Dudley, a Republican member of the state legislature who lived at New Bern, was chosen to head it. Only in his early thirties, Dudley was a cooper by trade and a Methodist by religion.[45]

Although the white Grand Lodge refused to admit black lodges or provide Dudley's Grand Lodge formal recognition, it did show some sympathy. "Believing the I.O.G.T. to be the best temperance organization known to us, and wishing the colored people to enjoy its full benefits," the Grand Lodge would help them so long as that did not mean accepting the social equality of the races. If the blacks could get lodge charters from other jurisdictions and form their own Grand Lodge, "we would interpose no legal objection, but bid them God speed." Chiding those whites who refused any cooperation, the official organ of the North Carolina Grand Lodge remonstrated: "If the negro has no soul, then take the Cross from him." The GWCT even arranged for Needham B. Broughton, partner in a large printing firm, to attend the New Bern convention. Broughton told the delegates that the white Grand Lodge rejected blacks as members merely out of "expediency." He wanted the black Templars to know that they "have our hearty sympathy in the cause of temperance."[46]

To this extent, blacks and whites managed to cooperate in North Carolina. In 1873 Dudley wrote the white Grand Lodge: "We have within three months organized fourteen lodges, with a membership of over three thousand, and have applications now for six or eight new lodges." The blacks needed rituals, degree books, membership cards, and other supplies: "Do help us; you have the power." The white Grand Lodge agreed to sell the blacks supplies at the standard prices as soon as the white officers became confident about the stability of the black organization. Some Templar rituals sold to blacks in North Carolina wound up in the hands of blacks in neighboring Virginia. When the GWCT of Virginia complained, Dudley protested that he had not authorized this resale.[47]

The debate on black access at the July 1873 RWGL session in London brought about a full-blown crisis, aggravated by confusion over the facts, which offered the United Friends an opportunity to supersede the IOGT in the South. Black lodges in North Carolina petitioned the RWGL for recognition as a duplicate segregated Grand Lodge on the ground that the white Grand Lodge would not admit them. The Committee on Memorials declined to recommend this kind of relief, since the Templar constitution precluded more than a single Grand Lodge for any geographical jurisdiction. Yet the committee sympathized and said that the white Grand Lodge of North Carolina was required to give the quarterly password to the black lodges if they had been legally instituted.

This report infuriated white southerners. Needham withdrew Kentucky's invitation offering Louisville as the site for the next RWGL meeting. Elliott of Alabama resigned a minor RWGL office. The London RWGL session was the first meeting held outside North

America, and there were only five southerners present. The first in-
dignant reports that they sent home gave exaggeratedly negative
accounts, so it is small surprise that the southern Grand Lodges got
in an uproar. Needham told the GWCT of Kentucky that the RWGL
had ordered North Carolina to give the quarterly password to black
lodges, "forcing upon our Grand Lodges the acceptance of the 'social
brotherhood of races,' or the abandonment of the Order, either of
which is terrible to contemplate."[48] Hickman, another Kentuckian
who had not attended the London meeting and so had a distorted
notion of what had happened there, telegraphed the various southern Grand Lodges to set up a convention to form a secessionist RWGL
South. Like Hickman, other southern Templars wanted to remain
Templars on their own terms. Alabama's *Crystal Fount* explained
that "because a parent is sometimes harsh and unjust to the son, it
does not cause the child to forfeit his name." The newspaper added
that the position of the white southerners had been misrepresented:
"We do not desire to withhold the benefits of Temperance Organization from the colored people, but on the other hand, have labored to
interest them in it."[49]

With the survival of the IOGT in the former slave states in
doubt, the United Friends seized the opportunity to win disgruntled
Templars over to their society. When the Grand Lodge of Georgia met
in September 1873, Searcy and Col. C.P. Crawford appeared as representatives of the United Friends to ask the Templars to join.
Spurning the United Friends, the leaders of the Grand Lodge did not
let themselves be outflanked. Judge Underwood, GWCT of Georgia,
advocated secession from the international RWGL, and a committee
that included a moderate named J.G. Thrower called for a sus-
pension of any connection with the RWGL until a conference of the
"Grand Lodges South" could meet to map strategy. They not only dismissed the United Friends as unscrupulous opportunists but cast
doubt on Searcy's personal integrity by charging that he had not
turned over the money entrusted to him while he had served as
Grand Lodge secretary.[50]

Other temperance societies in the South also looked down upon
the United Friends of Temperance as a collection of ambitious mal-
contents. A slightly older society with almost the same name, the
Friends of Temperance, declined to merge with the upstart United
Friends, in part over the cider question.[51] The (Nashville) *Good Templar* complained about the practice of "appealing to sectional feelings
and prejudices" and saw no future for a society of strifemakers. The
(Raleigh) *Friend of Temperance* hinted that leaders of the United

Friends "hoped to turn the thing to their good account pecuniarily" and sneered that "their policy seems to be to build up a new Order with the material prepared by other Orders."[52] Although the United Friends of Temperance at one point claimed 100,000 members, this rival quickly disappeared.

Despite Hickman's efforts, the South had trouble marching in step. The Grand Lodge of North Carolina showed little enthusiasm for secession in 1873, although it had been black lodges in its territory that had petitioned the RWGL. Shortly before the adjournment of the 1873 Grand Lodge session the GWCT received Hickman's communication asking that North Carolina attend his proposed conference of southern Templars. Meeting in executive session, the Grand Lodge voted to decline the invitation. Later, the outgoing GWCT got an urgent request from Hickman to attend a conference in Atlanta. He referred it to the incoming GWCT, who opposed "precipitate action" and concluded that this moment was not the breaking point. He hoped "to make the negro element a powerful auxiliary rather than impediment to our organization." A leading Templar in a neighboring state agreed: although declaring that "whites will never submit to a union with colored persons in their lodges," South Carolina's GWCT looked favorably on providing separate Templar Grand Lodges for the two races.[53] The Atlanta conference attracted delegates only from Georgia and Alabama.

Soon the storm over the RWGL session in England blew over. The situation calmed after details arrived from England and Hickman had a chance to confer with Hastings, the veteran leader who had been elected RWGT after being out of office for several years. Once Hastings had satisfied him, Hickman traveled from Grand Lodge to Grand Lodge in the South to preach unity. It turned out that the London meeting had left a loophole that enabled white southerners to escape their dilemma. Tallcott's black lodges in North Carolina had lost their legal standing by failing to pay their dues to the RWGL, and after the establishment of white Grand Lodges in most of the southern states there was no way that a black lodge could get a lawful charter. Under Templar law, then, there were no black lodges in the former slave states for the white Grand Lodges to recognize. Non-members had no rights.

Although Hastings was the old abolitionist who had spoken strongly for the rights of blacks in 1866, he appeased the white southerners throughout his 1873-74 term of office. He made it clear that the white Grand Lodges could deny charters to blacks who wanted to organize subordinate lodges: "Should an appeal come to me in a case of this kind, I should at once dismiss it for want of jurisdiction."[54] Despite his antislavery history, Hastings's concern over institutional unity and constitutional procedure made him content to compromise away the rights of the African Americans who lived in the South. At the 1874 RWGL session delegates learned that without consulting the full executive committee Hastings had spent IOGT funds to purchase rituals and constitutions for the black Order of True Reformers created by the Grand Lodge of Kentucky.

The changed relationship between Hastings and the South was dramatized in the RWGT's travels in the spring of 1874: he visited Templars in Kentucky, Tennessee, Alabama, Georgia, and North Carolina. In Montgomery he attended a lodge meeting where eighty-six white Alabamians were initiated. Impressed, Hastings said, "I never saw so many persons on the floor for initiation at one time." In Atlanta appreciative southerners honored Hastings with a banquet attended by about 700 Templars and their guests. He reported to his fellow northerners that the irritation over the London session "seems to have entirely subsided."[55]

Hickman of Kentucky had already seized the initiative in setting up a segregated black fraternal temperance society. In 1871, his Grand Lodge had affirmed the desirability of such an organization, and two years later the Grand Lodge of Kentucky published a ritual and named the society the United Order of True Reformers. Hickman envisaged it as a new order for blacks both inside and outside Kentucky. In October 1873 the Grand Lodge of Tennessee purchased True Reformer supplies for twenty-five "fountains," the name given to lodges in the black organization.[56]

The official connection between the IOGT and the True Reformers is not clear, but there is no doubt that to the extent of his authority to do so, Hastings, the RWGT in 1873-74, endorsed the new society. He even met with a True Reformer affiliate during his conciliatory southern tour. In one controversial instance Hastings directly chartered a black Templar lodge in a state where there was no Grand Lodge: in December 1873 Hastings issued Jacksonville blacks a charter for Triumph lodge. According to Hickman, Hastings provided the charter with the expectation that the lodge would reorganize as an affiliate of the black True Reformer organization, which was in the process of formation in Florida. During the pamphlet wars of the great schism there was a squabble over Triumph lodge's charter. Malins and others complained that it was a "mutilated" charter because the printed form had been altered in Hastings's handwriting to reduce the powers of the lodge. Eventually

Malins had to acknowledge that Hastings had used a Grand Lodge charter form because no printed subordinate lodge charter was available, and had modified the form to provide Triumph lodge with the powers appropriate for a subordinate lodge.[57]

The RWGL session of 1873, which once had appeared to be a disaster for white southerners, actually began a period when the former slave states exerted great influence in the IOGT. With satisfaction the official organ of the Grand Lodge of Kentucky advised its readers that the controversy over black membership had disappeared. "We are coming more and more to the conclusion that the good, sound, practical common sense of the North has solved the problem, and the real demands of the case are being so realised by them that they are at last consenting to leaving the matter to the management of the local Grand Lodges, where only it legally belongs."[58]

The white southerners had reason for satisfaction. At the 1874 session of the RWGL, held in the old abolitionist stronghold of Boston, Hickman of Kentucky was elected RWGT. He was reelected in 1875. From 1873 to 1880 Hickman's ally, W.S. Williams of Ontario, served as Right Worthy Grand Secretary. The alliance between Ontario and the American South provided the former Confederate states with a friendly newspaper in Canada, the (Napanee) *Canada Casket,* which was often quoted by the worldwide Templar press.[59]

Comfortable with Hickman and Williams in charge, southern whites tolerated with good grace the occasional black Templar they met in the North. The official organ of the Grand Lodge of North Carolina, mentioning that the former slave William Wells Brown had participated in the annual session in 1874, commented that "he was a gentleman and a scholar, so far as we saw, and knew his place, and did not offer offense in any manner." The (Raleigh) *Spirit of the Age,* pointed out defensively that blacks took part in other national conventions held in the North, such as recent Baptist anniversary meetings in Philadelphia.[60] Few of the blacks who appeared at RWGL sessions were delegates, however. Josephus O'Banyoun (or Banyon), who served on the Nova Scotia delegation, was the only black representative seated at the 1875 session in Bloomington.[61] There were no black delegates the following year at the session in Louisville, situated on the south bank of the Ohio River.

After Hickman was elected RWGT in 1874, he appointed James G. Thrower of Georgia as superintendent of the True Reformers for the transitional period when several white southern Grand Lodges were helping organize blacks into subordinate fountains and state Grand Fountains. A plasterer turned building contractor, the English-born Thrower had moved to Atlanta from Minnesota after the Civil War and organized Georgia's first Templar lodge. He was known as "a forceful and eloquent public speaker, endowed with a magnetic personality which made him a central figure everywhere." When Thrower published the text of the Reformer ritual, he boldly claimed that the Good Templar Order had organized the True Reformer Order, and he explained elsewhere that the Order had been "approved by the RWGT, through its Executive Committee."[62]

The True Reformer Order was for southern blacks, and so its creation did not prevent blacks elsewhere from joining the IOGT—a compromise unacceptable to Searcy but one that many white southerners worked vigorously to make a success. In the 1870s no Grand Lodge more adamantly resisted the admission of blacks to the Templar Order than Alabama's. It appointed its secretary, Alonzo S. Elliot, as state superintendent of the True Reformers and spent Templar money in getting the True Reformers started: "Philanthropy, as well as self-interest, demands that we, claiming to be the superior race, should do all in our power to bring up the colored race to a higher appreciation of its moral and religious obligations." A manifesto addressed "to the colored people of Alabama" asked for "the cooperation" of blacks "who desire to benefit their Race by teaching the doctrine of total abstinence from intoxicating drinks." Although the Grand Worthy Secretary did not seem comfortable in his mission to the black people of his state ("There was no one else who would accept the appointment," he explained), the Grand Fountain of Alabama was organized in 1875.[63]

In that same year J.G. Thrower of Atlanta reported that there were fountains in every state of the old Confederacy and the District of Columbia.[64] Virginia, Alabama, and Georgia had Grand Fountains. A year after its founding Georgia's Grand Fountain claimed more than 5,000 members. Other than Thrower's role as national superintendent, the True Reformers lacked a national organization and consisted of parallel state societies bearing the same name.

A North Carolina newspaper, delighted with the creation of a society to fight drink among black people, claimed that the IOGT "stretches its arms like seas to grasp in the world," though with "different arms for different classes": for white adults there was the Templar Order itself; for children, the auxiliaries called juvenile temples, and for blacks, the True Reformers. Each organization had its own ritual, but all were united in the battle against drink.[65]

Did blacks welcome or despise the segregated organization sponsored by white racists? Critics dismissed the United Order of True Reformers as a demeaning "kitchen order," an expression coined by Edward Dudley. William Wells Brown compared the True Reformers to the "negro pew" in the slaveowners' church and the Jim Crow seats in a segregated railroad coach. Answering such attacks, Hickman pointed out that to initiate 40,000 members in three years the whites "must have worked in concert with the coloured people." By 1875 blacks had taken control. For instance, the Grand Fountain of Virginia published its own ritual. After the True Reformers had disappeared elsewhere, this Grand Fountain developed into a fraternal insurance society that operated in many states.[66]

White southerners dismissed criticism of the new segregated organization. Hickman argued that getting blacks to take the pledge against drink mattered more than any ideological crusade "to establish the equality of man." Speaking at the time of the great schism, he pointed out that where blacks could join the IOGT, they had seldom chosen to do so. For instance, "the doors have always been open to them" in Philadelphia, where there was a large black population, but the two or three Templar lodges organized there for blacks failed to survive; they preferred "their own Temperance Orders." He described blacks who tried to get Templar charters in the southern states as politicians looking for "a question on which they can work on the credulity of their people, and thereby gain political power and influence."[67]

The triumph of the South had its limits. In 1874 the annual session of the RWGL refused to endorse the True Reformers. When Thrower proposed the creation of a committee to revise the True Reformer ritual, he was forced to withdraw his motion, so strong was the opposition to anything that would connect the IOGT with a segregated black organization. Denying that the executive committee had agreed to the purchase of the rituals and constitutions, Malins insisted that the officers return them to the Grand Lodge of Kentucky.[68]

The white southerners had to recognize the importance of the Grand Lodge of England. In 1874 Malins was elected to the second highest office as Grand Counsellor and like Hickman, was reelected in 1875. The Grand Lodge of England was the largest in the IOGT, and at their zenith the Grand Lodges of the British Isles had a total membership nearly matching the number of Templars in the United States. (The British wrongly assumed, however, that other Grand

Lodges throughout the British Empire from South Africa and India to Australia and New Zealand would act as their allies at the RWGL annual sessions.)

Another controversy that affected the race question and contributed to the great schism resulted from the proposals for multiple or duplicate Grand Lodges. At the London session James Black of Pennsylvania filed a year's notice for a constitutional amendment to be debated in 1874 at the Boston session.[69] Beginning in the late 1860s, Judge Black, a stalwart of the National Prohibition Party, had proposed modifying the exclusive jurisdiction of existing Grand Lodges, *if* they agreed. Some of the larger Grand Lodges in the United States, notably New York, considered subdividing their territory. If adopted, Black's amendment would permit segregated Grand Lodges for blacks in the American South, provided the white Grand Lodges consented.[70]

The British opposed duplicate Grand Lodges other than for differences in language and perhaps race. They said that such an amendment would encourage the inflation of the voting strength of the Americans, most of whose Grand Lodges were very small by British standards. When the Americans suggested that the British increase their own voting strength by dividing their large Grand Lodges into smaller ones, the British answered that they could not afford to send additional delegates to North America, the location for all RWGL sessions except the 1873 meeting. During the great schism the Americans and their British allies sneered that Malins and Gladstone simply wanted to keep their unwieldy Grand Lodges undivided to maintain their own prestige and power and, in the case of Malins, a generous salary. Minorities in England had argued in the early 1870s for what they called provincial grand lodges, and critics alleged that Malins wanted to "effectually squelch any agitation in England, and keep his kingdom intact."[71]

Black claimed that his amendment had been "prompted mainly by the desire to give the Order of Good Templars to the colored people in the way they wanted, and in the only way in which they will have it, and that is, as an institution of their own, to be seen and enjoyed by themselves, and yet to be equal in power and privileges with their white neighbors." He pointed out that he had first filed his amendment in 1868 and that it had been discussed for the first time in 1869, before the establishment of a Grand Lodge of England; he could not have been motivated by a desire to break up a Grand Lodge that did not yet exist.

At the Boston RWGL meeting in 1874 a representative from Wales amended Black's amendment to restrict duplicate Grand Lodges to situations where there was difference in language. This was passed, permitting separate Welsh-speaking and English-speaking Grand Lodges of Wales. According to Black, only the opposition of Malins had restricted the legislation to difference in language.[72] William Wells Brown filed a notice for an amendment to add race to language as a basis for creating duplicate Grand Lodges.

Black's original proposal was reconsidered at the 1875 RWGL session at Bloomington, Illinois, and his constitutional amendment carried by the required two-thirds majority, sixty-six to twenty-eight. This angered the British representatives. Malins had been reelected counsellor and George Gladstone of Scotland had been named chaplain; they resigned their offices and removed the regalia that went with them. To persuade Malins and Gladstone to resume their offices, the RWGL agreed to instruct its officers to provide duplicate Grand Lodge charters for Maryland and North Carolina only, thus allowing duplicate Grand Lodges in states where there were already a considerable number of black local lodges and not threatening English and Scottish unity.

Left to itself, the white Grand Lodge of North Carolina would probably have accepted the creation of a duplicate Grand Lodge, but the Grand Lodge of Georgia and other southern Templars persuaded the North Carolinians that accepting blacks as members of the IOGT anywhere in Dixie "will tend to retard, if not entirely annihilate, the Order of Good Templars in the Southern States." Later, the vice Templar of the white Grand Lodge presented a petition from 400 black Templars for a segregated duplicate Grand Lodge, but her request was ignored by North Carolina's Committee on Memorials.[73]

When blacks in South Carolina wanted Templar lodges, whites urged them to make do with True Reformer fountains. A black minister, S.C. Goosley (or Gooseley), who had emigrated from Canada, asked for help from Ontario, where he had joined the IOGT. The Canadian officer referred Goosley to Hickman who in turn referred him to the GWCT of South Carolina, Henry M. Mood. The white leaders offered to help Goosley if he would organize the blacks of South Carolina as True Reformers. A Templar newspaper in England published their correspondence with Goosley. In a letter 22 February 1875, Hickman called the True Reformers "the prettiest Temperance Order in existence" and said that he had paid for the printing of a thousand sets of supplies: "I assure you that nothing that I can do for the Coloured people shall go undone." On 4 April 1875 Mood made a symbolic concession: he agreed to remove from the ritual for instituting the True Reformer Order the statement that it was solely for blacks.[74]

In Florida too, black temperance reformers were shunted into the True Reformers. On 4 November 1874 Hickman told W.M. Artrell of Key West that he could not grant him a Templar charter because a white lodge objected. Hickman argued that this was not a matter of favoring one race over another but simply a case of priority. The existing white lodge had several hundred members, and Hickman had been told that it would break up if he chartered a black lodge; moreover, "I have been informed that the coloured people would have been well satisfied, had it not been for a few officious whites [from outside Florida]." As a result of this rejection, Artrell organized a True Reformer fountain and became deputy Grand Master of the Grand Fountain of Florida. Thrower quoted a letter from Artrell that sounded content: "Our members are very proud of the 'Order,' and are willing to do anything to help it on. Our Fountain Room presents a very respectable appearance now. We have our platforms, pedestals, and a beautiful banner, also desks for the different officers." He inquired whether there was "a juvenile organization in connection with our Order," as he hoped to obtain a charter for Key West children.[75]

Instead of organizing blacks in segregated duplicate Grand Lodges affiliated with the IOGT, then, the white southern Templars worked hard to persuade the few black Templars in the South to accept reorganization as True Reformers. In 1874, after a rebuff to his proposal for such a shift, Thrower asked Dudley, head of North Carolina's black Templars, to pray for guidance. Two years later, in March 1876, Hickman, his predecessor Hastings, and Broughton, head of the white Grand Lodge of North Carolina, conferred with Dudley to discuss the True Reformers and presented him with a copy of the ritual. But Dudley stood firm because he knew that the British planned at the May meeting of the RWGL to demand that the southern blacks be allowed to organize segregated Templar lodges.[76] By the time the great schism broke out in 1876, the unrecognized black Grand Lodge of North Carolina was barely clinging to life. Dudley said that of the twenty-six lodges that had existed three years earlier, only five remained in working order: "The last password issued by us, was 'Lord save us or we perish,' and it truly represents our struggling condition."[77]

A few blacks outside North America belonged to the Templar Order. In Trinidad nine-tenths of the members were nonwhite, and there were black Templars in Britain, mostly at seaports. In 1875 Mariner's Friend lodge, London, claimed three dozen black brothers and one black sister. About the same time a black man named King was a member of Divine Providence lodge, South Shields. When he complained that while he lived in New York a lodge had refused to admit him because of his race, all twenty-one lodges in the Templar district to which South Shields belonged responded by passing resolutions of condemnation. Jacob Christian, a timber merchant at Toxteth Park, Liverpool, had come from Africa at age fifteen. Later he joined the Wesleyan Methodists, gave up drink, and became a "devoted" member of the IOGT. In January 1877, when the GWCT of Scotland addressed a public meeting at Glasgow on the great schism, a black man named Brooks gave a pound note to help fund a mission to the African Americans in the former slave states; another black Templar named Haig seconded the motion of thanks. In 1880 the RWGL proudly pointed out that in the Australian colony of Victoria most of the officers of Pride of Permin lodge were "brethren and sisters of color."[78]

Despite such instances of nonwhite members around the world, tokens of Templar universalism, those who wanted to encourage black membership had to look to the American South, for it was there that most black men and women likely to join lived. And there the established white Templars did not want them in the IOGT. In reacting to outside pressure, however, southern white Templars did not always agree with one another on priorities and strategy. Although all insisted on racial separation and white supremacy, they interpreted these principles in more than one way. The most loyal to the Templar Order as an institution and the less rigidly racist were willing to make repeated concessions, but others either demanded corporate secession or quit as individuals. The southern white reaction varied from state to state. Unsurprisingly, Alabama was more militantly racist than North Carolina. Leadership in the Grand Lodge could make a difference: the influence of the English-born Thrower helped make Georgia in the Deep South more moderate than the border state of Kentucky. Often, other quarrels became involved. Some of the Georgians who fought Thrower over concessions on black membership also wanted the teetotal pledge restricted to the time one belonged to the IOGT and disliked the interpretation of teetotalism that banned sweet cider.

The controversy over black membership cost the IOGT dearly in the South, but it is unreasonable to assume that all the losses suffered in the former slave states and the decline in recruitment resulted from white dissatisfaction with Templar racial teachings. The IOGT also suffered losses in northern states where race was not a major question, and other factors—such as disagreement over the growing identification of the Templars with the National Prohibition Party—contributed to the problem. Moreover, in parts of the South the IOGT achieved brief revivals in the 1880s, after the RWGL had adopted in practice what the British had demanded at Louisville: segregated Grand Lodges for blacks in states where the whites would not admit them to their own Grand Lodges.

During the great schism the rival parties quarreled over what they were fighting about. Was it the RWGL's complicity in the exclusion of blacks from Templar membership in the South, or the British leaders' opposition to multiple Grand Lodges that would threaten their prestige and perquisites? It is clear that except in Maryland and perhaps Missouri the white Templars of the former slave states did not charter black lodges, and that most Templars outside the South condemned this as a violation of Templar universalism. To avoid isolation, the white southerners would have to make major concessions.

4

The Great Schism

The decade from 1876-86 saw angry declarations of principle, fumbled attempts at compromise, invasion and consolidation, pamphlet wars, bitterness, financial crisis and lawsuits, radicalizing of the demand for African American rights, brief-lived black Grand Lodges, frustration and indifference, and in the end new RWGL leaders eager to put the racial controversy behind them. During these years Templar membership shrank in both North America and Britain, but new Grand Lodges flourished outside the English-speaking world in Sweden, Norway, and elsewhere.

The motives and expectations of the British leaders in 1876 remain unclear. Since early 1874 the membership had dropped precipitously in England, and the Grand Lodge there staggered under heavy indebtedness, circumstances that might have counseled caution. What did the British leaders want and expect? To secure for blacks in the American South the opportunity of joining the IOGT, or to win new power in the RWGL and—by rallying enthusiasm at home—protect existing power in the English and Scottish Grand Lodges? To obtain a two-thirds majority at the RWGL session for a constitutional amendment, or to create a justification for secession? A short-lived split to put pressure on opponents to make concessions, or a permanent break?

Most likely, the racial question took priority for the British leaders. They were surprised at the extent of their defeat at the Louisville session in 1876, and they expected that in any schism many northern Grand Lodges would join them. They assumed that if anybody would be forced out, it would be the white southerners; the British did not anticipate a lengthy schism dividing the Templars not just on both sides of the Atlantic but around the world, with divisions appearing nearly everywhere.

Principles, illusions, and a sense of self-importance all influenced the British leaders. They disliked any kind of segregation within the Templar Order; it was only to win votes at Louisville that they offered to accept racially segregated local lodges and Grand Lodges. They expected that the black people in the former slave states would pour into the IOGT if charters were made available. There were four million blacks in the American South, "of whom five hundred thousand were communicants in Christian Churches."[1] The British believed that the North Americans needed them more than the British needed the Americans and Canadians. As early as 1871 Scotland's George Gladstone had been content for the British to go it alone: "Subordination to America is a mistake." Allegedly, in 1875 Malins had asked an associate privately, "What do you think if we threw the Americans overboard?"[2]

Late in 1875 the United Executives of the Grand Lodges of the United Kingdom devised their strategy. In a circular titled "Shall the Negro be Excluded from the Order?" they insisted that the Grand Lodges in the former slave states allow blacks in their jurisdictions to become Templars. Under the provisions of the British Manifesto, as it was called, the RWGL could organize black lodges in jurisdictions where the local Grand Lodges would not, or commission other Grand Lodges to do the work. At this point the British did not ask for the racial integration of subordinate lodges or even a common Grand Lodge, but the United Executives made clear in the Manifesto that the British would not accept defeat. If the RWGL did not adopt the Manifesto, the British Grand Lodges would join with like-minded Templars in a provisional organization to send missionaries to the American South.

On New Year's Day 1876 the British Manifesto was sent to all the IOGT's Grand Lodges. At the request of the GWCT of Scotland it was not published; he did not want a public threat to make it more difficult for the North American Grand Lodges to submit to the British demands.[3]

During the great schism, Malins's enemies asserted that he lacked authority to make rejection of the United Executives' demands the basis for the withdrawal of his Grand Lodge from the RWGL, since only District Lodges had seen the Manifesto prior to Louisville and not all of them. This argument lacks persuasiveness, for the annual meeting of the Grand Lodge of England had openly affirmed "that the brotherhood of the [human] race is one of the *fundamental* principles" of the IOGT and directed its RWGL representatives to support the Manifesto of the United Executives. Moreover, leaders of the other Grand Lodges and the RWGL certainly knew what to expect. On the evening before the Louisville session opened, Hickman and Thrower, "whom he introduced as his best helper," held "a long interview" with Malins. Hickman argued that the True Reformers met the needs of black people and "that time would settle all things if we would only be quiet."[4]

The document actually submitted by the British to the Louisville session was called the "Ultimatum." It differed from the Manifesto in one crucial respect. The Ultimatum asked that individual Grand Lodges, such as those in Britain, be authorized to organize blacks in jurisdictions where the local whites refused to do so. The Manifesto would have allowed the RWGL to commission a Grand Lodge to organize black lodges in some other jurisdiction but did not authorize such a Grand Lodge to take the initiative. Dudley, the black leader in North Carolina, had warned the British leaders that the RWGL executives would connive with the white southern Grand Lodges; hence, the innovation in the Ultimatum meant that the British did not trust the RWGL officers to act but would take direct responsibility to bring Templar membership to African Americans.

As few southern Grand Lodges would tolerate giving authority to outside Grand Lodges to enter the South for the purpose of organizing blacks, any delegate voting with the British had to be willing to risk a southern secession. Nor did most northerners accept the Ultimatum's innovation. Hastings told the Grand Lodge of Wisconsin that the British proposal would have passed had it not been for the "four words" allowing outside Grand Lodges to enter different jurisdictions without authorization from the RWGL.[5]

The debate at Louisville did not take the form of a direct confrontation between Malins and the white southerners; rather, because of the widespread hostility toward Malins, the comparatively obscure Scottish GWCT, George Gladstone, introduced the Ultimatum. He was a minister in the Evangelical Union, a small Presbyterian denomination that rejected the Calvinist doctrine of predestination.[6] Belief that God offered sinful humans universal salvation, if they repented and accepted His gift of grace, harmonized nicely with Templar universalism.

In the opinion of many North Americans, however, it was the pursuit of power, not principle, that motivated the British. And since it was bad tactics, contrary to Templar ideology, to fight the British by espousing black exclusion, the white southerners shifted attention to Malins's alleged ambition. After the great schism began, Georgia's Thrower argued that the question of black membership was a red herring: "We do not believe that the question of admitting the colored people into the Lodges South, was the real cause of the secession of the British Representatives at Louisville, but that this was used *by the leaders* as a pretext to cover up a deep laid scheme to obtain the control of the Order for Joseph Malins, Gladstone & Co."[7]

Opponents of the British proposal also stigmatized it as unconstitutional because of the failure to provide one year's notice, although nominally, the Ultimatum was an amendment to a very different proposal that *had* been filed in 1875. There was also resentment that the change in policy put forward took the form of an ultimatum—even though, as William Wells Brown later pointed out, the South had thrown down its own ultimatums, most obviously in 1873 after the London session of the RWGL.[8]

The British also felt misused. To curry favor with Canadian Orangemen a southern delegate introduced a resolution congratulating Queen Victoria on her birthday, a resolution using the new title created by the Tory prime minister, Benjamin Disraeli: "Empress of India." When one of the Liberal members of the English delegation, James Yeames, protested the use of the controversial title, his protest was represented by several Canadians as indicating lack of patriotism. In addition, the RWGL seated as a guest an Englishman ineligible to be present, J.H. Raper of the United Kingdom Alliance, who held only a Templar first degree and who "had scarcely ever entered one of our lodges since the night he was initiated." Raper had become friendly with Malins's American enemies while attending the National Prohibition Party convention in nearby Cincinnati, which had nominated for president a leader of the Kentucky Templars, Green Clay Smith.[9]

As it turned out, the Ultimatum never came to a vote. The debate shifted to the "Substitute," introduced by Oronhyatekha, a Mohawk physician representing the American South's old ally, Ontario.[10] Contemporaries regarded the substantially built six-footer as physically imposing, a clever debater, and ambitious. Was he a racist? According to William Wells Brown, Oronhyatekha disliked African Americans and had refused to have his photograph taken with Brown because the Boston doctor was black.[11] If so, Oronhyatekha's motive for allying himself with the white southern Templars was based on more than expediency and opportunism. In any case, his Substitute forbade Grand Lodges from rejecting applicants on the grounds of race or color, but at the same time allowed Grand Lodges to deny charters to new lodges without providing a reason. The southern Grand Lodges agreed to this compromise, which outlawed the principle of racial exclusion while protecting its practice.

Oronhyatekha's Substitute carried by a vote of eighty-seven to forty-eight. The majority included a number of votes from British Empire jurisdictions: Oronhyatekha's own Ontario, neighboring Quebec, and South Africa. Delegates from the places which had allowed slavery swelled the majority—Alabama, Arkansas, Delaware, District of Columbia, Georgia, Kentucky, Louisiana, Maryland, Mississippi, Missouri, North Carolina, South Carolina, Tennessee, Texas, Virginia, and West Virginia—but also supporting the Substitute were delegates from California, Colorado, Illinois, Indiana, Kansas, Maine, Massachusetts, Michigan, Nebraska, New York, Pennsylvania, Rhode Island, Washington territory, and Wisconsin. Representatives from Union Jack Grand Lodges made up the heart of the minority: Bermuda, British Columbia, England, Newfoundland, New Zealand, Nova Scotia, Scotland, South Australia, and Wales (Welsh-speaking). The minority also attracted votes from some Grand Lodges in the United States: Connecticut, Indiana, Iowa, Kansas, Maine, Michigan, Minnesota, Montana, Vermont, and West Virginia[12]—in several cases dividing the state's delegation. Ohio abstained.

The British-led minority that voted against the Substitute came from jurisdictions with a majority of the total membership of the IOGT but could not muster a majority of delegates. In part, it was a minority because of location. For instance, Scotland was authorized to send six representatives but could afford to send only two. Neither the Grand Lodge of Ireland, the English-language Grand Lodge of Wales, nor most of the Australian colonies were represented at all. In contrast, for the first time every American state, the District of Columbia, and three territories had Grand Lodges, and almost all had sent a delegation.

It is not clear whether the British had expected to win before they got to Louisville. On the one hand, they were right in anticipating that their arguments would persuade some northern Grand Lodges. The executive committee of the Grand Lodge of Minnesota and two of its representatives to the RWGL gladly signed the Manifesto: "It was one of the most high toned and consistent documents it has been our privilege to join in."[13] On the other hand, the United Executives let a shortage of money prevent them from sending all the delegates that the RWGL allotted them, negligence that raises questions about what the British leaders intended to accomplish. The Grand Lodge of England was careful to pay off its debt to the RWGL so that its right to vote would not risk challenge. Surely, the British could have raised a little more money to pay additional delegates' travel expenses if they had believed that a few more votes might provide the margin for victory. Did the British go to Louisville taking defeat for granted? After the fact, in the report to his Grand Lodge in 1877, Malins admitted that there had been no prospect of a two-thirds majority to amend the constitution, although "had all the Grand Lodges supporting our Manifesto been represented we might possibly have defeated the Substitute by majority vote."[14]

And why did the British leaders then decide upon an immediate break with the RWGL? They did not offer to compromise or to try again. By resubmitting the proposal in 1877 they might have won over at least those who had justified their opposition by the lack of a year's notice. Probably the British leaders thought they could win by carrying through on their the threat to take the largest Grand Lodges out of the IOGT; they had the precedent of 1875, when Malins's and Gladstone's resignation of their offices had forced the RWGL to retreat from its decision to allow duplicate Grand Lodges everywhere. The British appear to have assumed that the abolitionist legacy in the northern states and the loyalty to the United Kingdom on the part of the Grand Lodges in the British Empire would leave Hickman and his allies in control of only a rump organization consisting almost exclusively of white southerners. Instead, the RWGL gave Hickman an impressive victory over the British, re-elected him RWGT unanimously, and doubled his salary.

After the Substitute passed, the British delegations issued a formal protest and withdrew from the RWGL meeting. Anecdotes suggest that Malins, the dominant figure in the British section, was surprised by how one-sided the vote had been and experienced last-minute qualms about breaking with the RWGL; he lay exhausted on his bed while a Templar sister applied cold cloths to his brow and puzzled delegates milled around.[15] No detailed contingency plans seem to have existed. A ciphered message sent to England used the word "secession," an interpretation of what happened that Malins later repudiated.

Tim Needham of Kentucky met with Malins to dispel rumors that he had offered to admit blacks in order to forestall the British withdrawal. In a curious confession Needham argued "that the line was drawn in the wrong place; that the South ought to have separated and the North to have stood with [Britain]." He predicted that eventually the North and the South would quarrel over black membership and the southern Grand Lodges would leave the RWGL to operate "as an exclusively White Man's Order." Pleased with Needham's candor, the British presented him with a gold-headed walking stick.[16]

Fourteen delegates convened at Louisville's Masonic Hall to declare the existence of the "RWGL of the World" and elect its officers.[17] Many of the delegates who had voted against the Substitute were absent; either they rejected the decision to break with the old RWGL or, like the delegates from Minnesota, expressed personal sympathy but wanted to consult their Grand Lodge.[18] The only North American delegates who participated represented Nova Scotia, Newfoundland, Indiana, Ohio, and Iowa. Three of the four delegates from the United States were women; the fourth was Indiana's GWCT, Jeremiah J. Talbott, a native of Kentucky where his family had owned slaves.[19]

The supporters of the new RWGL of the World did not admit to having seceded from the old RWGL. Instead, the RWGL of the World claimed to be the only Good Templar Order, on the grounds that the original RWGL had forfeited its legitimacy: it had shown itself untrue to the fundamental Templar principle of brotherhood by its failure to protect the rights of prospective black members. Sensitive about the accusation that the Malinites could not claim the Templar name, the Grand Lodge of England purchased from the historian Isaac Newton Peirce the first IOGT-granted charter, dated 23 July 1852, as a symbol of continuity and legitimacy.

Under a rule that existed in 1876 the RWGT could not simultaneously serve a Grand Lodge as GWCT, so Malins, the principal figure in the RWGL of the World, did not take the highest office and instead became secretary. A comparatively minor figure, a Methodist minister from England named James Yeames, was elected RWGT. He was best known as an editor of the weekly *Templar* newspaper and as the officer in charge of England's juvenile temples. A few years later Yeames emigrated to Massachusetts, where he sank into comparative obscurity.

North American efforts to effect a reconciliation began at Louisville with the dispatch of a delegation consisting of Hickman, Oronhyatekha, and Amanda M. Way. The RWGL of the World refused to receive the delegation as an official body because the Malinites rejected the claim of the old organization to be the RWGL. In turn, Hickman allegedly threatened to prosecute Malins if he organized his Louisville hotel's black waiters, who had asked him to provide them with a Templar lodge charter.[20]

After the Louisville meetings in May, the scene shifted to Philadelphia in June.[21] Hickman asked Williams, the RWGL's secretary, to present Malins with a compromise: a promise that the white Grand Lodges in the southern states would volunteer to organize blacks in their jurisdictions in segregated Grand Lodges. Malins already had hurried home, but a few second-echelon delegates affiliated with the new RWGL of the World had lingered to visit Philadelphia for the exhibition commemorating a century of United

States independence and for the World's Temperance Congress being held in conjunction with the centenary. Also in Philadelphia were the majority of the RWGL's executive committee. Williams persuaded Hickman to leave a sick bed to join the negotiations.

Thrower of Georgia, also in Philadelphia to attend the World's Temperance Congress, took part as well. At first he "strenuously opposed" Hickman's plan of settlement, but he finally acquiesced. Soon afterward, while visiting Halifax, Thrower became convinced that the South had to offer some sort of compromise to prevent the secession of Nova Scotia and New Brunswick. Thereafter, he championed the Philadelphia scheme.

The Philadelphia proposal made it clear that segregated subordinate lodges for blacks would have no right of representation at the white Grand Lodges, but when black subordinate lodges became numerous enough, a separate black "Dual Grand Lodge" would be instituted. Hickman told the Grand Lodge of Pennsylvania that "the doors of the Order South are open to all mankind." He offered his word to guarantee that the white Grand Lodges would cooperate. The Malinite delegates "personally endorsed it and pledged themselves to use every honorable effort to procure its acceptance by their constituency."[22] Three of the four Malinites eventually joined the Hickmanite faction: Robert Simpson, a regalia maker who had served as a Grand Lodge of Scotland delegate, Nathaniel Smythe of England, and John Harding of New Zealand North. The fourth, the "singing evangelist" John Bennett Anderson of England, accepted reimbursement of travel expenses from the RWGL, a decision that made questionable his repudiation of its authority.

After receiving the text of the Philadelphia plan, the United Executives of Great Britain rejected the compromise on the grounds that the southern Grand Lodges had not yet approved it and that there was no guarantee that blacks would be admitted on terms of equality.[23] In fact, however, the Philadelphia plan collapsed because of lack of support in the white South, not because of hesitations in Britain. Thrower arranged from Nova Scotia for a special meeting of the Georgia executive committee to be held in his absence, but despite the presence of the ordinarily persuasive Hickman, the committee unanimously rejected the Philadelphia proposal. Capitulating to this vehement opposition, Hickman withdrew his scheme.

Returning to Georgia "to find the Order reduced one half, or nearly that much,"[24] Thrower together with Hickman called an emergency meeting on 21 September in Atlanta, which was attended by representatives of nearly all the southern Grand Lodges. Thrower still expected that the South would endorse Hickman's Philadelphia plan which had been published to the world, but Hickman was now advocating a rival plan promoted by Tim Needham. It was modeled on the declaration of Kentucky's executive committee: "We do hereby consent that, as between the Grand Lodge of Kentucky, and the R.W.G.L., *in so far as the Negro race is concerned,* Kentucky may be held and considered 'unoccupied territory,' and we invite the R.W.G.L. to occupy same at her pleasure, by chartering as many sublodges, composed of coloured persons exclusively, as she may deem fit, and then grant them a separate Grand Lodge charter when ready for it, just as though no Grand Lodge existed in this State."[25] Following the lead of Kentucky, the plan adopted by the Atlanta conference allowed the white Grand Lodges to stand aloof while the RWGL organized blacks into segregated subordinate and Grand Lodges.

Thrower was furious at Needham, whom he regarded as a well-meaning but ineffective meddler, and at Hickman for being weak-kneed. He took the occasion of his response to a letter from Hastings, congratulating him on his reelection as GWCT of Georgia, to vent his frustration. Discussing the Atlanta conference, Thrower snapped that "to my surprise I found another 'basis' had been prepared by our good but vacillating Brother Tim. Needham, of Kentucky, and strange to say, endorsed by you [in a letter read at the conference]." Needham, he said, "doubtless means to do right, but this great desire to accomplish something runs away with his judgment. This has been proved by his continually being prominent on this [black membership] question, yet producing no beneficial results." Thrower complained that "Brother Hickman fell into line, and this child of Brother Needham was to be heralded to the world as a wonderful concession. I *alone,* opposed it all day, and was called stubborn, but finally signed it under protest, giving my reason [at the end of the Atlanta document]." Thrower grumbled that Needham had withheld the signature and the reservations that accompanied it when he published the Atlanta declaration. Those reservations included the assertion that "the work of organizing the colored people of the Southern States, *if organized into Lodges of Good Templars at all,* should be done by the Southern people."[26]

Thrower took gloomy satisfaction in the subsequent failure of any Grand Lodge other than Kentucky to ratify the agreement signed at the Atlanta conference. He blamed Alabama's and Tennessee's intransigent rejection of any kind of black membership on Needham's ineptness "and the want of stability on the part of

Brother Hickman." Most of the Alabama members joined an openly racist new organization called the Templars of Temperance; in Texas, many enrolled in the Friends of Progress.

Thrower persuaded the members of his own Grand Lodge ("God bless them") that he was right and that Needham, Hickman, and the other people at the Atlanta conference were wrong. He insisted that if the white Grand Lodges decided to allow the organization of blacks as Templars, they should shoulder the responsibility of doing it themselves. He contrasted the Philadelphia or Hickman basis of settlement—"meaning immediate action on our part"—with the Atlanta or Needham basis, which, "while refusing to do the work ourselves, consents that it may be done by others, *which simply means nothing.*"[27]

Thrower assumed responsibility for organizing a Dual Grand Lodge in his own state. At the end of October he met with Georgia's Grand Fountain of True Reformers and, despite "considerable opposition" from the black Georgians, persuaded them to reorganize as Templars. The formal installation of the Dual Grand Lodge took place in December 1876. Thrower believed that the temperance agitation among the black population "must be done by the colored people themselves, and to this end [organizing blacks to help themselves] I will devote my time until the matter is accomplished." The white Templars in Georgia paid a dear price for the controversy over organizing blacks: between 1876 and 1882 the Grand Lodge lost two-thirds of its membership. On 12 May 1882 Thrower sent a circular to the RWGL delegates asking for help in organizing black lodges, an appeal endorsed by the governor of Georgia, the editor of the *Methodist Advocate,* and one of Atlanta's leading A.M.E. Church pastors.[28]

Outside Georgia, few southern blacks were organized into Templar lodges and Grand Lodges until well into the 1880s. The only other Dual Grand Lodge formed in 1876 was in Maryland where whites discontented with racial integration at the Grand Lodge level withdrew and formed a Dual Grand Lodge. The old Grand Lodge was mostly black, although whites held the major offices.[29]

A few subordinate Templar lodges for blacks were organized elsewhere. The Grand Lodge of South Carolina established a couple, the earliest situated in the hometown of the white GWCT, William H. Cuttino, who "assisted at its organization" and later "visited it frequently by request."[30]

At first nearly all southern white Templars resisted chartering segregated black lodges. Several southern Grand Lodges rejected outright the Atlanta scheme that their leaders had signed. North Carolina never organized a Dual Grand Lodge for blacks, even though its white Grand Lodge had been willing to contemplate sharing the state with a black Grand Lodge as early as 1873. In October 1877 the (Berea, N.C.) *Granville Good Templar* grumbled that "there is no making apples of plvms [*sic*]." The Grand Lodge did assent to a Dual Grand Lodge in 1881, but the state's black population failed to respond to the belated offer. Yet whites in North Carolina worked with blacks on behalf of prohibition and even attended a convention with them.[31]

The controversial Atlanta compromise was what Hickman offered to the British during a reconciliation conference held in London in October 1876, not yet knowing that the white Grand Lodges in the South had repudiated it.[32] Acknowledging southern white racism, Hickman insisted that time was necessary to change minds. He himself had "not been educated" to accept the idea of equal rights for blacks and whites.[33] Despite a destructive compulsion to quarrel over history and a climate of anger, suspicion, fault-finding, and personal abuse, the London conference nearly ended the great schism when it was only a few months old. The Malinites, though doubtful that the white southern Grand Lodges would live up to Hickman's promise of black access to a segregated Templar Order, were willing to give them a chance to prove themselves. But the London conference broke down over something unrelated to race.

The problem was that the beginning of a schism within the schism was dividing the British Isles. Some British Templars rallied to the side of the North American–dominated RWGL. Malins and his supporters insisted that the existing Grand Lodges must control all the lodges in their jurisdictions. They were willing to give up authority over the black lodges that the RWGL of the World had chartered in North Carolina, Florida, and elsewhere. In an ironic contrast, Malins and his allies showed much more sensitivity about the sovereignty and territorial integrity of their own Grand Lodges than they had offered the southern Grand Lodges that excluded blacks. Hickman and his party refused to withdraw the protection that the RWGL offered its British supporters. As a result of this disagreement over an armistice, the rupture continued with growing bitterness. Significantly, when the Malinites approached the RWGL about reunion the following year, they insisted on the elimination of Hickmanite organizations in the geographical jurisdictions of the breakaway Grand Lodges. The Hickmanite invasion of England outraged Malins.

The two RWGL representatives in Britain had been Hickman, partly incapacitated with a throat ailment, and Oronhyatekha, the author of the Substitute, who had become GWCT of Ontario in July after the incumbent relocated to a different province.[34] In a quarrel within a quarrel, Hickman and Oronhyatekha feuded. Illness delayed the Kentuckian, so the Canadian arrived in England alone and did not wait for the RWGT to take action: as early as September, he organized a Grand Lodge of the Isle of Man to spite "Jos Malins & Co." In contrast, until after the failure of the London conference, Hickman hoped to work out a deal with the adherents of the RWGL of the World and wanted to avoid provocation.

There were other grievances between the two. Oronhyatekha wanted to organize a black lodge in the American South as a symbol of the RWGL's ability to admit black members in the former slave states. Hickman regarded his ambitious lieutenant as a meddler and apparently worried about the impact that such a black lodge might have on the already restive white southerners. He complained about Oronhyatekha's plan, "Have I no voice in these matters?" In turn, Oronhyatekha was upset because Hickman "had no confidence in my judgement" but in England had relied on the advice of Samuel Capper of Liverpool instead. Oronhyatekha returned to the British Isles for a few months in the following year to help organize the anti-Malinite party, and in 1877 the quarrel became embarrassingly public during a dispute over travel expenses. Oronhyatekha spread his correspondence with Hickman before the RWGL session, and the letters were published in the *Journal of Proceedings* for all the world to read.[35] Further, Oronhyatekha moved the resolution that eliminated any salary for the office of RWGT.[36] As a result Hickman declined to be a candidate for reelection. Heavily indebted, the RWGL could not even pay him the money it owed him.

The quarrel between Hickman and Oronhyatekha was a minor complication in a larger story, the emergence of a Hickmanite party in the British Isles, which prevented the great schism from becoming an Anglo-American dispute. Occasionally, Templars in the United States played the patriotic card and accused the British of being British. South Carolina rejoiced: "For the second time in our history united America stood side by side against British aggressions."[37] But this kind of rhetoric was rare even in the year of the centenary of the Declaration of Independence. The RWGL did not want to offend its own supporters in the British Isles and throughout the British Empire by shortsighted appeals to American xenophobia.

Virtually no Templars in Wales joined the Hickmanites and only a few in Scotland, mostly in the Edinburgh district. But a majority of the Irish Templars supported Hickman, the only case in which the RWGL defeated the RWGL of the World in the British Isles. The Hickmanites benefited from Oronhyatekha's prominence as an Orangeman and, more important, the resentment aroused by John Pyper's aggressive Bible wine agitation.

Pyper had headed the Grand Lodge of Ireland since it was organized in 1871. Four years later he became president of the Irish Sacramental Wine Association, subsequently the Bible Wine Association.[38] Pyper alienated the moderators of the General Assembly and other Presbyterian divines when he demanded in vehement language the substitution of unfermented, nonintoxicating grape juice in place of wine in the eucharistic sacrament. The majority of Irish Templars, nearly all of them Presbyterians, agreed with Pyper, as did the paramount leader of the Hickmanites in England. It was not that Hickmanites and Malinites split on this question; rather, the quarrel among Presbyterians in Ireland provided the Hickmanites with a substantial minority of anti-Pyper Templars who got some Bible wine Templars to join them on the basis of other issues, such as Pyper's alleged mismanagement of Grand Lodge finances. Demonstrating Pyper's unpopularity was his replacement as president of the Irish Sacramental Wine Association, as chairman of the Belfast Ladies' Temperance Union, and as GWCT of the Grand Lodge of Ireland.[39] In 1877 his newly elected successor led the Grand Lodge out of the RWGL of the World and back into the RWGL. "The Bible Wine Question, and not the Negro Question," fumed Pyper, "was the real cause of that disruption."[40] He organized a rival Grand Lodge of Ireland affiliated with the RWGL of the World. Later he became a Congregational minister.

England, however, was the site of the most sustained and acrimonious battle in the Templar world. As a bemused Georgian pointed out: "In England, where the negro question was rather abstract than concrete, the controversy raged with far more bitterness than in Georgia, where the very life of the cause seemed at stake."[41] Nowhere did it produce a more learned polemical literature than the pamphlets published in 1876 and 1877, a time when both sides believed that arguments and historical evidence might persuade people.[42] Nowhere else did so many respected veterans of the temperance movement take opposite sides in the fratricidal conflict.

A substantial minority in England, including well-known and wealthy Templars, enlisted in the Hickmanite party. But although they shared the general Hickmanite condemnation of the Manifesto, the Ultimatum, and the RWGL of the World, the Hickmanites in England responded to a separate agenda involving grievances against Malins as leader of his Grand Lodge, whom they dubbed "one *Man* made a *God* with £400 per annum." For years his enemies had complained about "the imperialism and centralisation of the officers at Birmingham." An influential pamphlet alleged that "many of the best men in the movement have left it in disgust, or they have been cut off from the Order by the G.W.C. Templar." Another Templar complained that "a spirit of intolerance—and in some directions of despotism—has been shown, on account of which many have left the Order." Purges of suspected Hickmanites added to the bitterness. They proclaimed themselves "[f]ree men"—free from the alleged subservience of Malins's adherents. Most English Hickmanites favored replacing a single Grand Lodge with numerous smaller provincial Grand Lodges; for them, the international issues in the great schism mattered less than local organizational and personality disputes. In short, the Hickmanite movement in England was a rebellion against "Joseph and his Brethren."[43]

Although the United Temperance Association, an earlier breakaway organization, approached the English Hickmanites about reunion in 1877, few of those who had taken part in previous rebellions against Malins rallied to the Hickmanite cause. The regalia and ritual used by the old RWGL divided the two factions. Those who had fought Malins in the earlier rebellions also placed a low priority on internationalism and had little use for the RWGL and its complex administrative machinery. Yet Malins's old enemies enjoyed his discomfort. Charles Garrett, a well-known Methodist minister, declared: "If [Malins] were hired by the publicans to ruin Templary and to hinder the spread of Temperance he could not do more."[44]

A towering figure in the English temperance movement, Dr. F.R. Lees, became the leader of the Hickmanites. An erudite and prolific writer, Lees published his best-known book before Malins had entered his teens, the *Alliance Prize Essay; or, an Argument, Legal and Historical, for the Legislative Prohibition of the Liquor Traffic* (1856). His doctorate, like Hickman's colonelcy, was honorary. Rigid in personality and innocent of political tact, Lees had won notoriety for a quarrel with an equally famous reformer: he resigned his appointment as a United Kingdom Alliance agent in the late 1850s after he had attacked the character of the Anglo-American reformed drunkard John B. Gough, and the courts had found in Gough's favor in a libel judgment. In the words of his son, Lees was "plagued with pugnacities." By the time of the great schism he also suffered from depression and physical ill health.[45]

Like many other established temperance reformers, Lees had

become an ornament of Malins's Grand Lodge. He had joined the IOGT in 1869 while on a lecture tour in the United States. As part of the English delegation at the RWGL session of 1875, he had supported Malins in the fight against duplicate Grand Lodges, and he also helped draft the Manifesto of 1876.[46] In that year he did not seek reelection as the Grand Lodge's counsellor, the second highest office, because of overwork and ill health.

In England the fight between the Malinites and Hickmanites brought about a protracted and expensive legal case. Lees sued Malins to reclaim the charter of the Grand Lodge of England, a response to the attempt of the GWCT to register a copyright for the charter with the Board of Trade. Both sides saw the charter as symbolizing their claim to be the legitimate Templar organization. Malins rejected Lees's offer to let the Society of Friends mediate the dispute. In turn, Lees avoided the public debate that Malins requested. The expensive charter suit began in December 1877 and—with a brief interruption late in 1881 during reunion discussions—dragged on, dominating the great schism in England. Although he received a little money from the RWGL, Lees bore most of the financial responsibility personally. After he made a sneering comment about an earlier bankruptcy of John Kempster, editor of the *Good Templars' Watchword,* Kempster sued him for libel, and Lees countersued, adding to the legal entanglement and embarrassment for English temperance reformers.

William Hoyle, formerly treasurer of the English Grand Lodge, became another prestigious convert when, after a brief hesitation, he broke with Malins. Forced to work from the age of eight, Hoyle had made his fortune as a textile manufacturer. He earned an honored place in the temperance movement as an authority on the economic cost of drink. Every year his National Drink Bill was published as a letter in the *Times.* At the beginning of the conflict in Britain, both factions agreed that the much respected Hoyle should preside at the 1876 London reconciliation conference. Afterward he hoped to maintain membership in both the Hickmanite and Malinite organizations, but the Malinites would not tolerate this fence-straddling.[47] Hoyle published two much-cited pamphlets attacking Malins. His health failed in 1884, and his death two years later symbolized the decline of the Hickmanite party in England.

Among other well-known reformers in the Hickmanite ranks was Thomas Watson of Rochdale, a Gladstonian Liberal MP and generous contributor to the Methodist Free Church. A onetime spinning operative, he had made his fortune by inventing an imitation sealskin.[48] A number of Nonconformist ministers also held office in the English Hickmanite organization. Stephen Todd, a Congregational minister, became the first Grand Worthy Secretary. He was succeeded by a Methodist Free Church local preacher, Thomas Hardy, who in turn was succeeded by an ordained Methodist Free Church minister, Samuel Wright. At the time of reunion Thomas Olman Todd, apparently a son of Stephen Todd, held the same office, a sign of the inbred character of the dwindling band of English Hickmanites.

Lees, Hoyle, and many other Hickmanite stalwarts were prominent in the United Kingdom Alliance, the principal lobbying organization of the English prohibitionists. Malins quarreled with the Alliance over its patronage of his enemies through articles published in its weekly organ, the *Alliance News*. In 1880 some members of the Alliance executive tried to block his election as one of the numerous honorary vice-presidents.[49]

Although reliable statistics are not available, by 1877 perhaps 100,000 of the English Templar membership were supporting Malins and 13,000 backing Lees. The anti-Malins faction had only a few pockets of strength, such as Liverpool, and throughout the great schism the English Hickmanites diminished in numbers but refused to disappear. The fight was much harder than during previous rebellions against Malins in 1872-73 by advocates of provincial Grand Lodges, less ritual and regalia, and the elimination of Malins's so-called "spy" deputies who represented him at lodges.

Now much of the Templar elite attacked the GWCT. His own brother Clement helped turn the original Templar lodge at Birmingham, Columbia lodge, against him; he accused Joseph of having "an ambitious craving for pocket and power" and, to attain these ends, creating "a mass of corruption and wickedness." For a time Capt. Frank Schofield of the military lodges remained in the Malinite Grand Lodge—to fight it from the inside. William Barton had supported Malins in a recent dispute over whether the office of GWCT should be salaried or honorary and had purchased the *Templar* to back Malins and the RWGL of the World. Then Barton was converted to the Hickmanite point of view, and the *Templar,* already in a circulation war with the *Good Templars' Advocate,* became for several years the unofficial voice of the English Hickmanites. Despite subsidies from wealthy Hickmanites and a change of name to appeal to non-Templar temperance reformers, however, the newspaper died before the end of the great schism. The English Hickmanites denied that their small numbers discouraged them. They ridiculed Malins as "Pope Josephus," and the motto of the their official organ, *British*

Loyal Templar, defiantly proclaimed, "They are slaves who dare not to be, in the Right with two or three." [50]

The Hickmanites in England fulfilled the dream of many long-time critics of Malins by replacing the centralized Grand Lodge of England with numerous provincial Grand Lodges. Ironically, the principal argument against a single Grand Lodge of England—its very large membership—did not apply in the case of the Hickmanite organization. The new provincial Grand Lodges were no larger than district lodges in the Malinite organization. The Hickmanites' Grand Lodge of England survived as a mere shell, kept in existence to support the suit over ownership of the Grand Lodge of England charter. The military and naval lodges were organized into a separate Grand Lodge. The RWGL authorized a shadowy Worthy Grand Lodge of Great Britain and Ireland which Lees headed for several years, a regional organization situated between the Grand Lodges and RWGL.

Problems abounded. The provincial Grand Lodge of Yorkshire would not recognize the Worthy Grand Lodge, and the RWGL interpreted the powers of the Worthy Grand Lodge so narrowly that Lees protested; he was willing to head the Worthy Grand Lodge only if it became more than a name. He also complained about the quality of Hickmanite lodge meetings and officers. He wanted sound instruction, not entertainment: "Above all, we must have officers who can read, financial secretaries who can keep accounts, and chaplains who cannot swear."[51]

The controversy over racism took on special bitterness in England because the Hickmanites there claimed to share the commitment to black membership in the American South, although disagreeing on the means. An old abolitionist, Lees resented any insinuation that he countenanced racism. Shortly after he broke with Malins, he said that "if Alabama will not admit the Negro, then Alabama must go." Yet the English Hickmanites inevitably ended up justifying the racial policies in the American South. Lees defended the principle of equal rights for people of all races and at the same time the practice of segregation: "*I will never consent, never, to make any distinctions of race or colour;* but do you think that because we do not recognise the distinction in our paper declarations, we can ignore the fact? Do you think that you can make these races mix? Can you mix the proletariat of England with the nobility?" Lees urged the need for time and education to effect change, and the practical necessity of leaving policy to the whites who lived among the blacks. "I never will fight for abstract principles," he said, because "they must be interpreted by the facts of life."[52]

In 1881 the charter lawsuit led to serious peace negotiations under the neutral auspices of a senior barrister. On 27 October 1881 lawyers for the two sides agreed that both factions favored equal rights in the Templar Order regardless of race: "It is admitted that both sides are equally anxious to uphold the principle of the absolute equality of the White Man and the Negro as regards admission to the Order." Lees argued that the RWGL had eliminated whatever problems might have existed in 1876: in 1878 it had adopted a constitutional amendment allowing the international organization to charter black lodges in jurisdictions where a white Grand Lodge refused to do so—regardless of whether that Grand Lodge consented or not—and to institute a black Grand Lodge. Lees and his party argued that the dual system of segregated Grand Lodges was a practical way of dealing with the reality of prejudice until people overcame it. But by this time Malins and his faction had moved beyond their Louisville position; they insisted that reunion be on the basis of eliminating the color line in the IOGT completely and everywhere. [53]

The negotiations broke down on 30 December 1881, over a very limited aspect of the question of black membership in the former slave states: the right of local black lodges to have representation at the white Grand Lodge in those southern states where there was no black Grand Lodge. In concluding the abortive efforts to bring the two British factions together, the presiding lawyer, Alfred Wills, diplomatically characterized Lees's faction as embodying "the practical spirit" and that of Malins "the sterner exhibition of principle."

Whatever their original intentions in walking out at Louisville, the Malinites made antiracist policies the justification for the great schism. News reports from the American South and serialized fictional accounts depicting the injustices endured by African Americans competed with temperance agitation for space in the *Good Templars' Watchword*. The RWGL of the World moved steadily beyond the demands that the United Executives had drafted for the Louisville session. At the little caucus in 1876 that created the new organization the delegates had considered changing the constitution to eliminate any kind of separation of the races but refrained from doing so in the hope of facilitating reunion. In 1878, when the prospects for reunion appeared bleak, Malins gave the required year's notice for a constitutional amendment to eliminate duplicate Grand Lodges organized on the basis of race. The representatives of the four black Grand Lodges present at that session concurred, and Malins's amendment was passed at the RWGL of the World session in 1879. To save money, the RWGL of the World then adopted biennial sessions, so its next meeting did not take place until 1881. At that time a committee boasted that the RWGL of the World "has rubbed out the last vestige of a colour line, and neither makes provision for it, nor gives it any toleration."[54]

The most prestigious abolitionists in the United States, William Lloyd Garrison and Wendell Phillips, praised the RWGL of the World for its stand on equal rights. Garrison told William Wells Brown that "it is a shocking delusion to imagine that the best way to promote the Temperance Reformation, or any other righteous movement, is by erecting an insurmountable barrier of caste."[55] Phillips advised Professor F.W. Newman, Cardinal Newman's freethinking brother, that "any Temperance man who has been disciplined by our old Anti-Slavery experience must see the whole affair as you saw it."[56]

Were the Malinites racists themselves? Probably so, although their racism was moderate by the standards of the time. During the schism they often thought it necessary to mention the light skin color of black Templars in their organization, perhaps to challenge the reasonableness of the color line but perhaps to imply that African Americans of mixed ancestry were superior to those with darker skins. For instance, the wife of the head of the black Grand Lodge of Virginia, it was said, "would pass anywhere but in America as a white lady."[57]

The Malinites could be insensitive about racial epithets. John Kempster, editor of the Grand Lodge of England's newspaper, loudly opposed any compromise that might undermine the rights of blacks to Templar membership, but with scant apology he sang "Ten Little Niggers" for the entertainment of a lodge meeting whose guests of honor were ex-slave Joseph May and his daughter, soon to leave for missionary work in Sierra Leone.[58] At the annual session of the Grand Lodge of England in 1877, Malins joked about the first head of the Independent Order of Good Templars being named Coon, a remark greeted by laughter.[59]

The members of the RWGL of the World shared at least some of the racist assumptions and vocabulary of the late nineteenth century but with less rigidity. A Templar who emigrated from Liverpool to Brooklyn in 1879 said, "I must confess I always regarded the coloured race as inferior to the whites in point of intellect," but after a visit to an all-black lodge he acknowledged, "I have had occasion to alter my opinion."[60]

The Malinites in Britain sought to appeal to Templars elsewhere through an antiracist interpretation of universal brotherhood and sisterhood. Although Templar statistics for these years are obviously flawed, it appears that the old RWGL had more members than the rival RWGL of the World. The British had assumed that they would have support throughout the British Empire, but most Canadians opposed them, as did most South Africans and Australians, and a great many in New Zealand and India.[61] This must have surprised Malins. An Australian opponent acknowledged that before the split, Malins's name was "sufficient to cause any statement endorsed by it to be received with a firm faith in its truth" and added angrily, "We know better now."[62] When the Templars spread to Scandinavia, the RWGL of the World attracted a solid majority of the new membership, but a substantial minority supported the Hickmanites.

The biggest disappointment for the Malinites occurred in North America. Although the British failed to achieve a majority for their constitutional amendment in 1876, they had received considerable support from Grand Lodges in the United States and Canada and expected to win many of them over; in fact, they succeeded only in the province of Nova Scotia. After Louisville the first annual session for a Grand Lodge was held in Minnesota, whose RWGL representatives strongly favored affiliating with the RWGL of the World. Yet despite sympathetic speeches and votes, the Minnesota Grand Lodge did not break with the old RWGL.[63] Subsequently, Minnesota accepted Dual Grand Lodges as a solution to black Templar membership.

Other northern Grand Lodges too insisted on the importance of Templar universalism, sometimes criticized the RWGL, sometimes defended it, but never renounced allegiance. For instance, Pennsylvania unanimously adopted a resolution that tried to satisfy both the supporters and opponents of Gladstone's motion. Pennsylvania urged "immediate measures to secure the full benefits of the Good Templar Order to all, without respect to class, color, race or country that may desire it."[64] Ohio endorsed Gladstone's Ultimatum but not the split.[65] Rhode Island declared itself "loyal to the R.W.G. Lodge, but condemn[ed] its action" in depriving "the coloured people of the rights and privileges of all Good Templars."[66] The Grand Lodge of Maine dismissed as a pretext Malins's crusade on behalf of prospective black members, asserting that the RWGL "recognizes fully and unequivocally the great and Heaven-born principle of the Brotherhood of the Human Race."[67]

In the old abolitionist stronghold of Massachusetts the Malinites won at the semiannual meeting in September. Hastings, a former RWGT, came from Wisconsin to persuade Massachusetts. At a hotel he told a Nova Scotian visitor that he would convince the session in ten minutes. In fact, though he spoke for two hours, William Wells Brown's reply—"a masterpiece of argument and invective"— demolished Hastings's case. Brown charged Hastings with hypocrisy: "SHAME upon the Northern Representatives, who remained silent while the black man's rights and the principles of the Independent Order of Good Templars had to be advocated by foreigners." With one dissenting vote the meeting condemned the RWGL's action as "contrary to the principle of our Order, and of human liberty." It was a brief triumph. Since the attendance at the semiannual meeting was very light, the decision was postponed to the annual session in March 1877, where the Malinites lost decisively. A motion that the Grand Lodge recognize the RWGL of the World was defeated, as was a minority report of a special committee on "the color question" that hinted at support for the British-dominated organization. The majority report adopted by the Grand Lodge employed strong language on behalf of the protection of the rights of blacks, severely criticized the southern Grand Lodges and the leadership of the old RWGL, and made "future loyalty" to the RWGL contingent upon "its unqualified loyalty" in practice as well as principle "to the cause of universal humanity."[68]

This rhetoric warmed abolitionist hearts but left the practical allegiance of the Grand Lodge with Hickman's RWGL. Recognizing that they were beaten in the existing Grand Lodge, the Malinites organized their own. Massachusetts was the only state where they succeeded in establishing a durable, predominantly white Grand Lodge. It was very small.

Other things that the British did not anticipate were the (reluctant) willingness of white southerners to make the concessions that satisfied the conscience of white northerners, the widespread resentment over a major constitutional proposal without a year's notice, and the outrage over the great schism that ripped apart the Templar brotherhood and sisterhood. Although the Grand Lodge of Connecticut avoided a partisan tone, it condemned the means that the British took toward an honorable goal: "Our British brethren made a moderate and reasonable demand," but the Ultimatum was inexpedient, and from a constitutional viewpoint the British were "in error."[69]

J.J. Talbott, the only GWCT in the United States to support the RWGL of the World, was frustrated at his failure to win Indiana over to the new organization. By the summer of 1876 he slipped into drunkenness and, after repenting and being reobligated, died.[70] Talbott's fall and subsequent death was a serious blow for the RWGL of the World. Raised in Kentucky, he had a history of alternating drinking bouts with spells of temperance evangelism. Supposedly he was drunk when he wrote many of Hickman's stirring temperance orations.[71]

After 1877 or so the *Journals of Proceedings* of the annual sessions of the northern Grand Lodges seldom allude to the great schism except in the summaries of RWGL meetings. In North America most Hickmanites lived where there were no Malinites, so the great schism was remote and, for the rank and file, not very significant. Some Templars such as William B. Reed, appalled at white southern racism, accepted the RWGL's majority vote reluctantly: "Never did I feel so ashamed of my race." Although he conceded the practical necessity of racially segregated subordinate lodges, Reed condemned racially segregated Grand Lodges.[72] Isolated supporters of the Malinite causes, such as Emma Barrett Molloy in Indiana, withdrew from lodge life and worked for temperance through other organizations. Many Malinite leaders in North America were British-born and-reared, as were Jessie Forsyth in Massachusetts and William G. Lane in Nova Scotia; in general, however, British immigrants who had been members of the RWGL of the World in the United Kingdom showed no discomfort in joining Hickmanite lodges in the United States and Canada.

In North America the great schism was never as bitter as in Britain, perhaps because after a year or two the Hickmanites were comfortably in control throughout nearly all the New World. In 1878 Malins and other British representatives to an RWGL of the World session in Boston traveled southward to rally supporters and investigate conditions. In Annapolis a Hickmanite who had written against Malins initiated him into the Dashaways Reform Club.[73] In 1880 the Georgia Templars arranged for "Mother" Eliza Stewart to organize the WCTU in their state, even though the Ohio woman supported the RWGL of the World. Martha McClellan Brown was one of the original officers of the RWGL of the World, although her family circumstances made it impossible for her to contribute "aggressive work."[74] Yet in 1882, when she conducted a lecture tour of the South under the auspices of the National Prohibition League, she too was feted by white southern Templars. The GWCT of Kentucky met her outside Louisville; J.G. Thrower organized a reception in Atlanta; and in Alabama, second to none in opposition to black membership, the GWCT greeted her.[75]

Throughout the American South the white Grand Lodges greatly shrank after Louisville and their subsequent concessions on black membership, although in a few states there was a temporary recovery in the middle 1880s. If the RWGL had authorized a semi-autonomous Worthy Grand Lodge for the white population of the former slave states, analogous to that of the British Isles and Australia, white southerners might have acquired more confidence in their ability to remain Templars despite their disagreement with northern interpretations of the IOGT's universalism and the northern alliance with the Prohibition Party.

The weakness of the southern white Templars at home reduced their influence in the RWGL and led to the breakup of the Louisville-Napanee alliance, which in the 1870s had put a southerner in the office of RWGT and made a Canadian international secretary. In 1880 a Nebraskan, F.G. Keens, replaced Williams of Ontario as Right Worthy Grand Secretary, and in 1881 Hickman of Kentucky was ousted as RWGT. At first Theodore Kanouse of Wisconsin was elected to the post, but he refused because he could not devote time to an unpaid office, so George Katzenstein of California took over the leadership—retaining his well-paid office as secretary of his Grand Lodge.

The most important shift in leadership came in 1884 when John Finch, formerly GWCT of Nebraska, was elected RWGT with over two-thirds of the vote.[76] The charismatic Finch, reelected unanimously in 1885 and 1886, made rulings on the rights of blacks that met the spirit of the original Malinite demands, rulings that the RWGL sustained in 1886—ironically, during a session held in Richmond, Virginia.

As early as 1882 the reforms adopted by the RWGL, combined with the collapse of the London reunion conference, persuaded Harriet N.K. Goff to quit the RWGL of the World. She had been its vice Templar, but she concluded regretfully that the continuation of the split was caused by Malins's ego and that the Malinites had lost sight of the objective that had inspired them in 1876: organizing blacks as members of the Templar Order. In an open letter to Malins, published in African American newspapers in June 1882, she declared, "I joined your Order [the RWGL of the World] in 1878 solely for the purposes of laboring for the interests of the colored race, and because I believed it, at that time, the best medium for so doing."[77] She did not want the freedmen to be "the shuttle-cock of Good Templary." Before she joined the RWGL of the World, she knew that Malins's motives in the schism had been impugned but saw that as irrelevant and still did not doubt his sincerity. "But the long-continued law-suit for the charter of the Grand Lodge of England has wearied, annoyed and perhaps embarrassed you, and pardon me for adding, seems to have changed the animus from justice or benevolence to self-preservation."

Goff added another complaint: "The utter futility of any protests against the Kansas work entirely dissipated all my faith that extinction of race prejudice is the object sought, or if it is, that white American co-operation is desired." It perhaps brought enthusiasm in England to spend $500 of Quaker money on a black Grand Lodge of Kansas which fell "to pieces like a rope of sand," but for black refugees newly arrived from the South it poisoned relations with their white neighbors.

Goff regretted the separation of the races in the Hickmanite Order, but the Dual Lodges were represented at meetings of the RWGL, a step in the direction of ending the separation. She advised the black lodges that she had helped organize in New York to ally themselves with the white Grand Lodge.

When Malins responded to her letter, he said simply, "I stand for the complete and immediate fraternization of all races."[78]

As a result of the changes in the RWGL and the minimal success of the RWGL of the World among African Americans, the great schism became harder and harder to justify. This did not make ending it easy but did make it possible.

5

The Black Templars

In contrast to the abundance of information on how white Templars viewed black Templar membership, there is only skimpy evidence about the black Templars themselves and even less about how other blacks regarded the IOGT. Historians of African American organizational life almost never mention the Good Templars, and biographers of blacks who held high Templar office seldom explore this phase of their lives. The general neglect of African American fraternal societies and the black temperance movement helps explain this oversight. Moreover, much of the source material for the black Templars lies buried in British temperance newspapers, not the place where research on African American history is commonly conducted.

In recruiting black members the Templar factions were helped by prevailing African American ideologies and social organization. In the nineteenth century blacks often made the analogy between drink and slavery, temperance and freedom.[1] A tradition of temperance reform among the black community in the northern states dated from pre–Civil War times. Maine's Abyssinian Total Abstinence Society claimed 176 members in the early 1840s. The temperance movement spread to the former slave states after the abolition of slavery. In 1867, for instance, Missouri's Colored Temperance Society held a fund-raising Independence Day picnic near Columbia. Although there were exceptions, the black men and women who joined the IOGT did so for the most part as teetotalers or moderate drinkers, not as alcoholics seeking to save themselves from a drinking problem. A Templar in Tallahassee declared himself "a Temperance young man before I joined the Order" but added "I am stronger since I joined it."[2]

In the absence of well-developed African American temperance societies, the churches dominated the black temperance movement. Methodist conferences often called for restraint in drinking alcohol. A black Templar, not himself a Methodist, credited "chiefly . . .

ministers of the A.M.E. Church" for the growth of the IOGT among African Americans. He added praise for a presiding elder of the A.M.E. Zion Church, the other major black Methodist denomination.[3]

A.M.E. clergy and laity joined the RWGL of the World in disproportionate numbers. Admittedly, some of these Templar memberships were nominal like that of the celebrated Bishop Daniel A. Payne, but other Methodists joined the IOGT to work.[4] A future A.M.E. bishop was the first GWCT for the Malinites in Virginia. The Grand Lodge of South Carolina gained momentum when all the ministers at an A.M.E. conference joined a special lodge; at least three chiefs of this Grand Lodge were A.M.E. ministers. The A.M.E. weekly newspaper, the *Christian Recorder,* became the Malinite organ in the United States. It published a section of Templar news under the RWGL of the World seal, which displayed a black man and a white man shaking hands. Malins himself, in the United States for a meeting of the RWGL of the World in 1878, organized Fraternity lodge at the Philadelphia headquarters of the *Christian Recorder,* with its staff as the membership.[5] At a Templar meeting in Ireland the newspaper's editor, Dr. B.T. Tanner, rejoiced that "Good Templary brought all upon one platform." Initiated at Bedford lodge in London during an 1882 international Methodist conference in England were James M. Townsend of Richmond, Indiana, corresponding secretary for the A.M.E. missions; Joseph P. Shorter, who taught mathematics at Wilberforce University in Ohio, and the Josephus O'Banyoun (or Banyon), a Canadian minister and ex-Templar.[6]

The second largest Methodist denomination among African Americans, the A.M.E. Zion Church, also provided Templar activists. A Zion bishop headed the Grand Lodge of North Carolina. California's Zion bishop served as a proxy representative at an RWGL of the World session in Britain while he was there on a fund raising mission.[7] Eliza A. Gardner, a Boston dressmaker, earned a reputation as an outstanding "speaker and reasoner" in the racially integrated Grand Lodge of Massachusetts. A white friend added that Gardner, "but for the handicap of her color, might have held first rank among the noted women of the world."[8]

This is not to say that the black Templars lacked non-Methodist leaders. The same observer who lauded the Methodists for their contribution to the IOGT offered praise as well to Albert Lewis, a Baptist minister in Key West.[9] In 1879 a Baptist minister was elected GWCT of Virginia, and Baptist ministers headed several Dual Grand Lodges for the Hickmanites. Yet on balance, the black Templars appear to have numbered fewer Baptists among their leaders than might have been expected from the largest African American denomination.

For blacks as for whites, the war against drink combined religion with worldly ambitions. A white Templar organizer said that most African Americans accepted "the authority of the Bible," so "I use the Bible itself for my text-book, and prove my positions by it." At the same time the black critique of alcohol emphasized the material handicap imposed by drinking. A black Floridian insisted that "the colored man cannot *afford* to waste his *time* and his *money* with drink."[10] Temperance was seen as contributing to both moral and material self-betterment.

African Americans joined various fraternal lodges enthusiastically. It is unclear how much the black fraternal societies were derivatives of white ones and how much, as W.E.B. Du Bois argued in his pioneering works, West Africa provided an independent model, but there is no doubt that many Templars were active in other lodges as well.[11] For the Templars this enthusiasm for fraternal organizations was a mixed blessing. Since time and money were limited, there was competition for members. Templars had innumerable rivals "such as Oddfellows, Knights of Wise Men, Knights of Pythias, United Brothers of Friendship, Seven Stars of Consolidation."[12] Another competitor was the Good Samaritans, originally a white fraternal temperance society, which became a de facto black organization after the Civil War.

The distinctive features of the IOGT that set it apart from most other fraternal societies both hurt and helped the Templars in recruiting African Americans. Most black fraternal lodges acted as benevolent societies, providing financial relief at times of illness and burial, so the Templars' policy not to offer mutual insurance hurt them. Caleb A. Stevens's diary cites a black Templar in Washington who argued that the Templars would have to provide insurance to attract and retain members.[13] Other Templar characteristics helped. Unlike comparable white organizations, numerous black societies such as the Galilean Fishermen bore a biblical name, and like such black organizations the Templars gave witness to their Christian belief. Christ was present in Templar ritual and rhetoric. And black societies frequently admitted both women and men, which made African Americans comfortable with a Templar practice rare in white organizations.

The black leadership admired the RWGL of the World for its commitment to admitting members regardless of race, and its large international membership. Regardless of the local reality of racial segregation and white supremacy, black leaders could enjoy momentary equality at RWGL of the World sessions on both sides of the Atlantic. When Joseph E. Lee of Florida attended the 1878 international session in Boston, he rejoiced, *"For the first time in my life I took as a brother the hand of the Englishman, the Irishman, the Welshman, the Scotchman, the American, and the African, feeling that I was in truth a man."* Describing his visit to Liverpool for a subsequent international session, John C. Dancy of North Carolina declared, "It was there I breathed the pure air of liberty, reached the full stature of a man." Paralleling these jubilant remarks, the justification offered by a black leader for transforming the True Reformers of Georgia into a Dual Grand Lodge emphasized equality and internationalism: by becoming Templars they entered "upon an equal footing with all men and all civilized nations of the earth."[14]

The extreme poverty of most African Americans handicapped efforts to organize black Templar lodges. A temperance leader in South Carolina used whiskey bottles in the communion service until white benefactors in New England provided him with replacements. An organizer from Massachusetts lamented that Templars in the same southern state could not afford adequate lanterns or a fire at lodge meetings. Paying the $2.50 charter fee was often difficult, and organizers for the Hickmanites sometimes tempted blacks with free supplies such as officers' blank books necessary for record keeping. Members improvised their own regalia. Grand Lodges had to pay their members who served as organizers because few blacks could afford to take time from their regular work without compensation. A northerner who taught at a freedmen's school in Georgia described two of his students, both of them Templars, as having walked seventy-five miles at Christmas vacation, arriving home with badly swollen feet, in order to save fares that would have equaled several weeks' board. A black ex-sailor dispatched from England to organize western Tennessee ran out of money, so to pay what he owed for his lodging he washed buggies in a livery stable. Because "the work was hard and incessant from 5 A.M. until 9, 10, and sometimes 11 P.M., weekdays and Sabbaths alike," he could do little for the IOGT.[15]

To make a living even the partially educated elite had to struggle. After a change in party at the White House cost W.M. Artrell of Florida his federal customs appointment, he moved to another city where he worked as a school principal and a tailor. A Methodist minister in South Carolina served four small scattered congregations and taught school as well.[16] Except for the most committed, there was little time and energy available for the Templar lodges. The search for a livelihood forced many officers to relocate outside their jurisdictions and consequently abandon their Templar offices. Those motivated by opportunism quickly moved on to more profitable causes.

The lack of education was as much a stumbling block as the lack of money. Some lodges depended on a single literate member to read the ritual and collapsed if this person fell ill or resigned or moved away. Yet former slaves and children of slaves responded to the challenge of a fraternal temperance society designed for people familiar with books. One Virginian, who had turned down lodge office because "he could not read his part of the ceremony," hired a tutor and learned to read. He then accepted election as the head of his lodge. [17]

Ambitious Republican politicians, often occupying federal patronage jobs, played a large role in Templar leadership. For instance, the chief mail agent for the Charlotte-Wilmington district was Grand Worthy Marshal of North Carolina. Although for most such politicians fraternal temperance was a fleeting enthusiasm, a few politicians proved faithful to the Templar cause for years, such as state legislators George Teamoh in Virginia and Joseph E. Lee in Florida.[18]

Racism complicated the Templar missions. For the most part whites did not object to black temperance organizations, and there are instances in North Carolina and Florida of white Hickmanite officers attending black Malinite meetings. But organizing blacks could be dangerous for white Malinites regarded by local whites as outside agitators. In November 1876 Charlotte's mayor threatened to dash out a British organizer's brains with a fireplace log. In Texas another British-born Malinite organizer complained that "the whites threatened to kill us, swore to tar, feather and burn us." Severely injured in the Texas whiskey riots of 1882, he returned to England the following year. Blacks were reluctant to mix too much with the white Malinites who wanted to put them into lodges. A Massachusetts-born schoolteacher complained that he had become ill after spending a night in an unheated Georgia church; a black organizer would have received an invitation to the home of a black family.[19]

Other than dubious statistics published by the RWGL, there is little information about the black Templars who affiliated with the Hickmanites after 1876. The Hickmanite press offered nothing comparable to the Malinite weekly *Good Templars' Watchword*'s reports of black Templar lodges.

The halfhearted attempt by white southerners to recruit blacks took place out of expediency, to appease the conscience of white Hickmanites outside the South and to hinder the Malinites in their organizing efforts. Although at first the white Templars in Alabama,

Mississippi, and Tennessee rejected any kind of Templar membership for black people, eventually all white jurisdictions authorized segregated black Templar societies. For a brief period early in the schism the Dual Grand Lodge of Georgia claimed a couple of thousand members, as did Virginia's at the other end of the schism. Another half-dozen states established smaller, short-lived Dual Grand Lodges, and in some southern states there were isolated black subordinate lodges that reported directly to the RWGL. In Maryland, when white Templars withdrew to form their unusual Dual Grand Lodge, the original Grand Lodge of Maryland became mostly African American and by the mid-1880s retained only a single white lodge.[20]

Some blacks outside the South belonged to Hickmanite organizations. In 1877 Ontario claimed about fifteen black lodges in its western districts and a total black membership in the thousands. The Grand Worthy Secretary denied that any lodge had "refused admission to a Negro, Indian, or Caucasian, on account of color." The small band of English Hickmanites had no all-black lodges, but in 1881 Toxteth lodge at the port of Liverpool had at least twenty black members and in 1884 more than fifty. In the mid-1880s Hope juvenile temple in Utica, New York, was "composed almost exclusively of colored children," several of them severely handicapped.[21]

Most of the few surviving records for the Dual Grand Lodges are from Georgia, where the 1880 census reported 725,133 blacks, the largest number for any state. There the dominant figure in the white Grand Lodge, the English-born J.G. Thrower, championed the cause of segregated black Templary after 1876. Previously the grand superintendent of the True Reformers, Thrower hoped to dismantle the black temperance organization he had helped create and reorganize its members in the projected Dual Grand Lodges. It looked easier to take over a sizable organization than to win converts one at a time.

Georgia epitomizes the shaky foundations typical of black Grand Lodges and the importance of that scarce resource, leadership. Thrower admitted that he had difficulty in persuading the Grand Fountain of Georgia to reorganize as a Dual Grand Lodge. Some accounts say that he threatened the True Reformers. In 1877 a former Grand Worthy Master, William A. Pledger, grumbled that Thrower had persuaded the True Reformers only after telling them that the Hickmanites and the Malinites had settled their quarrel.[22] In 1878, after the new Dual Grand Lodge conciliated Pledger by electing him GWCT, he denied that the black Hickmanites were dupes and offered to debate a Malinite. In 1879, shifting to a third position, Pledger connived with the first GWCT's son to secede with a few lodges and affiliate with the RWGL of the World. Still in his twenties, Pledger then drifted out of the Templars and devoted himself to Republican politics and journalism.[23] What happened in Georgia also illustrates the way black Templar lodges in other states shifted from the Hickmanites to the Malinites and vice versa in a kind of civil war that benefited the temperance movement not in the least. After Pledger's desertion Georgia's Dual Grand Lodge collapsed. Thrower blamed a white infiltrater from Massachusetts, Charles P. Wellman. In the mid-1880s, with the help of black preachers, the determined Thrower reconstituted the Dual Grand Lodge, but it fell apart again almost immediately.

The Malinites believed that the Hickmanites enrolled more blacks: the RWGL of the World's secretary calculated in 1887 that "our American friends had last year at least double the number of colored lodges and members in the southern States that we had."[24] An enemy's compliment is hard to dismiss, but the published statistical evidence, for what little it is worth, fails to establish Hickmanite numerical superiority other than at the end of the great schism before a new Hickmanite black Grand Lodge of Virginia had had time to collapse. To justify its own failure, the RWGL of the World overestimated the advantage that the black Hickmanites obtained by sharing territory with the white adherents of the RWGL.

The relationship between black and white Hickmanites was an uncomfortable one. Local southern whites appear to have done little to help beyond persuading True Reformers to reorganize as Templars. The black Hickmanites had fewer problems getting Templar supplies, but in most other regards seem to have been as isolated as the Malinites in the former slave states. Fear of forced socialization strained relations. The Grand Lodge of West Virginia reassured its white members that if blacks were allowed to join the IOGT "our Lodges will not be required to allow them to visit unless they so desire." The head of the white Grand Lodge of South Carolina pointed out to his members that the black Templars made no embarrassing attempt to visit the white lodges. In 1886 the *Alexandria Gazette and Virginia Advertiser* reported that when a representative of the Dual Grand Lodge of Virginia dared to attend a county Templar meeting in northern Virginia, "the [white] Wood Grove delegation left."[25]

Probably few blacks cared very much about the quarrel between the rival RWGLs and took for granted that local lodges would be racially segregated. Wanting only respect and cooperation, they would work with the Hickmanites if the Hickmanites would work with them. A letter from a Methodist minister in Missouri, J.C. Owens, to the (Philadelphia) *Christian Recorder* both illustrates this pragmatic attitude and exemplifies the obstacles to cooperation. The head of the Hickmanite Grand Lodge of Missouri had organized the first black lodge in the state in February 1878 with the minimum ten charter members and Owens as Worthy Chief Templar. Within five months it grew to fifty members, and twenty-five other black lodges were also organized, comprising nearly three hundred members. The day before the Grand Lodge met in St. Louis in July 1878, a caucus of black Templars decided to stick with the Hickmanites if the whites made it possible. When the blacks joined the whites at a public meeting, Owens wrote, "so harmonious was the occasion that several times during the evening I was made to wonder, is this St. Louis, Mo." The next morning the black representatives were allowed to take their seats at the Grand Lodge session, but in the afternoon whites began "wire pulling and trickery" to challenge their credentials. After a racist faction introduced a resolution challenging the legality of the black lodges, a committee recommended a separate black Dual Grand Lodge, but the Grand Lodge voted to keep the blacks in the same organization as the whites.[26] Despite this decision, a Dual Grand Lodge was organized in Missouri the following year.

The international Hickmanite organization made a few respectful gestures. The RWGL hired a black Baptist minister from Louisville to organize segregated lodges in Kentucky—which he did with modest success—and bestowed minor international offices on several blacks. A prosperous African American restaurant owner, a member of the integrated Grand Lodge of Maryland, was appointed Outer Guard (later styled "Sentinel") in 1877. The Kentucky organizer obtained the same office in 1883. In 1881 Rev. D.A. Williams of the Dual Grand Lodge of Mississippi became Grand Worthy Chaplain, an office carrying more prestige, though some white southerners derided the apparently portly Methodist minister as the "Elephant." He was selected at the session in Topeka, Kansas, but did not show up at the next RWGL session in Charleston, South Carolina—an awkward site for attempting a racially mixed meeting. Black Hickmanite organizers seem to have been cautious reformers. One black GWCT declared, "Our aim is to avoid making ourselves troublesome to anyone."[27]

Although there are only fragments of information about the black Malinites, they left more evidence than the Hickmanites. In order to encourage support for the RWGL of the World, the weekly newspaper of the Grand Lodge of England published excerpts from letters and meetings, as did smaller Templar newspapers. In addition, the memoirs of Jessie Forsyth offer a unique look at black participation in the Malinite, predominantly white Grand Lodge of Massachusetts, where relatively few African Americans lived (at the 1880 census Massachusetts had only 18,697 blacks but a strong abolitionist heritage). The Boston lodge to which Forsyth belonged, Joseph Malins lodge, "for several years had a membership of over one hundred, about equally divided between white and colored." At the time of reunification a Nova Scotia–born black minister headed the lodge.[28]

The celebrated author William Wells Brown, a onetime fugitive slave who had settled in Boston, organized lodges in Virginia, West Virginia, and Tennessee. Brown's story provides a good case study of the Malinite organizer in North America. The RWGL of the World thought that it had found a shortcut to organizing blacks as Templars when the True Reformers in Virginia asked to be accepted as Templars.[29] As one member explained, "We, the coloured people of Virginia, did not join the United Order of True Reformers because we liked it so well, but because we could get no other."[30] The secretary of the Grand Fountain, W.H.L. Coombs of Richmond, had previously applied to the Hickmanite RWGL, which put him off with a promise to consult the white GWCT of Virginia.

Coombs exemplifies the handful of black leaders who circulated among rival organizations. He had been one of the first blacks to be admitted into the National Division of the Sons of Temperance and in February 1873 was elected the first Grand Worthy Patriarch of Virginia's black Grand Division. After joining the Templars, apparently through the black lodges in North Carolina, he had organized lodges in Virginia and West Virginia which, under pressure from white Templars had reorganized as True Reformer fountains.[31]

Although the True Reformers wanted to become Templars immediately, the RWGL of the World, preferring that the transformation be done "carefully and lawfully," dispatched Brown to make arrangements. In October he attended the session at which the Grand Fountain of Virginia voted to disband. Its last password had been "We mean to be Good Templars." He visited subordinate fountains, instructed them, and gave them Templar charters. It was a busy time. Brown, who was over sixty, rode "a hard trotting horse" early in November to institute lodges nine miles apart and returned the same night to take the train to Richmond. On 14 November 1877 a Grand Lodge was organized at Samaritan Hall, Richmond. Brown described the officers as "more or less coloured persons [some being of mixed race], the whites holding aloof of course." Three days after the institution of the Grand Lodge, Brown presented a lecture under the auspices of Britannia lodge on the African general Hannibal, a reminder both of the alliance with the British Templars and the racial pride of the black Templars.[32]

Several threats confronted the new Grand Lodge. A few True Reformer subordinate fountains refused to dissolve, and rumor had it that a former Grand Master would try to set up a new Grand Fountain. Moreover, another rumor indicated that the white Grand Lodge of Virginia, like the Grand Lodges of Georgia and South Carolina, might permit blacks to have their own Templar lodges affiliated with the Hickmanite RWGL rather than let the "Britishers" succeed. Brown complained about the low quality of the membership of the True Reformers recruited into the IOGT and reported being told that no respectable black wanted to have anything to do with Coombs.[33]

Hickman's claim to be an old friend of black people infuriated Brown. He pointed out that when Hickman organized the True Reformers, each fountain had to pay the white Grand Lodge of Good Templars ten dollars for its charter and outfit, whereas eight dollars was enough for a charter and outfit for a white Templar lodge: "The black man was robbed of his rights and his money."[34]

The RWGL of the World's Mission Committee lacked the funds to keep Brown in Virginia for more than a few weeks. He returned to Massachusetts, where he became a leader in a small but lively Grand Lodge, which he instituted on the last day of 1877. His wife was elected its first secretary. In spring of 1878 the honorary secretary of the Mission Committee, Catherine Impey, visiting from England, stayed at the home of the Browns.[35]

The hurriedly constructed Grand Lodge of Virginia, like so many black Grand Lodges, quickly fell apart, but the Mission Committee located the money to send Brown back in 1879 for four months of repair work. Brown found the Grand Lodge in "terrible condition": the secretary had left the State, and the local lodges had received no quarterly password in eight months. A few despairing lodges had petitioned the white Grand Lodge of Virginia for reorganization in a segregated Dual Grand Lodge, but "the Hickmanites refused them a charter" as punishment for quitting the True Reformers for the RWGL of the World.[36] Only a half-dozen lodges survived in the eastern part of the state, the Norfolk-Hampton-Portsmouth district.

George Washington Bain, popular temperance lecturer.

S.B. Chase, Pennsylvania lawyer responsible for transforming Templar rules and regulations into a system.

John B. Finch, charismatic orator and architect of reunion.

See Acknowledgments for illustration sources.

Jessie Forsyth, editor of *Temperance Brotherhood.*

Oronhyatekha, controversial Mohawk physician from Ontario.

S.D. Hastings, champion of African-American rights who became an ally of white Southerners.

Col. J.J. Hickman, Kentuckian who headed the RWGL at the beginning of the great schism.

Joseph Malins in regalia, 1880.

Delegates to the Boston Union Conference, 1886. First row: Jessie Forsyth, William Ross, Francena C. Bailey; second row: William M. Artrell, W.H. Lambly, William G. Lane, John B. Finch, Joseph Malins, Oronhyatekha; third row: William P. Hastings, Charles L. Abbott, William W. Turnbull, N.B. Broughton, N.T. Collins, George A. Bailey; not pictured: W. Martin Jones.

Eliza A. Gardner, officer in the Grand Lodge of Massachusetts.

F.G. Keens, Nebraskan whose visit to Birmingham began the reunion process in 1886.

Morton's Chapel, Birmingham, where the first English Good Templar Lodge meeting was held.

Dr. F.R. Lees, leader of the English Hickmanites.

Bishop J.W. Hood of North Carolina.

John Pyper of Ireland, "Bible wine" enthusiast.

S.C. Goosley of South Carolina.

Joseph E. Lee of Florida.

Harriet N.K. Goff, a Malinite who defected.

James G. Thrower of Georgia, an Englishman in Dixie.

William Middleton Artrell of Florida.

Dr. William Wells Brown, the most celebrated African-American Good Templar.

Catherine Impey, honorary secretary of the Mission Committee.

Brown did not minimize the drink problem among black Virginians but praised their willingness to join the temperance agitation through the Templars. He lamented that he lacked sufficient ritual books and charters. When he instituted a lodge with sixty-eight members and had no charter to give them, "they felt badly about it, because they like to have their authority hanging on the wall." It was hard for blacks to find the money for the charter fee, since many were out of work, "yet I think it best they should pay something where they can, for people appreciate a thing more highly if they have to pay something for it." He succeeded in instituting a new Grand Lodge. Both the new Grand Worthy Chief Templar and the new secretary were Richmond men, the former a Baptist minister and the latter a post office clerk.[37] At the beginning of April 1879 Brown said he would leave Virginia with thirty lodges organized, four with more than a hundred members and—except in Richmond where there were numerous small lodges—none with less than forty. He had found all the churches friendly; the legislature had granted the Grand Lodge a charter, which the governor signed; and other than the Hickmanites, the whites were well disposed and lent halls for black temperance meetings.[38]

The Hickmanites provided a less flattering view of Brown's work in Virginia. J.N. Stearns, editor of the *National Temperance Advocate,* sneered that Brown had organized his most recent Grand Lodge "in a kitchen on Leigh Street [in Richmond]" and complained that he had advanced "bad men to positions of honor." Stearns alleged that Brown's first GWCT was a forger who had fled to New York in order to avoid prosecution, that one secretary had used Grand Lodge funds for his own purposes, and that another subsequently served a sentence in a state prison. Coombs, who changed sides and became secretary of a Dual Grand Lodge organized by the Hickmanites, accused Brown and the Malinites of exploiting Virginia's black people: "Give us back our dimes and dollars that they robbed us of in 1878 and 1879." Brown dismissed Coomb's charges as slander by a renegade who was "in fact only the tool of men who can ill bear the independent spirit the colored people have shown."[39]

In 1879 Brown worked in West Virginia as well as Virginia. He told the Mission Committee that West Virginia "has been an expensive state to travel through, owing to the great distance between the towns where enough coloured people could be found to form a Lodge." He organized his first lodge in Charleston and named it Old Hero after John Brown, who had won immortality through his 1859 raid at nearby Harpers Ferry. This lodge had as its vice Templar a young woman whom the militant abolitionist had kissed when he was on

his way to the gallows and she was a slave child. To make strong
lodges, W.W. Brown said: "I pick out the men and women for leaders";
fortunately, a black college in West Virginia had graduated many
teachers and preachers. Delegates at a Baptist quarterly conference
founded a lodge, named in honor of the radical Republican senator,
Charles Sumner. Brown discovered a few black ex-Templars: when
he instituted a lodge at Clarksburg "they shewed me the charter
of Sheridan Lodge, No. 15, granted June 1871. Password withheld
in 1874; died in 1875." In May 1879 he instituted a Grand Lodge of
West Virginia at Wheeling. Of the thirty-one representatives from
ten lodges, thirteen were ministers; one had traveled three hundred
miles to take part. Seven of the delegates were "educated coloured
women," three of whom were elected to the Grand Lodge Executive.[40]
The Grand Lodge of West Virginia died within the year.

The heat of summer forced Brown to retreat to Boston. For reasons of health and weather he had to resist the entreaties of friends
who wanted him to organize in Tennessee. In the autumn, Tennessee
became practicable: "Yes," he told Catherine Impey, "I will return to
the South as early as the 1st of October [1879], upon the same terms
as last winter." Five clergymen offered their churches, and a white
printer provided Brown a place to live in Nashville and free printing.
That winter his letters appeared in the organ of the Grand Lodge
of England. Brown faced competition from Hickman, however. On
20 November 1879 the Grand Fountain of Tennessee voted to dissolve and be reorganized by Hickman in a Dual Grand Lodge. Yet
almost immediately the Dual Grand Lodge officers became disillusioned and, after the arrival of Brown, affiliated with the RWGL of
the World. Brown's work in eastern and middle Tennessee produced
a Grand Lodge that cheered morale in Britain, but its organization
was too hasty to endure. Some of the subordinate lodges met only
"once or twice" after they were instituted.[41]

Brown had not spent the money of the Mission Committee to
enjoy a late autumn and early winter holiday in the Tennessee
mountains. In February 1880 he wrote Impey from Boston, "I have
not yet recovered from the chills" contracted in late 1879. Angrily,
he told his English friend, "With all the hotels and other places of
accommodation closed against me—made to pay for a first-class
ticket, and forced for the poorest possible excuse, into a second-class
car; often going hungry, because niggers [sic] are not allowed in the
most common eating-houses; walking long distance from depots (railway stations) on account of the rules not permitting niggers to ride
in public conveyances; frequently waiting in the cold for a train, and

not allowed in the railroad waiting-rooms, and other obstacles too numerous to mention; make me feel rather blue in the South."[42]

After his Tennessee campaign Brown remained in the North. The next Grand Lodge institution in which he took part was for New Jersey in 1880. He worked hard for his own Grand Lodge of Massachusetts. He helped foil a Hickmanite effort to take over a new lodge in Winthrop. He contributed to the little Templar newspaper *Temperance Brotherhood,* published in Boston. He denounced the RWGL: "That once grand old Order which has done so much for humanity, now trails its banner in the American mud, with scarcely a black face to mourn its downfall." In 1884 he died at age sixty-eight, a faithful Templar to the end. A year earlier he had argued that "a large proportion of the coloured men and women in the Northern States are recently from the South, and need the Temperance pledge and the spelling book more than they do advice on politics."[43]

Since the Malinites had separated from the old RWGL to protest the exclusion of blacks in the American South, their missionary activities centered on recruiting blacks in the former slave states and it was important for the RWGL of the World to show that African Americans wanted to join Templar lodges. What little money was available came from British Quakers, many of them not members of the Templar Order. As honorary secretary, Catherine Impey—a well-off member of the Society of Friends—directed the work of the RWGL of the World's Negro Mission Committee, later renamed the Mission Committee to make clear that it also welcomed whites who accepted the principle of universal brotherhood and sisterhood.

Whites born outside the South played a large role in the Malinite strategy. On two occasions the RWGL of the World paid whites from Britain to organize in North America: Henry William Parsons of England in 1876, and George H. Fea of Scotland in 1882. Parsons, chosen for his "known capacity for rough pioneer work," spent most of his time in North Carolina, which from the late 1860s supported a few struggling black Templar lodges. Fea appears to have spent his time in the North, where he accomplished nothing.[44]

Otherwise, for its work in the South the RWGL of the World chose to hire people already resident in the United States. Some were white teachers at black schools in the former slave states. For a couple of years the principal organizer was a recent graduate of Boston University, Charles P. Wellman, who taught at black schools in Georgia until ill health sent him back to his native Massachusetts to die. For a time he was GWCT of Georgia. He also founded the *Temperance Brotherhood* newspaper. Next William P. Hastings, a middle-aged Quaker formerly of Iowa, who conducted a school in eastern Tennessee to train black teachers, served as the Mission Committee's principal agent until it ran out of money. A.G. Marment, British-born but ordained in the A.M.E. Church, worked in Texas and the Indian Territory, almost out of sight.

The Mission Committee engaged a couple of whites who did not teach in black schools. During an exodus of former slaves from the southern states Mary E. Griffith of Ohio, a protégé of Martha McClellan Brown, tried to organize both races in Kansas. Near the end of the schism the Mission Committee contracted with Caleb A. Stevens, GWCT of Massachusetts, to revive the lodges in South Carolina. During this venture Stevens kept a diary that was serialized in a Malinite newspaper.

Other whites served without pay. Harriet N.K. Goff tried to organize a de facto black Grand Lodge in New York City. Jessie Forsyth served as the North American agent for the Mission Committee and edited the monthly *Temperance Brotherhood*. George Phillips, an English immigrant, labored to keep the Templar Order alive among New Jersey blacks, mostly around Camden. An English-born Methodist minister, George S. Williams, tried to organize black lodges in northern Kentucky and southern Indiana. He had been converted to the Malinite cause after mail from the RWGL of the World was delivered to him by mistake.

One of Hastings's letters, describing his work during a twenty-four-hour period, offers a fair example of a full-time organizer's life of constant travel and reveals his own lack of confidence in his local supporters. After instituting a lodge in Jonesboro, Tennessee, Hastings got to bed an hour past midnight. Up at 3:30 A.M., he took a train to Bristol on the Virginia border, thirty-three miles away, and then slept briefly at his new hotel. After breakfast he met with black temperance advocates, who told him they had announced that he would speak that evening. "Fearing that it might not be generally known, I sat down and filled out 100 handbills, and paid a young man a dime (5d.) to distribute them."[45] Hastings took for granted the need for white supervision: "It will take another generation to train the average negro to manage business as well as it should be managed." Although optimistic about the generations born in freedom, whose possibilities "are unlimited by anything except the decrees of God," he regarded the former slaves as "dull intellectually," as well as "selfish and sensual."[46]

Hastings's negativism and paternalism notwithstanding, African Americans carried the main burden of organizing their own people. Two blacks from outside the South were paid to organize there. One was William Wells Brown. The other was an obscure American-born sailor, Henry Hammond, who headed a London lodge at the time that he accepted his assignment and who for many years had lived under the British flag on ship and in port. His discouraged letters and diary entries record dismal failure in western Tennessee. He managed to organize only a couple of lodges in Memphis.

More important than organizers dispatched by the RWGL of the World were the local black officers. In Florida the establishment of the black Templars was a "spontaneous growth" that owed nothing to British money.[47] Pleased, the Mission Committee subsidized the head of Florida's Grand Lodge to organize a new Grand Lodge in Alabama.

Some of the black leaders in the southern states might be regarded as black carpetbaggers. James W. Hood of North Carolina and Joseph E. Lee of Florida were born in Pennsylvania. A surprising number were born under the Union Jack: S.C. Goosley of South Carolina in Nova Scotia, W.M. Artrell of Florida in the Bahamas, W.B. Derrick of Virginia in the West Indies. All five headed Grand Lodges in jurisdictions where they were newcomers.

The RWGL of the World honored black Templars with office when they managed to attend its sessions. At the Glasgow session in 1877 William Wells Brown of Massachusetts was elected Right Worthy Grand Counsellor, and two South Carolinians were elected to the same prestigious office in the two following years. Other black Templars were appointed to minor offices. A member of Morning Glory lodge, Halifax, Nova Scotia, was appointed guard at the 1877 session.[48] In the following year the head of the Grand Lodge of North Carolina was named Right Worthy Grand Chaplain and the heads of the Grand Lodges of Virginia and Florida were appointed to minor offices, as was another Virginian in 1883. No blacks from North America attended the biennial RWGL of the World session in distant Stockholm, Sweden, in 1885, however, so no African American held international office during the final years of the great schism.

Joining with whites on a basis of equality appears to have mattered a great deal for leaders and common members too. S.C. Goosley joined the IOGT in Canada. When the A.M.E. Church assigned him to South Carolina, he was unable to get the white Templars there to allow blacks to join the IOGT; as an alternative, Hickman and the head of the white Grand Lodge of South Carolina tried to get him to organize blacks as True Reformers. Goosley speculated: "These sanctified whites . . . would refuse to enter heaven if they thought a 'nigger' could get there."[49] In 1886 Catherine Impey, honorary secretary of the Mission Committee, visited Philadelphia, where she attended a lodge meeting in the parlor of a Yorkshire emigrant who served as lodge deputy: "One of the coloured members, speaking of his Lodge, was heard proudly describing it as the one place where he could forget he was black, unless he chanced to look down on his hands."[50] Scattered among the varied names chosen for black lodges are some political allusions and others that speak to black pride: for instance, Emancipation and Fred Douglass in Georgia.

Among blacks who rejected racial segregation was W.M. Artrell of Florida. Explaining his temporary acceptance of True Reformerism, he said, "I was always opposed to a separate organisation for coloured people, and only made the best of it for the good of my race." With many biblical references he rejoiced in the defeat of the southern white Templars through the establishment of black Good Templary: "The Southern whites remind me forcibly of Pharaoh of old." He added that "the uplifting of the human race is a work in which angels would delight to partake, and for us to be able to do this work is a privilege that we should prize." He pointed out that "we not only teach Temperance but morality."[51] On 16 September 1878 he wrote the *Christian Recorder* to express his pride that a newspaper "conducted by colored men" had become "a mouthpiece of the R.W.G.L. of the World." He pointed out that the racism in the Good Templar Order existed in the North too: "The south, it seems, is willing to do all the dirty work, while the north quietly acquiesces"; "Prejudice against the colored man is *the* great sin of the United States of America." He praised the British for fighting for equal rights and insisted that American blacks had a "bounden duty" to enroll.[52]

The RWGL of the World wanted to make it possible for blacks to join the Templars anywhere but as a result of racism the Malinite policy of opening membership to both blacks and whites had the effect of creating lodges in the former slave states composed exclusively of black people. The Spanish-speaking lodge at Key West served Afro-Cubans. Even in the North, integration of local lodges was rare.

The Malinite mission to African Americans covered much of eastern North America. The RWGL of the World chose not to organize blacks in Maryland and Missouri—since at least part of the time the Hickmanites in those two states chartered segregated local lodges and allowed black lodges representation at integrated Grand

Lodge sessions—but claimed to have organized black lodges in virtually every other former slave state, with Grand Lodges in most of them.[53] Malinites also claimed a handful of black lodges and Grand Lodges outside the South. The predominantly white Grand Lodge of Nova Scotia boasted seven completely or mostly black lodges and five temples for black children.[54]

Most of the African American lodges and Grand Lodges died almost immediately. For instance, helped by the endorsement of the A.M.E. Church, membership in South Carolina quickly grew from nothing to 5,000—and evaporated just as quickly. Often, commitment to the Malinite cause was non-existent; a black lodge in Louisiana, for example, "afterwards joined another temperance organization."[55] Late in 1879 a Hickmanite sneered that the RWGL of the World had instituted only twenty-nine black lodges over three years. Malins answered that the correct total was more than a hundred—itself a modest number to justify a schism.[56]

Templar lodges fared best when existing leaders of local African American communities made the IOGT a favorite cause and persisted in their efforts, as in the Norfolk-Hampton-Portsmouth district in eastern Virginia, Wilmington in eastern North Carolina, and the widely separated Florida cities of Jacksonville and Key West. Elsewhere there appears to have been only enough energy to organize lodges, with none left over to make them living institutions.

The Grand Lodge of Florida was fortunate to have W.M. Artrell, a devoted and talented Templar, and an impressive specimen of a local and state leader, whom the *New York Freeman* described as "a gentleman of rare eloquence and intensely in earnest in temperance work."[57]

Like many black Templar leaders he was an outsider.[58] Born in the Bahamas in 1836, William Middleton Artrell was one-quarter African and three-quarters European in ancestry. As a result of the Bahamian depression that followed the end of the American Civil War, he gave up schoolteaching at Nassau and relocated to Key West in 1870. In 1876 he began a new career in the United States Custom Service. Artrell served as an inspector, then as a statistical and marine clerk—a post previously not available to blacks—at a $1,200 annual salary, and still later as an impost clerk at $1,500. In 1880, refuting criticism of Artrell, his supervisor described him as "the peer of any colored man in Florida."[59] After the Democrats won the presidency, he lost his government job and relocated in Jacksonville in 1885, where he served as principal of a black grade school until 1894 and augmented his school salary by working as a tailor. After a

long interval out of federal employment, he returned in his sixties
to Key West and appears in the 1900 city directory as merchant
tailor and deputy collector of internal revenue. He died no later than
1906.[60]

Artrell's temperance career began late in 1874. Previously a
moderate drinker, he embraced teetotalism and prohibition for his
own sake and out of distress at seeing how many blacks were slaves
to alcohol. He wanted to organize black abstainers in a fraternal
temperance society. When Hickman refused him a Templar charter,
Artrell organized a True Reformer fountain and became deputy
Grand Master of the Grand Fountain of Florida. Early in the great
schism, on 16 October 1876, Artrell's old fountain was reorganized as
Oscar Carter lodge, with seventy-five members, all formerly True
Reformers. Artrell described Carter, a black man killed because of
his teetotal principles, as the first temperance martyr.[61]

Artrell was the indispensable figure in the Grand Lodge of
Florida and helped make it one of the few indisputable successes
recorded by the Malinite Templars. When the Grand Lodge was
organized in 1878 he began a long period of service as secretary.
He became Grand Chief Templar in 1885-89 amid controversy: supporters of his predecessor claimed that Joseph E. Lee had been
elected.[62] In 1886 the Grand Lodge began publication of a brief-lived
bi-monthly newspaper, the (Jacksonville) *Florida Templar,* the only
black temperance newspaper in North America.[63] The black Grand
Lodge of Florida never had a membership much over 1,000, but it
was remarkably durable, surviving into the 1930s.

About half the Florida membership consisted of women, and
women seemed to make up a larger proportion of the membership
of the black Malinite lodges than in the Templar Order as a whole.
The Grand Worthy Secretary of Virginia described the membership
in that state as "mostly sisters," many of them domestic servants. A
Good Samaritan chapter in Massachusetts, "consisting of more than
seventy women, nearly all of the African race," voted to affiliate with
the Malinites to support the RWGL of the World's defense of the
rights of black people. In 1886 women held all the offices in Queen
Esther lodge, Wilmington, North Carolina. The black Grand Lodges
almost never elected sisters to any office other than the traditionally
female ones of Grand Worthy Vice-Templar and superintendent of
the juvenile temples; this sexism paralleled the southern whites'. The
Grand Lodge of Alabama was an exception: "With so many estimable
ladies among the officers, woman's suffrage is not forgotten."[64]

Most of the black women Templars remain anonymous, but
there are scraps of information about a few. For instance, Rachel

Thomas, Grand Worthy Vice-Templar in North Carolina, taught school at Rocky Mount.[65] In Florida, Victoria Artrell participated actively in her husband's missionary efforts and, like many women Templars, devoted much of her time to the juvenile temples.

Lucy Wooden (or Woodin) of Norfolk was elected to a couple of offices in the Grand Lodge of Virginia. The surviving bits of her correspondence with Jessie Forsyth testify to her temperance work among children. Forsyth also published fragments of her speeches. In her welcoming address at a Grand Lodge session, Wooden said, "We find that strong drink has brought about a slavery in this free land of ours that enslaves not only the body but the mind, the conscience and soul." After a lecture tour in a nearby agricultural county, Wooden paid tribute to the spirit of the rural lodges: "I saw persons in my audience, male and female, who had come many miles, on foot, just to hear what I could say on Temperance." She praised little Sewell's Point, which supported two lodges totaling 196 members.[66]

In the 1880s a handful of blacks such as T. Thomas Fortune flirted with the National Prohibition Party, and in a few southern states white advocates of local option sought support from African Americans. Other white prohibitionists favored black disenfranchisement as a means toward moral reform, so it is not surprising that the black Templars in the South for the most part remained detached from any political agitation for prohibition of the sale of drink.[67] Although Templar leaders in Florida and elsewhere endorsed local option campaigns, prohibition does not appear to have dominated what were essentially moral suasion organizations.

Instead of political involvement, the black Templars busied themselves with a routine similar to that of black churches and fraternal organizations: weekly local meetings, less frequent district and state meetings, and sporadic campaigns to win new supporters and solidify the allegiance of old adherents. Like the Red Queen in *Alice in Wonderland,* Templar organizers and officers had to run as fast as they could to stay in the same place and even faster to move forward. Many black Templars sacrificed themselves in this critical work. W.M. Artrell described one exhausting expedition that he and his wife, Victoria, undertook in order to institute a new lodge in an out-of-the-way Florida village on a wintry evening in 1886. St. Nichols lay across the St. Johns river, four miles from Jacksonville. L.C. Fleming, a young woman recently returned from school in North Carolina, had "lectured from church to church" and persuaded twenty-seven people there to sign a charter petition. After the Artrells crossed the river by steam ferry, a mule-drawn dray carried them to meet the new recruits at a Baptist church. On the return journey through the pine woods they endured a pouring rain, followed by a wait in the chill for the ferry, which was late. They got home at two in the morning and had to rise at six to begin a new day's work.[68]

Like other black organizations the Templars held parades to demonstrate their vigor before the public. During the 1879 session of the Grand Lodge of Florida, 500 Templars "all in full regalia" and 300 children belonging to the local juvenile temple, "headed by the Key West Silver Cornet Band," paraded through the city. The following morning, led by a fife-and-drum corps, the children marched "armed with a plate and spoon" apiece. In the same year, with the aid of a twelve-piece band, the Templars in Camden, New Jersey, marched a hundred strong, white and black together. On another occasion New Jersey Templars marched without music but wearing regalia, two abreast, and dressed in dark suits and white gloves. At a parade in Key West in 1883, the women wore white and the men black, with white vests and white gloves, while the paraders carried banners of white, blue, purple, and scarlet in honor of the seventh anniversary of Oscar Carter lodge.[69]

The strength of the black Templars, to the extent that it existed, was only local. By 1887 the RWGL of the World identified only two working black Grand Lodges in the United States: Virginia's and Florida's each claiming about 1,000 members.[70] At the 1880 census Virginia had a black population of 631,616, while Florida had 126,690. Elsewhere there were a few scattered black lodges and a measure of racial integration in the tiny Grand Lodge of Massachusetts. Toward the end of the great schism the Mission Committee spent most of its meager funds in supporting the publication and distribution of a hundred copies of *Temperance Brotherhood*.[71]

At the end of the great schism the Hickmanites claimed more black members than the Malinites but could point to only one healthy Dual Grand Lodge: Virginia's with about 2,000 members. In 1886 the RWGL's secretary conceded in his annual report that the North American–dominated organization had better success in organizing black lodges than in keeping them: "We have never had a prosperous colored Grand Lodge." He blamed the scarcity of "sufficiently educated" southern blacks.[72]

The study of black fraternalism provides a glimpse into important but neglected community structures. In the case of the Templars they were fragile structures, so their story is often one of failure or at best marginal success. Yet even though only a fragmentary account of the black Templars has been possible, it offers glimpses of

African American life otherwise unavailable and draws attention to previously unknown black leaders, as well as adding a new dimension to the history of some already familiar figures. The rank and file, alas, can be seen only murkily. Except for a few locations such as Norfolk in Virginia and Jacksonville and Key West in Florida, the Templar impact on local black communities seems to have been modest. The black Templar lodges may best be seen as moral reform auxiliaries to the black churches, especially the Methodist denominations.

The opinion of black people as to what had been accomplished is hard to reconstruct, but this much is undeniable. Some 10,000 to 15,000 black men and women had worked through their own lodges for the uplift of their race, and at a time when most religious denominations were completely segregated, they had done so in an organization in which whites predominated at the international level. Integration required white participation.

From the standpoint of white Templars, the dream of organizing African Americans had failed. For the old RWGL this was frustrating. For the Malinites the failure mattered much more: it made the great schism irrelevant.

6

The Reunion

After Louisville the quarrel that sustained the great schism became increasingly complicated to explain and difficult to justify. The anger and the distrust remained obvious, but not so the underlying principle in the dispute. Sometimes it seemed only a legalistic excuse to keep fighting. The RWGL and reluctant white southerners made compromises that satisfied nearly all white members in the northern American states and Canada and many other Templars around the world, but not the leaders of the English and Scottish Grand Lodges or their African American allies.

At the London conference in October 1876, Hickman offered segregated black lodges and Grand Lodges in the American South, and Malins accepted in principle. This settlement failed over a secondary question: the status of the Hickmanite lodges in Britain during the months intervening between the London conference and the proposed simultaneous meetings of the rival international organizations.

After rejecting an RWGL of the World olive branch in 1877, the old RWGL changed the Templar constitution in 1878 to promise African Americans the right to membership through separate organizations. This concession came too late to appease the Malinites. In 1879 the RWGL of the World adopted a radical new policy of rubbing out the color line, to use a popular propaganda phrase, by prohibiting any kind of segregation.[1] This insistence on racial integration made it much more difficult for the Malinites to accept a settlement that the Hickmanites could accept too. Ironically, the few lodges that the RWGL of the World managed to organize in the American South were de facto segregated.

In 1881 the Hickmanites and Malinites negotiated for a second time. These London talks, which sought to terminate the expensive charter suit, included the leaders of the rival English organizations and their legal counsel. In December the negotiations broke down over a narrow question: the Malinites' demand that black lodges in the former slave states be accorded the right to representation at the white Grand Lodge annual sessions when a black Grand Lodge did not exist.

Negotiations revived in the mid-1880s. There was a false start. In 1884 Hickman suggested that the two factions restrict themselves to the Eastern and Western Hemispheres respectively, share passwords, and recognize each other's clearance and traveling cards. Under this proposal the RWGL of the World would surrender a very few members, mostly in Nova Scotia, while the RWGL would abandon many viable Grand Lodges from Ireland and Scandinavia to South Africa and Australia. When Malins asked Hickman's successor as RWGT if the suggestion was an official one, the answer was an emphatic no "in language that was rather more curt and less courteous than might have been desired."[2]

Another private intervention got negotiations going in earnest. In March 1886 a former secretary of the Hickmanite international organization, F.G. Keens of Nebraska, visited Malins at Birmingham. The GWCT of New York, W. Martin Jones, had written Malins to ask him to see Keens.[3] Although Keens had voted for Oronhyatekha's Substitute, he had supported the British at Bloomington in 1875, and when he had received a copy of the Manifesto he said he expected that Nebraska's executive committee would support it.[4] Now, Malins suggested that Keens consult Dr. Lees, the most prestigious figure among the Hickmanites in England, and Stephen Wright, head of the Worthy Grand Lodge for the British Isles. This proved impossible because Keens was scheduled to leave England almost immediately. The failure to consult with Lees and Wright contributed to the subsequent sourness about reunion among the English Hickmanites. To supplement the brief interview, Malins sent Keens a letter, in care of Jones, to present to John Finch, the head of the old RWGL.

At first Malins minimized his interest in reunion and his willingness to make concessions. He told Keens that although he and his associates were "willing for a reunion, if it can be justly arranged," they did not "crave it." He insisted that the RWGL of the World, having eliminated the color line in its own organization, "cannot go back to the suggested compromise of 1876." He thought the only justification for the dual system would be a black organization's fear that it would be excluded from sharing power in an amalgamation. Despite his caution, Malins left the door open for negotiations: "We are doing very well as we are, yet we think the [temperance] cause might be advanced by unity." He added that "we must treat as absolute equals."[5]

It was Finch who took responsibility for making the negotiations succeed. For him the division appeared senseless after the organization of the Dual Grand Lodges in the former slave states. Finch opposed revisiting the origins of the quarrel, any rehearsal of history on the lines of the acrimonious London conference of 1876. He insisted that there were only two questions to consider: was union desirable? was union possible? Finch pointed out that "a great majority of our members were not in the Order 20 years ago [when the controversy over black membership began]. They are in the Order to-day to fight the liquor traffic, and not to keep alive the quarrels and bickerings of 20 years ago."[6]

Finch helped the cause of reunion by his rulings in favor of the rights of black members and prospective members: subordinate lodges could not reject prospective members or visitors on the basis of race. Nor could a Grand Lodge deny a charter on the basis of race. The RWGL confirmed these interpretations of Templar law in May 1886. Shortly after the adjournment of the RWGL session, Finch ruled that a Grand Lodge could not exclude black lodges from its annual session unless there was a Dual Grand Lodge in the same geographical jurisdiction. Moreover, a lodge that uniformly rejected black applicants and a Grand Lodge that uniformly refused to charter black lodges would be investigated by the RWGL on "the presumption of conspiracy to violate the fundamental principles of the Order."[7]

The letters that Finch exchanged with Malins, the dominant figure in the RWGL of the World, and with William G. Lane of Nova Scotia, its nominal chief as RWGT, led in a few months to a reunion conference on the American side of the Atlantic. In July, Lane proposed a conference at Boston and provided a tentative list of his delegates. In August the RWGL executive committee authorized Finch to send a delegation.[8] The meeting was held in late September 1886. Templars called the meeting the Union Conference, not the reunion conference. The name and the conference itself refused to look backward.

The plan had been to omit the most controversial leaders from the conference, but as the only member of the Grand Lodge of England who served on the executive of the RWGL of the World, Malins could not be excluded. With Malins invited, it was decided to admit a controversial figure on the other side, Oronhyatekha of Ontario. At the Boston meeting the two old adversaries transformed themselves into conciliators.

Finch led the RWGL contingent, which consisted entirely of North Americans. It included W. Martin Jones, the New Yorker who had persuaded Malins to see Keens. N.B. Broughton of North Carolina represented the white southerners. The English Hickmanites, still bitterly anti-Malins, did not receive an invitation.

Lane of Nova Scotia headed the other delegation. William Ross, a Free Church minister, and W.W. Turnbull spoke for Scotland and Malins for England. Several delegates represented the scanty ranks of the Malinites who lived in the United States: Jessie Forsyth of Massachusetts, editor of *Temperance Brotherhood;* William P. Hastings of Tennessee, previously an agent of the Mission Committee in the South; and W.M. Artrell of Florida, the sole African American present. The only participant who lived neither in the British Isles nor in North America was N.T. Collins, a Massachusetts-born member of the Grand Lodge of New South Wales. Added by the Malinites at the last minute, the Australian appears to have been in Boston on the way home after presenting a paper at a temperance conference in London.[9]

In her memoir Jessie Forsyth describes the tension when the RWGL delegates failed to appear at the time the RWGL of the World expected them; nevertheless, the negotiations turned out to be amicable and took little time.[10] All the formal votes were carried unanimously. Although many minor differences in organization and ritual had developed over the decade, the central problems confronting the Boston conference remained those of 1876: black membership and multiple Grand Lodges. On race the crucial provision was the second proposition, declaring that difference in race could be the basis for a temporary division between what were styed a Senior Grand Lodge and a subsequently chartered Junior Grand Lodge. For the most part, the Junior Grand Lodges would be black organizations. According to this controversial compromise, "a charter may be issued, or continued, to a Junior Grand Lodge, in order to provide for the successful prosecution of the work of the Order in a jurisdiction where it is necessary temporarily to overcome differences of race or language." The Boston basis for union also promised that no other new duplicate Grand Lodges would be created—long a demand of the large English and Scottish organizations—with the promise supplemented by an expectation that when they occupied the same territory, rival Grand Lodges not based on race or language would merge within twelve months of ratification.[11]

The split had meant quarrels in jurisdictions from Norway to New Zealand and from South Asia to South Africa. With some patriotic discomfort, for instance, the Grand Lodge of Tasmania had barred from lodge meetings British sailors from visiting warships because the Grand Lodge supported the RWGL and the seamen were affiliated with the RWGL of the World.[12] Despite the importance of such incidents to local Templars around the world, what mattered from the standpoint of the international organizations was the division between the North American and British lodges. This rupture had separated the countries where most Templars made their homes. The territorial configuration of the great schism reduced its practical effect for most Templars. In the United States and Canada few Templars ever met a Malinite, whereas in England and Scotland the Malinite organizations had many times as many member as the Hickmanite lodges. The security of the Hickmanites in North America and of the Malinites in Britain reduced the incentive for ending the schism and yet facilitated reconciliation once leaders regarded international unity as worthwhile. By the early 1880s the Malinites and Hickmanites had won the battles in their own parts of the world; neither faction could destroy enemy strongholds. For the most part the rival Templar Orders were geographically complementary, so a deal did not undermine the personal position of most leaders.

Both international organizations had lost membership in their core areas and suffered financially. Although losing the taxes previously paid by the Malinites had crippled the Hickmanite international organization, the old RWGL had the allegiance of a majority of Templars at the end of the great schism. It claimed nearly a 100,000 more adult members than the RWGL of the World (287,000 as compared with less than 196,000). In England, however, Malins's Grand Lodge had about 66,000 adult Templars, the Hickmanites fewer than 4,000.[13]

Why did the leaders of the RWGL and the RWGL of the World settle their differences after more than a decade of bitter strife? In 1887 W.W. Turnbull listed a number of reasons. The Scottish officer began with the need for unity to promote the cause of temperance. He added as his second and third reasons "the difficulty of maintaining a *raison d'être* for continued separation" and "the demoralising tendency of internal strife." The fourth reason that he cited overlapped with the second, "the effect of time in modifying opinions, changing the *personnel* of our membership, and leading to a widespread indifference." Turnbull then described the frustrations of the Malinites over organizing African American lodges.[14]

Although Turnbull's analysis is accurate, a more nuanced answer distinguishes between the old RWGL and the RWGL of the World, between Finch and Malins. For Finch it is fairly straightforward. A newcomer from the West, Finch carried none of the baggage of Louisville. He lacked a sense of personal grievance against Malins and the RWGL of the World. Finch could accept the fact that the RWGL of the World was firmly entrenched in England and Scotland, and after its session at Stockholm in 1885 he must have recognized the greater success of the Malinites in Sweden and Norway.

Moreover, since the RWGL no longer shied away from an aggressive policy of promoting black membership, Finch had little need to curry favor with white southerners. Although in North Carolina and Alabama there was a temporary recovery in the middle 1880s and Virginia achieved its peak membership in 1886, in general the white southern Templars had shrunk in numbers during the great schism. After becoming RWGT in 1884, Finch moved decisively to protect the rights of African Americans. His rulings in 1886 satisfied the substantive demands that the British had made at Louisville ten years earlier, and the Malinites recognized that the RWGL leadership had established a new policy on black membership which, had it existed in 1876, would have forestalled the great schism. According to Malins, "the latest decisions of Bro. Finch and of his R.W.G. Lodge constituted the pivot upon which the whole [reunion] conference turned."[15]

Calling the supporters of the North American–dominated RWGL Hickmanites throughout the great schism obscures the transformation in its leadership and policies. Finch wanted a strengthened IOGT in order to serve larger temperance objectives. A leader in the National Prohibition Party, he hoped that a reinvigorated Templar Order could bolster the third party with votes on election day. In contrast, southerners such as Hickman had been cool toward a separate Prohibition Party, and for Canadians like Williams United States politics were irrelevant, whereas Finch saw the Templars as the foot soldiers in the service of the National Prohibition Party general staff. He may have been looking for black voters when he helped organize African Americans in Templar lodges. After Boston, Finch estimated that the IOGT could recruit 200,000 blacks "within ten years."[16] In the 1880s many blacks still retained the franchise in the southern states.

Like other Templar leaders, Finch regarded international unity as a vital dimension of Templar universalism. All Templars were proud that the IOGT had become an international organization with an effective central policymaking structure, something almost unknown among the voluntary societies founded in the United States before the WCTU.[17] In 1884, on the day of his election as RWGT,

Finch told a close friend that he was determined to see the IOGT unified before he left office.[18] Enormously popular in the RWGL and accustomed to success, Finch was not inclined in his mid-thirties to play safe. He wanted a resounding triumph.

For the RWGL, reunion actually posed few risks. Only the white southerners and the English Hickmanites, for very different reasons, might regard a compromise settlement as injurious to their interests. Small in numbers, they were marginal to the success of the IOGT, so their defections alone would not offset the benefits of reuniting with the Malinite Templars. Nor was there danger of a rank-and-file revolt, because a largely youthful and transient membership had invested little in the quarrel. The practical problem for the RWGL leadership was to prevent a combination of white southerners and English Hickmanites from aligning with the old guard in the northern American states and Canadian provinces, veterans of Louisville who detested Malins and his supporters as seceders and who demanded their humiliation as a price for reunion. Oronhyatekha's support symbolized Finch's success in winning over at least a part of the old guard.

Malins also wanted reunion but was sensitive about the risk of a rebuff. Since 1876 the supporters of the RWGL had denounced Malins and the RWGL of the World as seceders who would have been more honest if they had stopped calling themselves Templars. Union with the RWGL would undermine the RWGL of the World's assertion that *it* was the only true Templar Order, that by violating the principle of brotherhood and sisterhood the Hickmanites had ceased to be Templars. Reunion required both sides to set aside more than a decade of legalistic debate about the legitimacy of the rival organizations.

Committed to Templar internationalism, Malins proved willing to make sacrifices for unity.[19] He had done more than any other Templar in promoting missions to new parts of the world. During his early twenties he had lived in the United States and joined the IOGT there. The schism appears to have pained Malins almost physically. After the reunion, the English chieftain said that "for years I have been subject, not to depression, but to illness, and the physicians have said that the only thing that would cure Malins was union."[20] Not yet forty-two when the Boston meeting was held, he became one of the dominant figures in the reunited IOGT and at the turn of the century served as its RWGT.

At the time of the negotiations, however, British politics distracted Malins. Unlike most prohibitionists, he had taken the side of

Joseph Chamberlain and the Liberal Unionists against William Gladstone and the Liberals, who favored Home Rule for Ireland. Chamberlain, an MP from the Templar headquarters in Birmingham, resigned from Gladstone's cabinet in March 1886, the same month that Keens visited Malins. The split beneath the surface in the United Kingdom Alliance—the most influential prohibitionist organization—between Malinites and Hickmanites handicapped the temperance movement at a crucial moment of political confusion and ambiguity, danger and opportunity.

Moreover, ending the great schism had practical advantages for Malins. The status quo was unpalatable. The English Hickmanites irritated Malins more than the white Malinites in Nova Scotia, Ontario, and Massachusetts bothered Finch. The charter suit was an expensive embarrassment. Finally, the effort to recruit southern blacks had proved quixotic. Organizing African Americans in the former slave states had been the justification for the existence of the RWGL of the World, and failure was humiliating. In a gloomy retrospect Malins contrasted the expectation of many "thousands of blacks . . . glad to flock into our Lodges" with the reality of perhaps 10,000 who "had passed through" organizations that repeatedly collapsed like houses of cards. And despite the Malinite principle of racial integration, "we had not in these Lodges initiated 10 white folk." Yet the Malinites had spent about $15,000 on these futile missions.[21]

Where available, statistics were dismal, and often the RWGL of the World received no figures at all. Malins reported at the end of the great schism: "I am unable to say almost anything satisfactory regarding our work in the United States. I must candidly confess that it has been most disappointing, and the almost entire absence of reports is disheartening."[22] At the time of reunion the largest total membership of a black Grand Lodge for the Malinites was in Virginia with 922 adults and 638 children. Florida had over a hundred more adults but fewer children. Grand Lodge memberships in Georgia, North Carolina, and Alabama were even smaller. South Carolina had fallen to 47 members, and the RWGL of the World no longer claimed any members at all in Tennessee or Texas.[23] Malins became frustrated too with the black leaders in the United States, most of whom only spasmodically devoted time to the Templar Order. At the end of great schism he complained that only one of them could write a decent letter—a remark that speaks more to his exasperation than to the facts.[24]

At the same time, the old RWGL had moved vigorously to organize African Americans. The *National Temperance Advocate* published many articles on the white responsibility to support the temperance movement among southern blacks. Like the Malinite black Grand Lodges, the Dual Grand Lodges were small and unstable, but in some states the Hickmanites enjoyed relative success. Near the end of the great schism southern white lodges and Grand Lodges occasionally tolerated the presence of a black visitor, and in 1886 a black delegate named Bourbon attended the session of the RWGL that met at the old capital of the Confederacy, Richmond, Virginia.[25]

Although Malins was indispensable to the reunion, he was not alone among its partisans in the RWGL of the World leadership. W.W. Turnbull, a former railroad clerk who was secretary of both the Grand Lodge of Scotland and the RWGL of the World, provided a revealing retrospective analysis of the reasons for reunion. Contemptuous of the fumbled organizing efforts in the American South, he reported "a growing dissatisfaction with the work of our 'Negro Mission Committee.'" Turnbull underscored *Negro* because of the failure to recruit southern whites. He objected to the fact that the RWGL of the World had inadvertently supported a segregated society. Expensive organizing work "frequently consisted in merely turning over another temperance organization [such as the True Reformers] into ours by giving them free materials" and then watching them switch to still another society when a fresh organizer arrived. Or, he said, in an unfair jab at paid organizers, "it might be employing some one to go on a tour during his holidays at the expense of our 'Negro Mission Fund' with *carte blanche* to give away charters and rituals wherever he could find people willing to take them." Turnbull said that he "began to *dislike* the whole affair, when neither reports of institution nor returns of membership were sent to me, and most of the communications I received were requests for money." He did acknowledge that Florida had established itself without outside help, and that Virginia, like Florida, did "good work." Otherwise, the southern Grand Lodges organized by the RWGL of the World "have been very evanescent." Turnbull also pointed out the irony that after its change of policy the old RWGL welcomed blacks.[26]

Malins had more to gain than Finch from reunion. He also risked more. By demonizing the southern white Grand Lodges and, for countenancing their practices, the RWGL itself, the RWGL of the World had made any kind of compromise appear immoral. Malins did not have to worry about most of the RWGL of the World. The potential resistance centered in his own Grand Lodge of England. Probably the rank and file, most of them always newcomers, cared very little. Instead, Malins had to risk fighting his closest colleagues in the English leadership, men and women who regarded the repudiation of racism as a matter of sacred principle. The Grand Lodge of England might reject the concessions that he would have to make to the RWGL, or the Grand Lodge might be crippled by the withdrawal of influential members.

The Union Conference in Boston in the autumn of 1886 had been surprisingly easy. To complete the task, the RWGL and the RWGL of the World agreed to meet in May 1887 at Saratoga Springs, a popular spa in northern New York state. The various Grand Lodges and the two international organizations had to ratify the Boston basis of union, and Jessie Forsyth's memoir draws attention to a stratagem that the Union Conference employed to circumvent opposition. Between the time of the Boston and the Saratoga meetings the RWGL and the RWGL of the World issued identical passwords and so allowed visitation between Hickmanite and Malinite lodges. "The result of this was that in jurisdictions where the two branches existed, the union had, to all intents and purposes, taken place among the subordinate members, before the question could be considered in either Grand Lodges, or R.W.G. Lodge."[27]

Most parts of the English-speaking world received the proposal for reunion enthusiastically. Lane described the Malinites in his own Nova Scotia, isolated from the main body of the RWGL of the World, as eager for it. In Ireland and Australia the reunion was consummated soon after Boston without waiting for ratification at Saratoga Springs. Finch predicted that if the international organizations did not ratify the "Boston basis," Hickmanite and Malinite Grand Lodges would both secede to form an exclusively Australian Templar Order.[28]

The basis adopted at Boston was ratified by the various Grand Lodges despite contradictory interpretations of the reunion language. For instance, did proposition two mean that the RWGL of the World would tolerate racial segregation, or did it mean that the old RWGL would accept racial integration after a brief transitional period? How temporary was temporary? What was the future for the English Hickmanites once the end of the great schism made their separate existence irrelevant? Must they submit to being absorbed by Malins's Grand Lodge of England?

The two international organizations first met concurrently at Saratoga Springs and then met as a single RWGL. To avoid disputes over constitutional technicalities, only Boston's major propositions were made part of the legislation for reunion. Nevertheless, old controversies over duplicate Grand Lodges and black membership flared up again.

The RWGL's informal discussion of the Boston propositions, the day before the annual session was convened, was not reported in the published *Proceedings*. When the official deliberations began, Hickman announced his opposition to the first proposition: that ordinarily there be only one Grand Lodge for a state or province or other major division of a country. He also asked that the RWGL vote on the Boston propositions separately, not as a package. A representative of the English Hickmanites sought assurance about charter rights. Despite a speech of almost an hour by Finch, the old RWGL insisted on the charter rights of duplicate Grand Lodges, meaning in practice the Hickmanite organizations in England. A daily Templar newspaper published during the convention quoted Finch in support of this legalistic position, which defended the right of the Hickmanites in England to defy Malins indefinitely.

Upset, representatives of the RWGL of the World spoke with Finch privately. He pointed out that although he had said what appeared in the published report, he had gone on to argue that a united RWGL should have the power to compel duplicate Grand Lodges to merge. Finch agreed that the RWGL of the World could incorporate in its ratification of the Boston basis an explanation that demanded the union of duplicate Grand Lodges not based on race and language. When the RWGL of the World did so, this apparent alteration in the terms of reunion caused "a considerable commotion" in the other RWGL.

After further private meetings, the RWGL accepted the explanation of the RWGL of the World that it had not asked for the revocation of charters but wanted the RWGL to influence the Grand Lodges to *agree* to fusion. What this meant remained unclear, but most Templars eager to reunite appeared willing to hope that such problems would work themselves out at some later time.[29] The strong leadership of the popular Finch prevented a revolt in the old RWGL. He insisted that the RWGL accept his interpretation of charter rights or be responsible for the failure of reunion.[30]

The main problem remained that of race. Interpretations of the Boston terms of union never reached a clear consensus. White southerners and the RWGL of the World had different understandings and misunderstandings of where Finch stood. In February 1887 the executive of the Grand Lodge of Virginia met with Finch, and the Virginians' published report of this interview assured their members that segregation was safe. Later, Finch repudiated this account.[31] In his report at Saratoga he said that "on the race question there is no change of our law."[32] This was questionable, and the head of the

Grand Lodge of Virginia questioned it after the reunion had taken place. He asked whether blacks would get charters directly from the RWGL or through the white Grand Lodge when one existed—and, where there was a black Grand Lodge but not a white one, whether whites would have to apply to the black organization for charters. Finch answered that when there was a single state Grand Lodge, it would have to provide charters for people of both races and allow all subordinate lodges representation at its sessions until a Grand Lodge for the other race was organized. The white southern Grand Lodges vehemently reacted against the prospect of integrated Grand Lodge sessions.

In 1887 the power of the South at the RWGL session was only a shadow of what it had been in 1876. The lusty Grand Lodge of Maine counted as many Templars as the combined numbers for the white lodges in the eleven southern states that had seceded to form the Confederacy. Even when counting those in the former slave states that had not seceded, the South had only five hundred lodges. A few years earlier Kentucky alone had had over four hundred.

The white southerners had a chance of successful resistance because Finch's answer to Virginia's GWCT amounted to a constitutional amendment that required a two-thirds vote for ratification. Moreover, the southerners could appeal with some success to the concern of northerners and Canadians that Finch's ruling undermined the traditional autonomy of Grand Lodges over their own membership. It was one thing to say that blacks had a right to become Templars, another to say that their lodges had a right to representation at what previously had been white Grand Lodge sessions. Although R.S. Cheves, a former GWCT of Kentucky and onetime Confederate colonel, led a handful of white southerners in voting for Finch's interpretation of the constitution, without the votes of the representatives from the former RWGL of the World, Finch would have faced defeat.[33]

On the last day of the Saratoga meetings the head of the Grand Lodge of South Carolina urged that the RWGL take on the responsibility of recruiting blacks and that any black lodges not part of a Junior Grand Lodge work directly under the RWGL rather than become affiliated with their state's white Grand Lodge. He said that although white southerners "love" the black people, they must deal with them on a basis of racial separation: "We will work for them and build them up in separate Lodges, but do not destroy the Order in the South by compelling the two races to associate." Finch rejected such arguments: "There has been too much gush in this body over this Southern question."[34] He was determined to reunite the North American- and British-dominated RWGLs, which together claimed over 623,000 adult and juvenile members.

Despite his sarcastic tone at Saratoga, Finch acknowledged a few months later that "things in the South are very 'sore.'" Defeated at the RWGL, the remnant of white southerners retained two final weapons: corporate secession and individual withdrawal. After years of commitment to the IOGT, southern leaders still hoped to retain a segregated Templar Order in their region. Virginia's GWCT told his Grand Lodge that "we are not going out, neither are we going to submit to *mixed* Lodges." When representatives of the Grand Lodges of Florida, Georgia, South Carolina, and Virginia met at Atlanta in October 1887, they did not decide upon secession; rather the Grand Lodge of Virginia decided to ask the RWGL to create a semi-autonomous Worthy Grand Lodge for the southern states.[35] But this did not happen, the white rank and file solved the problem by voting with their feet, and their Grand Lodges disappeared.

After Saratoga, England turned out to be the major trouble spot. The Hickmanites there considered themselves abandoned. Prior to the Boston conference Lees had been asked to stay the proceedings in the charter suit. After Boston the RWGL executive sent Lees the minutes of the conference and a request that the Worthy Grand Lodge executive ratify the terms of reunion. Lees reported this to his fellow English Hickmanites at Leeds on 3 November 1886. The delegates complained that the Boston agreement put Lees and his supporters under Malins, an arrangement that was "illegal and an unwarrantable attack upon our liberties." If the RWGL implemented the proposed treaty it would be "the deserter of its friends." The head of the Worthy Grand Lodge grumbled, "Not only have we been altogether ignored, . . . everything for which Mr. Malins seceded has been conceded without him giving an iota in return."[36] Lees himself stayed at a distance from the fight.

Thomas Olman Todd published a special number of the *British Loyal Templar* that was less than loyal to the leaders of the RWGL. He printed the correspondence between Finch and various English Hickmanites, attacked Finch personally, and denied that the RWGT had authority to conduct the reunion negotiations. Although this number of the *British Loyal Templar* seems not to have survived, its contents can be reconstructed from a summary printed in the *Irish Templar* in April 1887.

Answering the English Hickmanites, Ireland's John S. Lytle explained why the RWGL's *Journal of Proceedings* made no reference to a grant of authority to conduct the negotiations. Lytle himself had

made a motion that such a delicate matter be excluded from the published record, and no more than six or eight delegates opposed the
call for secrecy "or more correctly silence." Even Samuel Wright, who
represented the English Hickmanites at the meeting, had supported
Lytle's motion.[37]

The English Hickmanites were slow to surrender the charters
of their small Grand Lodges. Malins teetered on the brink of a serious quarrel with the RWGL, perhaps even a new schism, not over
black access to the IOGT but over what he understood had been
promised at Boston and Saratoga: the incorporation of the Hickmanite organizations in England. Adding to his discontent, the RWGL
tried to force his Grand Lodge to change its constitution and by-
laws, which denied subordinate lodges direct representation at
annual sessions.[38]

The biggest battle in England was fought among the Malinites
themselves. A red-haired Quaker with strongly held humanitarian
principles led the opposition to Malins. Aged forty in the year of the
reunion, Catherine Impey had been a Templar since 1871. She was a
Poor Law Guardian, a Band of Hope worker committed to training
children in temperance principles, and a member of a prosperous
Somerset seed-growing family. A vegetarian, she lived a life of near
austerity. For several years she had been in charge of the Mission
Committee of the RWGL of the World. A visit to the United States in
1878 convinced Impey that "in the deliberate and systematic separation between those differing in colour lay the root and core of race-
prejudice with all its inhumanities to the dark race and attendant
moral degradation of the white." In 1886 Impey returned to North
America to attend a national convention of the WCTU. She regretted
that with few exceptions black women were restricted to segregated
WCTU societies, and she grieved that in the United States the notion
prevailed "that persons of colour are somehow different from ordinary human beings."[39]

The fight over Malins's new policy began in 1886—as soon as
the Boston terms of reunion became known—and continued through
the annual session of the Grand Lodge of England in 1887, the
Saratoga session of the RWGL of the World later in the same year,
and the Grand Lodge sessions of 1888, 1889, and 1890, when it finally sputtered out. A prestigious minority of English Templars complained that the Boston terms of reunion tolerated racism. They were
more Malinite than Malins.

Black people played a supporting role in this controversy. The
one African American with the prestige to challenge the Boston basis
effectively, William Wells Brown, had died earlier. In his absence a

few blacks unsuccessfully tried to persuade the RWGL of the World and the Grand Lodge of England of the error of their ways. The whites did not want to think of themselves as racists, but, fortunately for their self-esteem, there was no unanimity among black leaders. Other leaders of the black Grand Lodges saw little advantage in a futile, symbolic fight and chose to have faith in the favorable interpretation that Malins put forth. When the white Malinites divided into factions, both sides could quote black Templars in their support.

Before the Saratoga meeting the RWGL of the World published endorsements of the Boston terms of reunion by many black officers in the *Good Templars' Watchword* (28 March 1887). H.K. Freeman, Grand Worthy Secretary of Alabama, claimed to be "highly pleased." The Grand Lodge of Florida's executive committee voted unanimously in favor of the work of the Boston conference, to which its leader, W.M. Artrell, had been the only black delegate. E.L. Hammett, a Methodist minister who served as GWCT of Georgia, rejoiced: "Thank God for the union of the two great Orders!"

Other black Templars were more wary. At the Grand Lodge of North Carolina session on 16 November 1886, the delegates hinted at the need for caution. Union must be "on a basis giving equal rights to all races and creeds." On 30 March 1887 the Grand Lodge of Virginia expressed approval of the reunion but added, "We would respectfully recommend that every Good Templar north, east, west, and south remember the foundational principles upon which this Order was first founded."[40]

In the most dramatic moment for black participation in the debate, T. Thomas Fortune and Dr. (later Bishop) Benjamin T. Tanner made the journey to Saratoga. The editors of the *New York Freeman* and the (Philadelphia) *A.M.E. Review* hoped to dissuade the RWGL of the World from endorsing reunion on the Boston basis.[41] As a nonmember, Fortune was not allowed to speak. (According to some accounts, he had once been a Templar; others deny that he had ever belonged to the Order. Ironically, in the previous year he had been the host of Artrell en route to the Boston conference). With reluctance the RWGL of the World did allow Tanner to speak. After being in and out of the IOGT, he had rejoined most recently in October 1886.[42] At Saratoga he argued that if there had to be separate lodges, the separation should be on the basis of condition, with ignorant and uncultivated blacks in one category and the whites and educated blacks such as himself in the other.

The reaction was chilly. Jessie Forsyth, the London-born woman who edited *Temperance Brotherhood,* reminded the RWGL of the World that Tanner had dropped out of the IOGT three times and that Fortune had "backed our opponents" in his newspaper. Discouraged, Tanner failed to present the memorial adopted on the previous Sunday by 2,000 people at a leading New York black church.[43] Later, he characterized the Boston terms of reunion as "a complete surrender" and urged his English friends to "oppose this covenant with hell."[44] In an editorial on 4 June 1887, Fortune's *Freeman* called upon black Templars to form their own society. In response, Artrell labeled Fortune's attacks upon the British "ingratitude" and described them as "odious."[45]

Fortune's *Freeman* (11 June 1887) scolded John C. Dancy, J.C. Price, and George C. Scurlock of North Carolina, W.M. Artrell and John R. Scott of Florida, and J.J. Spellman of Mississippi for their "profuse hallelujahs" on behalf of terms of reunion that would help give "a victory for American colorphobists." On 16 June the (Salisbury, N.C.) *Star of Zion* uneasily replied that it had written on the basis of the reports available, which said that the reunion terms disregarded the color line. Dancy, editor of the *Star of Zion,* reminded his readers that he had served the Grand Lodge of North Carolina as secretary for six years and had attended RWGL of the World sessions in Boston and Liverpool. At its most recent session, he said, the Grand Lodge of North Carolina had voted unanimously in favor of union, "but not on terms that will violate or sacrifice any principle which has been gained for the Negro by the disruption at Louisville." Dancy defended the British: "What was told [the British] before the disruption, that the Negroes would not join the order—has proved only too true"; the A.M.E. editor Tanner "has just woke up to the situation so far as concerns Good Templars." Dancy explained that it was understandable that the British, "finding their favors unappreciated," became "willing to accept some terms of compromise, in order to continue the work of reform everywhere."

Another North Carolinian argued that the black Templars had to make the best of a situation that was not ideal. Despite this glum realism, Scurlock, writing in the *Star of Zion* on 23 June 1887, expressed admiration for Catherine Impey of England and John Pyper of Ireland, the two white delegates at Saratoga who resisted the Boston agreement. "We frankly confess that our [other] British friends yielded some ground in the fight."

English opponents of the terms of reunion quoted complaints by black Templars.[46] Walter S. Wilson of Virginia was the most active of these black critics. He had held a minor international office and served for several years as his Grand Lodge's secretary and GWCT. At Saratoga he had seconded Impey's motion against segregation and any insinuation of black racial inferiority. On 24 February 1888 he denied that blacks could be comfortable only in segregated lodges; blacks welcomed whites to their lodges. Wilson said on 15 March that his Grand Lodge of Virginia accepted the reunion only "as a half loaf." On 4 April he added that "we do not seek social equality as charged, but we do want the full rights of the Order regardless of our colour. I feel sorry that I took any part in the Saratoga session at all." On 29 August he complained about the abandonment of the black Templars: "We feel that we are out in the cold."

Impey implied that Jessie Forsyth, during a trip to Virginia, had twisted arms to compel the Malinite black Grand Lodge to merge with the black Hickmanites. Repudiating her old friend's accusation, Forsyth retorted that Wilson had changed his mind about reunion out of failed ambition: he was not elected to the top office in the Junior Grand Lodge when it was organized in December 1887. Earlier, in a letter of 27 July 1887, Wilson had praised Finch and added, "I trust that God will spare our dear Sister Impey to realize this view of mine."[47]

Other black leaders showed unease. Scurlock complained on 31 August 1887 that the British paid too much attention to Artrell, who had misrepresented black opinion. Scurlock lamented that "the manhood of the race is considerably crushed." He considered the fight hopeless but told Impey he was "glad that there is still a strong minority [in England] who think as you do respecting the status of the coloured people in the Order." Even the Artrells were not unequivocal supporters of Malins. Victoria Artrell thanked Impey for her help "in our fight for the rights of the coloured people," while Artrell himself acknowledged in February 1888 that Impey was "right in principle." He personally favored racially integrated Grand Lodges but doubted that anybody could "find a colored Grand Lodge in the South that is willing to merge itself into one Grand Lodge with the whites."[48]

Turnbull assembled quotations from black Templars in support of the compromise.[49] Lucy Wooden, head of the children's auxiliary of Virginia's Junior Grand Lodge, acknowledged on 14 February 1888 that "the time for mixed Lodges has not come yet." Senator J.J. Spellman, the secretary of Mississippi's Junior Grand Lodge, contended on 19 March 1888 that "the colored people enjoy the same desire for race separation, which obtains amongst other nations who, in this country, develop and cling to their own national organizations." Bishop J.W. Hood declared on 3 April 1888 that "in the present state of feeling in this State [of North Carolina] nothing else than separate

Subordinate Lodges [for blacks] and a Grand Lodge of their own is suitable." E.R. Carter, head of the Junior Grand Lodge of Georgia, pointed out on 10 May 1888 that "the masses had rather be in their own Lodges." He explained that blacks "haven't any confidence in the white men of the South."

In the late 1880s many of Malins's closest allies joined Impey in denouncing the Boston basis. Those who took this position included John Kempster of the *Good Templars' Watchword,* many members of the Society of Friends, and wealthy business entrepreneurs such as James J. Woods. As Grand Counsellor, Woods occupied the second highest office in the Grand Lodge of England.[50]

Part of the quarrel concerned the separation of races in general, but most of it hinged on the incompatibility between the racial inequality within the IOGT and its principle of universal brotherhood and sisterhood. His own idealistic rhetoric of the late 1870s and the early 1880s, contemptuous of compromise, came back to haunt Malins. He argued that he never had opposed voluntary separation. After all, his Grand Lodge included separate lodges for London Scots, for Quakers, for the military, even for brushmakers: "I have never strenuously objected to birds of a feather flocking together."[51] His critics questioned that blacks in the American South had much say over whether there would be separation. They regarded Malins as guilty of surrendering the rights of blacks in order to bring about unity on ignoble terms. George Dodds, a northern England radical, protested: "Was this expediency principle not the rock upon which [in 1876] the Order was split?"[52]

Before the Saratoga meetings Impey sent out a memorial to collect signatures from all who had been officers of the Grand Lodge of England since its institution or its representatives to RWGL sessions, as well as other leading British Templars. Sympathizers circulated similar memorials in Ireland and Scotland.[53] Malins's Scottish partner in 1876, George Gladstone, also questioned the Boston terms of reunion. But Turnbull, Malins's new Scottish ally, organized a countermemorial throughout the British Isles and got two former senior officers of the Grand Lodge of England to change sides in the war of memorials.[54]

Shortly before the Saratoga meeting the Grand Lodge of England held its annual session and, in a spirit of conciliation, elected Impey to the office of Grand Worthy Vice-Templar. She declined because of the prior defeat of a resolution asking that the Grand Lodge try to amend the RWGL constitution to eliminate the color line.[55] Kempster offered to resign the office to which he had been elected,

Grand Electoral Superintendent, but he was persuaded to remain. He also agreed to muzzle himself as editor of the *Good Templars' Watchword* and, at Malins's request, close its correspondence columns to further controversy over reunion.[56] (Malins later complained that Kempster did not keep his word.)[57] In the ballot for representatives to the RWGL of the World session Malins finished second to Impey, a sign of the widespread respect for her antiracism.

At Saratoga, Impey challenged the Boston basis despite the general eagerness for reunion: "She felt sick at heart about this reunion, because she felt that it had been determined to consent to a dual Order on the ground of race, not literally, perhaps, but in fact—not in law, but in practice." The hope of advancing temperance reform failed to justify violating the fundamental Templar principle of brotherhood. She denied that she was "trying to force social equality." She simply wanted equality within the Templar lodge room and Templar work. She complained that the reunion was being rushed without the membership having time to understand its terms and without many Grand Lodges meeting to discuss them. She lamented that the racial division in the United States was becoming more rigid, despite the growth in education of black people there: "The whole system of separation was false and wrong." She disagreed with the argument that blacks preferred separate institutions; rather, they had little choice. She quoted Eliza Gardner, a black officer in Massachusetts, on the isolation of African Americans who dared join white churches: they endured "treatment such that they could not, without loss of proper self respect, remain."[58] Defeated, Impey left Saratoga for Canada without attending the united RWGL session.

Although Impey was the only RWGL of the World delegate to vote against reunion, she was not alone in some of the unrecorded preliminary votes. The published record lacks detail, but according to Impey herself, John Pyper of Ireland and several black delegates joined her in voting to amend the terms of reunion to leave out anything that permitted separation on the basis of race and anything contravening the equality of the races.[59]

After Saratoga, Malins argued that "the American theory in the South was race separation; the British theory was race amalgamation; the intermediate theory was equal rights to all to enter, or form any Lodge, regardless of colour; with permission for senior and junior Grand Lodges as a temporary necessity to overcome difficulties arising from difference of race—as had previously been allowed [in Wales] where differences of language prevented united working." He acknowledged that one or two former slave states interpreted the

Boston basis of reunion in a racist fashion, but he pointed out that when the British protested, Finch insisted that all Grand Lodges follow the British interpretation. Malins justified temporary segregation on the grounds that both races wanted it (an argument that he had ridiculed when the Hickmanites had used it during the great schism): "The negro GLs all desired to be left intact."[60]

A few months later, in November 1888, Malins made another statement that contrasted with what he had said during the heated schism years: "Those who split from our Grand Lodge in England were as fully in favour of equal rights to the negro as we were, but they dissented from the methods we adopted in relation to the matter."[61] For Malins, the priority now was conciliation. Similarly, the first head of the RWGL of the World, James Yeames, denounced Impey for accusing the American churches of un-Christian behavior in their toleration of racism.[62]

The fight in the Grand Lodge of England dragged on. Prominent supporters of Impey signed a protest published in the *Good Templars' Watchword* on 29 August 1887 to answer charges that the Malins faction raised against her, and another on 26 September 1887. James J. Woods, Grand Counsellor, headed a list of those who issued still another protest at the time of the Grand Lodge session of 1888. Woods minced no words: "We had such faith in our leaders who attended the Boston Conference because they led us straight in the past, that we accepted the proposed settlement without reading between the lines." By the time Woods and others had awakened to the danger, Malins persuaded the district lodges to instruct their representatives to vote for the Boston basis. "Personally at last G.L. Session I was undecided; it was Bro. Malins' speech that led me to think that in the desire for re-union the colour question was [for him] a secondary matter." It was not a secondary matter for Woods. He complained that once any compromise with racism was permitted, there was no clear place to draw the line. Even if the Malinite Grand Lodges in the American South lacked integration in practice because of the failure of whites to join them, it was not the blacks who refused them entry. In April 1888 Woods moved a resolution to modify the RWGL constitution to protect "those fundamental principles of Christian Brotherhood which know no distinction of race or class in the great work of human reclamation."[63]

In seconding Woods's resolution, Impey argued that after the split in 1876 "further experience taught us that not only exclusion but that separations and distinctions between race and race were inconsistent with the principles of a brotherhood." She complained that

Malins had misused a letter of hers to accuse her of having opposed the amalgamation of the races. She opposed the admission only of those whites who rejected the brotherhood of all races within the IOGT. The commission that Malins had given to a missionary agent in the former slave states in 1881 instructed him "to extend the fellowship of the Order among the previously excluded coloured people" and "also enrol such white people as recognise the Brotherhood and equal rights of mankind, and do not countenance any 'colour line' in our fraternity." This remained her position.[64]

Speaking at the 1888 Grand Lodge session, John Kempster acknowledged that he had favored Dual Grand Lodges in 1876, but since that time the scales had fallen from his eyes. The widespread existence of racial prejudice did not justify tolerating it in the RWGL constitution: "They might as well, because of the universality of sin, attempt to put the Divine sanction of sin in the New Testament." In reply, Malins criticized Kempster for changing his position on the Boston terms after the beginning of 1887. "He went wrong when he began to read between the lines. The lines were right. It was what Sister Impey wrote between them that was wrong."[65]

Catherine Impey was losing hope. Once again in 1889 a race memorial was presented to the Grand Lodge of England on behalf of amending the RWGL constitution.[66] When the Grand Lodge declined to do so, she quit the Templar Order. Impey questioned "the right of majorities to rule where moral principles are concerned."[67] Shortly before that, Impey had begun a little magazine called *Anti-Caste* to continue her fight against racism.[68] In 1894 an organization that was "practically her own creation," the Society for the Recognition of the Brotherhood of Man, created another journal to combat racism, the *Bond of Brotherhood*.[69] Later, when Impey quarreled with the new organization, she revived *Anti-Caste*.

Virtually all other members of the minority in England who opposed the Boston terms of reunion as racist nevertheless remained in the IOGT. They tried as late as the Grand Lodge session of 1890 to press Malins to demand racial integration for the IOGT in the United States, but he rejected their pleas.[70] In his opinion, it was not the terms of reunion that had brought about racial separation, and the blacks in the South did not want any change. In 1891 Kempster was forced out as editor when the Grand Lodge took over direct control of the *Good Templars' Watchman* and moved its editorial offices from London to Malins's Birmingham headquarters.[71]

While Impey and her friends fought their rearguard battle in the Grand Lodge of England, the leadership of the united IOGT shifted from Chicago to Glasgow, and the best chance of a Templar revival in its homeland ended. The charismatic John B. Finch died of a heart attack at age thirty-five late in October 1887. At Saratoga he had been elected RWGT by acclamation. At first the office of counsellor had gone to W.G. Lane of Nova Scotia, the last head of the RWGL of the World, but he had withdrawn his acceptance when nobody from Britain was elected to the executive committee. The office then went to William W. Turnbull of Scotland, who, upon Finch's death, succeeded to the office of RWGT. Like Katzenstein a few years earlier, Turnbull retained his salaried office as secretary of his Grand Lodge.[72] In his new international office Turnbull appeased the North Americans and offended his old ally Malins. Like Finch, he questioned the legality of a Grand Lodge session that denied subordinate lodges direct representation—the situation in England under its district lodge scheme.

Jessie Forsyth, the vice Templar, had the right to move up to the office of counsellor but declined the post, to the cheers of the British Malinites, who regarded it impolitic to exclude the Hickmanite half of the reunited Templar Order from the two most senior offices. Consequently, Oronhyatekha was elected counsellor. The Canadian had once been a bitter enemy of Malins but since Boston had championed conciliation. As one sign of a new alignment of Oronhyatekha with Malins, the latter supported the extension to England of Oronhyatekha's Canadian-based fraternal insurance organization, the Independent Order of Foresters. In contrast, Kempster, who opposed the Boston terms of reunion, editorially praised a rival English-based Foresters society when it canceled the charter of an American affiliate for prohibiting blacks from joining: "We were never more disposed to be proud of our English working men."[73]

Malins remained emphatic that he stood for racial equality. In 1894 the *Good Templars' Watchword* reported a meeting at Wolverhampton that unanimously condemned the lynching of blacks in the American South. In the same year the Templar newspaper carried an advertisement, "Lynch Law and the Negro," seeking donations to pay for travel to the United States by Peter Stanford, "England's Coloured Preacher." In 1901 Templars in England were asked for money and clothing to help the black Templars of Jacksonville, Florida, where fire had destroyed Triumph lodge and the homes of many members. Alone among the black Grand Lodges, that of Florida had limped into the twentieth century.[74]

Malins took the lead in fighting racism in his own city of Birmingham and in the British capital. In 1909 an American-owned skating rink refused admission to a West African studying at the University of Birmingham. Malins caused legal notice to be served on the manager that the County Council would oppose renewal of his business's music license. The apologetic manager promised that there would be no further racial discrimination.[75] In 1910, after the *Daily News* reported a hotel in Bloomsbury that would not accept nonwhite guests, Malins asked for the name of any discriminating hotel.[76]

After the conclusion of the great schism the controversy about nonwhites in the Templar Order shifted to colonial Africa. In South Africa the response of whites to the question of black membership differed only in detail from that in the American South. South African whites promoted a separate fraternal temperance society for black people, the True Templars, but in contrast with the strictly segregated True Reformers, whites held the principal offices. The presence of a few white Good Templars dominating a mostly nonwhite organization made the True Templars analogous to the Juvenile Templars, a society separate from the IOGT but incorporating a few adult Templars who controlled this auxiliary organization.

The Independent Order of True Templars took shape in the mid-1870s. In 1874 the Grand Lodge of South Africa appointed a committee to devise a ritual for blacks, and in 1875 the first IOTT temple was organized. By mid-1876 the True Templars had over a thousand members. Apparently there was no actual legislation prohibiting nonwhite members in the Good Templar lodges, but few if any joined.[77] In contrast, during the great schism, when the Grand Lodge of South Africa allied itself with the Hickmanites, the local Malinites organized a Grand Lodge of the Cape Colony which sought out black members. Nearly half its lodges were racially mixed, and one was a former True Templar affiliate.[78]

The True Templars became distinct from the Good Templars. In 1890 the True Templars organized a Grand Temple as their central organization, and they adopted a strictly Christian basis in the late nineteenth century when many continental European members of the IOGT were calling for a secular reconstruction of the Templar ritual. The True Templars' white leader, Theo. Schreiner, denounced the trend toward "Christless" Good Templary.

Although by the early 1900s the IOGT had become a mostly northern European organization, there was reluctance to drive the South Africans out of the Templar Order on the grounds of local racist policies. An editorial in the *Good Templars' Watchword* explained that "in such matters as race prejudice and caste distinction 'force is no remedy.'"[79] When an Englishman who held a commission from the international society organized Good Templar lodges with nonwhite members, the True Templars and South African Good Templars protested.[80] It was only in 1969, however, that the Good Templars and True Templars became formally affiliated. At that time a woman of mixed race headed the IOTT, which claimed a membership of more than 91,000 men, women, and children.[81]

The end of the great schism had been irrelevant in continental Europe. For example, the reunion of the IOGT was brief in Sweden and Norway; most ex-Hickmanites in these Scandinavian kingdoms broke away to set up national Templar orders in 1888. With some exaggeration a Danish observer explained the divisions in Sweden and Norway as disagreements over the question "who should reign." Actually, the quarrel was more complicated than that. The largest Swedish and Norwegian seceding groups considered the official Grand Lodges insufficiently Christian, while a subsequent working-class break-away organization in Sweden, the Verdandi, considered the IOGT too religious. In Denmark, where the IOGT was much weaker, numerous rival Templar organizations sprang up, partly because of disagreements over the acceptability of low-alcohol-content beer. Whatever their basis, the divisions in Scandinavia after Saratoga had nothing to do with unhappiness over the racial aspects of the reunion. The same was true in Germany, where a schism resulted from "a protest against the leadership of Hermann Blume, the almighty Grand Chief Templar."[82] In Scandinavia and Germany the new Templar organizations were national societies. Some had a few affiliates among people who had emigrated to North America, but none aspired to international status.

The reunion of the Templar Order in 1887 was more surprising than its division in 1876. Fraternal societies often split and resplit; they seldom reunited formally, although when splinter groups died out there might remain only one principal survivor—a kind of unity. This was what happened in 1852 when the Independent Order of Good Templars broke away from the original Order of Good Templars and the parent organization disappeared.

The great schism had not been about racism alone, but racism had made it possible, and the schism had encouraged antiracist idealism. As a result of the frustrations endured by both parties during 1876-87, the terms of reunion rejected the doctrinaire and the idealistic. Above all, the practical spirit at Boston and Saratoga meant that the RWGL of the World accepted the RWGL's policy of segregated Grand Lodges as a solution to black membership in the

American South. This kind of moderate racism was deemed tolerable. Because the priority of the negotiators was international unity, not racial brotherhood and sisterhood, the terms of reunion combined a diluted antiracist principle and a diluted racist practice, through black access to segregated subordinate lodges and Grand Lodges. Within a few years Good Templary among African Americans had virtually disappeared.[83] Within a few decades the white Grand Lodges in North America collapsed as well.

Ironically, the Junior Grand Lodges remained important. They allowed Scandinavian immigrants to create their own organizations with difference in language as the justification. When the English-speaking Grand Lodges faded away, Scandinavian lodges made up most of the Templar remnant in the country where the IOGT had had its beginnings.[84] Appropriately, the national headquarters for the United States is located today at Minneapolis. Louisville has no Good Templars.

In retrospect, one can see that internationalism had been a prerequisite for the great schism. Internationalism also helped bring about reunion. British and American leaders valued the international character of the IOGT and paid a price for it. Black people also paid a price. The "temporary" separation of the races in Senior and Junior Grand Lodges lasted as long as there were African Americans in the IOGT—no surprise to most people. Although blacks in the former slave states could join segregated Grand Lodges, such a redefinition of Templar universalism sacrificed ideals of racial brotherhood and sisterhood on the altar of internationalism.

Conclusion

This book has pursued multiple objectives, the most fundamental of which has been to make the Good Templars visible. It also establishes that studying the IOGT can contribute to a variety of historical discourses: temperance, race and gender relations, internationalism, social class, and the African American experience. The nineteenth-century Templars reflected the search for a new, universal, reformed world order based on human equality of race, gender, and class. The Templars deserve a place in the subject matter of the new social and cultural history.

In the introduction I spoke about writing the book as a voyage of discovery. Such a voyage maps the coasts and occasionally ventures a landing and risks a short march into the interior. Other researchers, making use of local sources and a variety of methodologies and languages, must explore the hinterlands. Why, for instance, did the Templars thrive in Sweden and Norway after their appeal had collapsed in North America and declined in Britain? More relevant here, why did white southerners regard keeping their place in the IOGT worth making some concessions about race relations? Southern Baptists and members of other regional churches did not think it necessary for their religious denominations to embrace the English-speaking world; if churches could be geographically limited, why the powerful attraction of a fraternal temperance society with a national and international membership?

Although as a work of reconnaissance this book does not answer all the questions that it raises, I have tried to make the Templars identifiable as well as visible. They varied from region to region, country to country, and generation to generation, but a few characteristics seem clear. In the nineteenth century most Templars were young and remained members of the Order for only a short time. Most were of modest circumstances, although officers tended to be middle class. Perhaps a third of the rank and file were women, and nearly all were devout Protestants. Sociability dominated Templar lodges, but Grand Lodges called upon members to promote temperance politically. In the last decades of the nineteenth century the IOGT became identified with political parties: in the United States, the National Prohibition Party; in Britain, the Liberals.

Templars valued the Order's universalism, which in theory welcomed all those committed to total abstinence and prohibition. A major contention of this book is that the principle and practice of universal membership made the IOGT distinctive. The meaning of this universalism often changed, however. For instance, after the early decades the welcome to repentant drunkards cooled in English-speaking countries. The welcome to women remained but diminished in significance after the founding of the WCTU in 1874. The zeal for gender equality faded when the IOGT spread beyond its old northeastern and midwestern heartland to the American South and overseas.

Pride in the IOGT's internationalism came to dominate the universalist ideology. By the end of the nineteenth century, internationalism had become so important that the IOGT conceded to the Grand Lodges discretionary authority that forestalled secessions, which might have pitted local people against the central organization. In the early 1900s a brief schism led by Swiss and Dutch Templars created the Neutral Order, which opposed the use of a quasi-religious ritual, but it was a not very important exception to the absence of international conflict. Typically, the little schisms following the great schism were national splits—such as those that fragmented Templar ranks in Scandinavia—rather than global divisions.

Most of this book focuses on another aspect of universalism, the welcome to people of all races. In the years between the American Civil War and the turn-of-the-century disintegration of the IOGT in North America, many members regarded a welcome to African Americans as indispensable to Templar universalism, although for others it was irrelevant or, in the case of white southerners, unacceptable. There was never a consensus on the role of blacks in the new social order created by the War between the States and by nearly two generations of transatlantic, evangelically inspired moral reformers.

Even in the South the response to the question of black membership varied. Southern white racism showed more complexity and flexibility than some historians acknowledge. W.E.H. Searcy, the ultra-racist Georgian, objected to black membership anywhere in the

Order but asked the IOGT to help African Americans start a separate society. Most white southern Templars, or at least their leaders, tolerated blacks in the Templar lodges outside their region, on the principle of local autonomy, as well as an occasional black delegate or visitor at international meetings. These whites preferred that blacks living in the American South confine themselves to a separate fraternal temperance society, but to preserve the unity of the IOGT they eventually conceded a segregated Templar membership. The white leaders paid a dear price for the resulting Dual Grand Lodges: the loss of much of the white membership, obsessed by fear of racial contamination. Even the question of who should organize African Americans—local whites or the international organization—touched raw nerves, as the debate over the Philadelphia and Atlanta plans demonstrated.

Outside the former slave states many Templars insisted that blacks had a right to join the IOGT regardless of where they resided, but most took for granted that the races would not mix in local lodges, and most accepted some kind of official segregation. In contrast, a few whites such as England's Catherine Impey insisted that the IOGT could not tolerate segregation.

In principle black leaders dreamed of complete racial integration for the Templar Order—this ideal made the IOGT dear to them— but they accepted segregated lodges and Grand Lodges as the best deal they could get. Moreover, blacks feared that in amalgamated southern organizations they would become powerless.

Although not an accident, the great schism could have been avoided. It would be heartwarming to say that a passion for human dignity and equality, intolerant of any expedient compromise with intolerance, motivated the Malinites. Unfortunately, that would be an unhistorical exaggeration. Although uncomfortable with white supremacist racism, most supporters of the RWGL of the World wanted to cut a deal over human rights for the sake of the unity of the IOGT. Such a compromise was possible. Although the supporters of the old RWGL managed to live with racism, most of them regretted it. A majority of the people on either side of the divide agreed on what kind of black access and restrictions they found tolerable. Nor did most transatlantic cousins need the incentive of ending a decade-old split to accept the compromise embodied in the Boston agreement. That the split was not inevitable is an interpretation implicit in its end in anticlimax.

The quarrel over the rights of blacks did not by itself suffice to bring about the great schism. Other disputes and human frailties helped turn an agonizing debate over the morality and expediency of Templar racial policies in the American South into a British-initiated rupture of institutional unity. The British leaders feared the precedent of duplicate Grand Lodges, and Malins bridled under the North American domination of the IOGT. Moreover before and after 1876, white northerners such as Hastings tried to paper over problems, not confront them, and Hickman lacked Thrower's tough-minded realism.

It is conceivable that if Malins and Gladstone had lingered in the United States following their departure from Louisville, the RWGL of the World might have dissolved a month after its formation. Malins and Gladstone preferred an IOGT with the color line rubbed out, but if they had participated in the negotiations that produced the Philadelphia plan, they might have gambled on Hickman's promise that the white southerners would implement it. If Malins and Gladstone had endorsed Hickman's Philadelphia plan, it is possible that the white southerners would have been hesitant to reject it and thereby assume the responsibility for dividing the IOGT.

Is it realistic to imagine that the white southern leaders might have conceded in 1876 what they conceded later? Did it take a prolonged schism to make them act? Might Hickman have made a difference if he had showed more determination and a willingness to accept the secession of the most militantly racist white southerners?

Speculating that changes in circumstances could have prevented the great schism or ended it quickly does not mean that it did not matter. Once the great schism began, it put pressure on the supporters of the old RWGL to adopt the objectives of Gladstone's Ultimatum, although not the method of allowing a Grand Lodge to organize lodges in the jurisdiction of another Grand Lodge. It also stimulated the supporters of the RWGL of the World to adopt more radical views of racial integration. During the late 1870s and the 1880s a few whites in Britain moved to a position of uncompromising commitment to equal rights within the IOGT for people of all races. The concessions that Malins yielded in order to end the great schism should not obscure the fight against them led by Catherine Impey.

The Templar Order was not an inward-looking sect isolated from the world. The history of the IOGT is part of the larger social history of the peoples from whom Templar lodges recruited men and women, brothers and sisters. In their attitudes and behavior they responded to the contradictory values of Templar universalism and late nineteenth-century white racism. The importance of the Templar struggle with the meaning of universal membership lies in the fact that it happened at all.

Templar trumpets failed to topple racist walls. In the twilight of twentieth-century reformism, more than a hundred years after the great schism, many of those walls still stand. Yet thousands of Templars, to their enduring credit, refused to avert their eyes and keep silent in the presence of injustice. Their attempt to achieve a world order pledged to universal equality deserves a chapter in the history of Anglo-American moral reform.

Appendix

On 20 September 1876, at the semiannual session of the Grand Lodge of Massachusetts in North Adams, William Wells Brown argued the case for the Right Worthy Grand Lodge of the World. In the abolitionist tradition, he accused his opponents of hypocrisy. He also made use of personal invective, directing insults at Kentucky's white population and Canada's Indian peoples and "low French." Brown's speech was published, as follows, in the *Good Templars' Watchword*.[1]

Grand Worthy Chief Templar,—We have listened for an hour-and-a-half to P[ast].R.W.G. Templar [Samuel D.] Hastings, in his defence of the actions of the R.W.G.L. at its late session in Louisville [Kentucky], where that body practically re-affirmed its former policy of permitting the exclusion of coloured persons from our Order in the Southern States. He has tried to prove to you that the R.W.G.L. has always been on the side of giving justice to the negro; that it has never sanctioned the exclusion of the blacks from our Order in the South. Let us see how far his assertions are correct.

For ten years the coloured people have been excluded from our Order in the South. They are excluded *to-day*. Somebody has done it. Who is it?

As early as 1866 the G.L. of Kentucky put in her Constitution, that no person in that State would be admitted into the Order except those of "pure white blood;" a most ridiculous proposition, since there is no such thing as "pure white blood," and if there is, Kentucky is about the last State in the American Union that should make such a claim, for it is a historical fact that during our colonial times England transported a large number of convicts to her American possessions, and landed them in Virginia and Maryland, and many of them afterwards emigrated to Kentucky. The blood of these transported convicts courses through the veins of the present white population of Kentucky. So much for the "pure blood."

This exclusion of the blacks by the Kentucky G.L. was well known to the R.W.G.L. and sanctioned by it. At the Madison [Wisconsin] Session, in 1872, this exclusion on account of colour came up, and here the Southerners declared that the negroes would not accept our Order; that they *would* not become Good Templars; and it was this positive assurance on the part of Southern Representatives that induced Joseph Malins to reluctantly consent to the blacks having the Temperance cause presented to them in another way than that of Good Templarism. And now the Southerners claim that Bro. Malins— whose amendment was *lost*—was the author of the "U.[nited] O.[rder] of True Reformers." A greater falsehood never was circulated.

In North Carolina the blacks had subordinate lodges before the whites, and yet when Col. [J.J.] Hickman, as R.W.G. Coun.[sellor], went to North Carolina to organise a Grand Lodge he ignored the coloured lodges, and took in only the whites. And yet the P.R.W.G. Templar Hastings says the R.W.G.L. knew nothing of exclusion?

Among the decisions given in his report at the London Session in 1873, R.W.G. Templar [John] Russell gave this:—

"The action of the R.W.G. Lodge, at its late session, relating to Lodges of our Order among the coloured population of the Southern States, gives to all Grand Lodges now existing, or hereafter to be organised, full power over that question within their respective jurisdictions, even to the discontinuing of Subordinate Lodge Charters previously granted by this R.W.G. Lodge."

This shews [*sic*] most clearly that the American leaders of the R.W.G.L. not only knew that the blacks were excluded from our Order in the South, but that the R.W.G.T. committed them to the mercy of the Southern G. Lodges, even to the right of taking away their charters.

But in England the Representatives saw through this transparent veil, and demanded that something should be done for the negroes, and this demand caused the passage [in 1873] of the following:—

"That all Subordinate Lodges, within the jurisdiction of any Grand Lodge, whose Charters have not been revoked or suspended for a violation of the Constitution, Laws or Rules of the Order, are entitled to be recognised and receive [the] quarterly Password, and that the refusal thereof, because of race, colour or condition, will be a violation of duty and obligation."

This action of the London Session so exasperated the Good Templars of the Southern States that they at once began to arrange for withdrawing from the R.W.G. Lodge altogether.

But the majority of the R.W.G.L. Executive were *Conservative* men—men who were accustomed to bow to the behests of the old Slaveocracy, and down they went upon their knees. Hear what the then R.W.G. Templar Hastings said in his report to the Boston Session in 1874. I am glad he is present, so that if I misrepresent him he can correct me:—

"The Order at the South"

"On my return from London in September last, I found an intense feeling of excitement prevailing in several of these States, growing out of misapprehension of the action of this body touching the question of lodges for the coloured people at the South. It was evident to my mind that unless something was done speedily to allay the excitement, several of the Southern Grand Lodges would be *lost to the Order.*

"With the most efficient aid of our worthy brother, J.J. Hickman, P.R.W.G. Coun., who at his own expense went from one Grand Lodge Session to another, explaining the real situation of matters and urging moderation, the matter was finally understood and perfect harmony and good feeling restored.

"A Council to decide what action should be taken by the Southern Grand Lodges was convened at Atlanta, Ga. on the 12th November, 1873. Delegates were present from Kentucky, Tennessee, Alabama, and Georgia. The whole matter was laid before the Council in a most able and lucid report by Bro. Hickman, when the following resolutions were unanimously adopted:—

"After a careful examination of the explanation by the R.W.G.T. (S.D. Hastings) of the action taken by R.W.G. Lodge, at its recent session in London [England], relative to the subject of negro lodges, we, as a Council of the southern Grand Lodges, submit that the R.W.G. Lodge having disclaimed all intention to detract from the rights guaranteed to us, and that we have full protection under our charters and laws; therefore be it *Resolved*—That there exists no further cause for disagreement between the Southern Grand Lodges and R.W.G. Lodge.

"*Resolved*—That we recommend to the several Grand Lodges represented by us that we *retain* our relationship with the R.W.G. Lodge as heretofore."

A gentleman who was present at a meeting in the South where Col. Hickman was pledging that the R.W.G.L. Executive would not enforce the London resolution, said he was ashamed that he was a

Good Templar when he saw the depth of degradation to which the head of the Order had descended.

And yet Bro. Hastings tells us that the R.W.G.L. has always been on the side of justice to the negro! At the Boston [Massachusetts] Session I placed upon the journal the notice of a change in the Constitution so as to give the negro the Order by separate G.[rand] Lodges.

This was called up at the Bloomington [Illinois] Session in 1875, and we were again cheated.

Then came the Louisville Session of 1876, which is familiar to you all.

The demand of Representative [George] Gladstone, of Scotland, was *just and reasonable,* and was the thing needed to settle the question.

But the Southern Representatives were determined in their opposition to the rights of the negro, and nothing but the continued exclusion of that race from the Order in the South would satisfy them.

The substitute offered by Dr. Oronhyatekha, filled as it was with a mess of high sounding phrases about human liberty, the well-understood fundamental principle of the Order, and the equality of all mankind without regard to race or colour, was ridiculous in the extreme when we take into consideration the fact that his was only a subterfuge to keep the blacks out of the Order. And this is clear enough when we come to the conclusion of Dr. O[ronhyatekha]'s substitute, which is a mere play upon words. Resolved—

"That any provision in the Constitution or Bye-laws of any Grand Lodge that in any manner contravenes this well understood fundamental principle of the Order, is absolutely null and void, and this R.W.G. Lodge is prepared at any time to revoke the Charter of any Lodge that may persist in violating this or any other law of the Order."

This concoction reminds us of a town's meeting called in New Hampshire to consider the subject of building a new poor-house, and where the votes were about equally divided as to the propriety of going to the expense of erecting the new building. The committee reported as follows:—"1st, *Resolved*—That we build a new poor-house, 2nd, *Resolved*—That we build the new house where the old one stands. 3rd, *Resolved*—That we keep the paupers in the old poor-house till the new one is built!!"

Before the adjournment of our opponents at the Louisville Session, they felt that it was a duty to take a little glorification to themselves, and to tickle Dr. O[ronhyatekha] and the Southern delegates, so the following deliverance was adopted:—

"The substitute offered by the Representatives from Canada, a country that has always offered a refuge to the oppressed of all nations, be they bond or free, and accepted by the Representatives from the South, practically demonstrated that in this great humanitarian work, in this great moral work, this Order knows no North, no South, no East, no West, no nationality, no race—the world is our field, our subjects mankind."

The work was finished; the negro was still successfully kept out of the Order; the South was safe; and one of the Southern Representatives proposed that the R.W.G.L. have a season of prayer!! Thus they "steal the livery of the courts of Heaven to serve the devil in."

While it is true that Canada was the land of refuge for the slave during the existence of that institution here, we are not so much indebted to the people of Canada as to the *home* Government of Great Britain, which made "Freedom" the watchword in all her colonies.

The population of Canada is still made up largely of low French and Indians, and in parts of Canada prejudice against the negro is as rampant as in the Southern States.

And Dr. Oronhyatekha has that combination of instincts which have distinguished him for his hatred to the negro.

While at the Boston Session in 1874 an English Representative [Joseph Malins], who had for the first time seen a negro initiated into the R.W.G.L., thought that it would be a capital thing to carry back to his own country a picture of a white, a negro, and an Indian Good Templar in a group. He therefore asked the Doctor if he would sit. His reply was to the effect that he did not object to be taken with a white man, but he would not be taken "WITH A NIGGER." Of the two races the negro is infinitely above the Indian in this country, and if either had cause to object it should have been myself, for I was the person referred to.[2]

P.R.W. Templar Hastings finds great fault with the British Representatives for coming here with an ultimatum. Does Bro. Hastings forget that the Southerners have for the past ten years presented their ultimatums for the continued exclusion of the negro? This ultimatum they have passed at some session of the R.W.G.L., and when beaten at the London Session, the Kentucky Representative [Tim Needham] withdrew the invitation extended the day previous for that body to hold its next session in Kentucky; while the Representative from Alabama [Alonzo S. Elliott], who had been elected to an office in the R.W.G.L., resigned his position; so that it was to meet a Southern ultimatum that the R.W.G. Templar, on his return to America, hastened to the South and assured them that the London enactment should not be enforced. Talk no more of the British ultimatums!

But SHAME upon the Northern Representatives, who remained silent while the black man's rights and the principles of the Independent Order of Good Templars had to be advocated by foreigners.

Then the motives of the British Representatives have been called in question by Bro. Hastings. He says that "Malins was ambitious and immovable, and that Gladstone would not accept any modification to his amendment; and that an alteration of four words would have satisfied the South." Yes; but the alteration of the four words which they proposed would have taken from the negro the justice that the English demanded.

For one, I thank God that He put it into the hearts of the English and Scotch people to send over here Joseph Malins, George Gladstone, and James Yeames—men with backbone, who to-day enjoy the respect and esteem of the liberty-loving people of this entire continent.

These men had been misled in 1872, cheated in 1873, deceived in 1874, and swindled in 1875. They prepared for 1876, and, thank God, they stood by their ultimatum.

P.R.W.G. Templar Hastings finds fault with the British delegates for re-organising the R.W.G. Lodge. He says they are *not* a R.W.G.L. Let me tell Bro. Hastings here to his face that the R.W.G.L. of the World occupies a position to-day infinitely higher than Col. Hickman and his associates. The re-organised body is *in the right;* numerically it has two-thirds of the Order, and above all, it presents the Order to the coloured people, and has made glad hearts among the millions in our Southern States whom Col. Hickman has laboured so diligently to keep out of the Order.

And where stand Col. Hickman to-day and *his* "R.W.G.L."?

You have there on your table, Grand Worthy Chief Templar, a letter from Col. Hickman, asking this G.L. to endorse the act of the Louisville Session; and he insists that, should Massachusetts fail to endorse the doings at Louisville, it will very much impede his work in England; and he hopes this G.L. will give him a letter of introduction to the Good Templars of England.

Now I tell Bro. Hastings that this G.L. will not endorse the work done at the Louisville Session, nor will it give Col. Hickman a recommendation to the English, simply because he does not deserve it.

He and his Southern associates have torn this noble Order to pieces; driven out the good and brave men and women of this country, of Europe, of the West Indies, the East Indies, and wherever they can appreciate justice. He has pandered to these low, mean instincts of an unholy prejudice of colour which have cast a blight upon one of the greatest of reforms.

P.R.W. Templar Hastings says that "four hundred subordinate lodges in England have resolved to join us." Let me tell Bro. Hastings that I don't believe there are that number of fools in England. I regret that P.R.W.G.T. Hastings has come here to-day in such a bad cause.

He has begged this G.L. not to pass the vote of censure upon the ex-R.W.G.L.! ["ex-" because Brown regarded it as no longer the legitimate international Templar organization]. He has almost shed tears in behalf of Col. Hickman and his Southern friends. But it is all of no avail.

Unfortunately for the cause of justice this semi-annual session of our G.L. is held in North Adams, nearly 200 miles from the capital of the State, which makes the attendance so small.

But for the respect I have for the large number of lodges which are not represented here to-day, I would move a resolution that our G.W. Secretary be at once instructed to send to England for her supplies [and so accept the authority of the new Right Worthy Grand Lodge of the World].

I regret that this question must go over to our annual session. We want to show where this G.L. stands upon this important subject. I know where I stand, and I know where I shall go, whether this G.L. goes or not.[3]

Here, you see, I have a handful of letters from black men at the South, asking my opinion. I tell every one of them that the R.W.G.L. of the World is their only hope, and I advise them to apply at once for charters for subordinate and Grand Lodges.

Notes

Introduction

1. See David M. Fahey, "Temperance and the Liberal Party—Lord Peel's Report, 1899," *Journal of British Studies* 10 (May 1971): 151, 154-56.

2. José Harris, *Private Lives, Public Spirit: Britain 1870-1914* (New York: Penguin Books, 1994), 4 n.

3. The Templars themselves did not adopt the terms "universalism" and "the great schism," which I use throughout this book.

4. In 1869 one Grand Lodge explained the absence of certain reports: luggage containing the papers and clothing of the Grand Worthy Secretary had been stolen at the St. Paul railway depot, according to GL of Minnesota, *Proceedings* (1869), n.p. (final page).

5. GL of Georgia, *Proceedings* (1875), 22. Even worse than official figures, private estimates could be pure invention. At the beginning of the twentieth century a South Carolinian estimated that his Grand Lodge had a hundred lodges with 4,500 members. Joel E. Brunson to the editors of the *Baptist Courier,* 4 Aug. 1902, cited in Frederick M. Heath and Harriett H. Kinard, "Prohibition in South Carolina, 1880-1940: An Overview," *Proceedings of the South Carolina Historical Association* (1980), 128 n. 3. In that year the International Supreme Lodge, *Proceedings* (1902), 25, reported that South Carolina had no Grand Lodge and only two working subordinate lodges.

6. Benjamin F. Parker, in RWGL, *Proceedings* (1886), 41. On the first mention of a person ordinarily identified by initials and surname, I provide the full first name when I know it.

1. The Templars

1. For brevity's sake, I generally call the Good Templars "the Templars," but there were other contemporaneous organizations with similar names, such as the Templars of Honor and Temperance.

2. See the chapter on the Sons of Temperance in Charles Chester Cole, *Lion of the Forest: James B. Finley, Frontier Reformer* (Lexington: Univ. Press of Kentucky, 1994).

3. Donald Weldon Beattie, "Sons of Temperance: Pioneers in Total Abstinence and 'Constitutional' Prohibition" (Ph.D. diss., Boston Univ., 1966).

4. The best introduction to temperance efforts in the United States is Jack S. Blocker Jr., *American Temperance Movements: Cycles of Reform* (Boston: Twayne, 1989). The Alcohol and Temperance History Group publishes the *Social History of Alcohol Review* and sponsors an Internet Listserv group and a World Wide Web site.

5. Joseph R Gusfield, *Symbolic Crusade: Status Politics and the American Temperance Movement,* 2d ed., (1963; Urbana: Univ. of Illinois Press, 1986); John J. Rumbarger, *Profits, Power, and Prohibition: Alcohol Reform and the Industrializing of America, 1800-1930* (Albany: State Univ. of New York Press, 1989).

6. Richard J. Carwardine, *Evangelicals and Politics in Antebellum America* (New Haven, Conn.: Yale Univ. Press, 1993), 101-02; Curtis D. Johnson, *Redeeming America: Evangelicals and the Road to Civil War* (Chicago: Ivan R. Dee, 1993), 124-34.

7. George Thompson Brake, *Drink: Ups and Downs of Methodist Attitudes to Temperance* (London: Oliphants, 1974).

8. Sidsel Eriksen, "Drunken Danes and Sober Swedes: Religious Revivalism and the Temperance Movements as Keys to Danish and Swedish Folk Cultures," in *Language and the Construction of Class Identities,* ed. Bo Sträth (Gothenburg, Sweden: Dept. of History, Univ. of Gothenburg, 1990).

9. For a handy introduction, see Jonathan Zimmerman, "Dethroning King Alcohol: The Washingtonians in Baltimore, 1840-1845," *Maryland Historical Magazine* 87 (Winter 1992). See also Ruth M. Alexander, "'We Are Engaged as a Band of Sisters': Class and Domesticity in the Washingtonian Temperance Movement, 1840-1850," *Journal of American History* 75 (Dec. 1988).

10. W.S. Harwood, "Secret Societies in America," *North American Review* 164 (May 1897): 617, 620. Mary Ann Clawson, "Nineteenth-Century Women's Auxiliaries and Fraternal Orders," *Signs* 12 (1986): 42 n. 4, points out that "in 1910 the Masons and the Odd Fellows each had memberships of over 7 percent of the total population of adult white males of native birth."

11. Alvin J. Schmidt, *Oligarchy in Fraternal Organizations* (Detroit, Mich.: Gale Research, 1973).

12. Mary Ann Clawson, *Constructing Brotherhood: Class, Gender, and Fraternalism* (Princeton, N.J.: Princeton Univ. Press, 1989); Mark C. Carnes, *Secret Ritual and Manhood in Victorian America* (New Haven, Conn.: Yale Univ. Press, 1989); Anthony D. Fels, "The Square and Compass: San Francisco's Freemasons and American Religion, 1870-1900" (Ph.D. diss., Stanford Univ. 1987); Lynn Dumenil, *Freemasonry and American Culture, 1880-1930* (Princeton, N.J.: Princeton Univ. Press, 1984). See also Christopher J. Anstead, "Fraternalism in Victorian Ontario: Secret Societies and Cultural Hegemony" (Ph.D. diss., Univ. of Western Ontario, 1992); the review of Carnes's book by Peter N. Stearns in *Journal of Ritual Studies* 4 (Winter 1990); and Dumenil's review of the books by Carnes and Clawson in *Journal of Interdisciplinary History* 21 (Winter 1991).

13. Alvin Schmidt and Nicholas Babchuck, "Trends in U.S. Fraternal Associations in the Twentieth Century," in *Voluntary Action Research: 1973* (Lexington, Mass.: Lexington Books, n.d.); Clifford Putney, "Service over Secrecy: How Lodge-Style Fraternalism Yielded Popularity to Men's Service Clubs," *Journal of Popular Culture* 27 (Summer 1993); Jeffrey A. Charles, *Service Clubs in American Societies* (Urbana: Univ. of Illinois Press, 1993), chap. 1, "From Fraternity to Service"; Gail Bederman, "'The Women Have Had Charge of the Church Work Long Enough': The Men and Religion Forward Movement of 1911-1912 and the Masculinization of Middle-Class Protestantism," *American Quarterly* 41 (Sept. 1989).

14. Tomkins County, N.Y., 1850 census, fol. 227. Curtis was listed as aged forty-nine, with $1,500 worth of real estate. The best authority on the IOGT's origins is Isaac Newton Peirce, *The History of the Independent Order of Good Templars* (Philadelphia: Daughaday & Becker, 1869).

15. Ben D. Wright in Clarence True Wilson, ed., *The Pocket Cyclopedia of Temperance*, rev. ed. (Topeka: Temperance Society of the M. E. Church, 1916), 149; Frederick Wagstaff, "The Relationship of the I.O.G.T. to the Drunkard," (London) *Templar*, 29 May 1873, 388.

16. In (Chicago) *Our Paper: For the Good of the Order*, 4 March 1863, 1, an Illinois lodge with a membership of seventy-one reported that forty-two were away in the army.

17. California and Virginia did not peak until the 1880s, but the northeastern and midwestern Grand Lodges reached their greatest membership in the late 1860s and early 1870s.

18. Peirce, *History,* 498-503.

19. Genevieve G. McBride, *On Wisconsin Women* (Madison: Univ. of Wisconsin Press, 1993), 79.

20. Of the 275 men and 53 women identified with the temperance and prohibition movement in the Lisle Abbott Rose database at George Washington University, 6.4 percent were Templars. Of the Templars, 71.4 percent also belonged to the Prohibition Party. Gail Sylvia Lowe, "A Bio-Bibliography of American Reformers, 1865-1917, with a Case Study of Temperance-Prohibition" (Ph.D. diss., George Washington Univ. 1992). 80, 88.

21. Sharon Anne Cook, *"Through Sunshine and Shadow": the Woman's Christian Temperance Union, Evangelicalism, and Reform in Ontario, 1874-1930* (Montreal and Kingston: McGill-Queen's Univ. Press, 1995), 17.

22. For instance, in 1877, with the support of a Fante schoolteacher who later helped found the Aborigines' Rights Protection Society, "the General Superintendent of the Wesleyan Mission and the Commanding Officer of the Castle garrison" organized the first Templar lodge in the Gold Coast colony. David Kimble, *A Political History of Ghana: The Rise of Gold Coast Nationalism, 1850-1928* (Oxford: Clarendon Press, 1963), 147.

23. J. Dawson Burns, *Temperance History,* 2 vols. (London: National Temperance Publication Depot, 1889), 2:279.

24. From a Templar songbook compiled by J.W. Hopkins, quoted in *National Good Templar,* July-Aug. 1993, 1.

25. Joseph Malins, "The Rise of Good Templarism," *Australasian Templar,* Jan. 1876, 136. Later the term "Good Templary" superseded "Good Templarism."

26. Disunity often crippled the Templars. In 1870, for instance, Ohio's secretary accused the GWCT J.A. Spencer of trying to destroy a new Templar weekly for the benefit of the National Prohibition Party newspaper, edited by Spencer and published by his brother and brother-in-law, "a nice family arrangement." J.B. King in (Dayton) *Temperance Times,* 10 Feb. 1870.

27. For the number of members in the early 1990s, see Helge Kolstad, *IOGT Handbook* (Oslo: International Organization of Good Templars, 1990), 13.

28. James H. Morrison and James Moreira, eds., *Tempered by Rum: Rum in the History of the Maritime Provinces* (Porter's Lake, Nova Scotia: Pottersfield Press, 1988), 24, 29.

29. *Obligations of the Independent Order of Good Templars* (Owego, N.Y.: Owego Times, 1875), Keir Hardie diary, 7 Jan. 1884, cited in Fred Reid. *Keir Hardie: The Making of a Socialist* (London: Croom Helm, 1978), 72.

30. Secretary's Book of Dublin Lodge, Dublin, Ind., 12 Sept., 30 Oct. 1863, fols. 4, 6-7, Earlham College.

31. Thomas Whittaker, *Life's Battles in Temperance Armour* (London: Hodder & Stoughton, 1884), 312.

32. GL of Connecticut, *Proceedings* (1874), 19.

33. Joseph Malins, "Good Templary in England," (London) *United Temperance Gazette*, March 1898, 29. In fact, the Odd Fellows provided the model for the early ritual.

34. Jessie Forsyth to George F. Cotterill, 2 Sept. 1903, in *The Collected Writings of Jessie Forsyth, 1847-1937: The Good Templars and Temperance Reform on Three Continents,* ed. David M. Fahey (Lewiston, N.Y.: Edwin Mellen Press, 1988), 460-61; "The Hindoo Memorial," *GTW,* 10 May 1880, 297-98. A handful of practicing Roman Catholics belonged to the Templar Order, such as P.J. Connell of Michigan, an Irish immigrant. George W.E. Hill, *Some Good Templars I Have Known: Brief Biographies of Our Most Eminent Members* (Grand Valley, Mich.: Valley City, 1893), 252-54.

35. For Willie Gallacher, see William Knox, ed., *Scottish Labour Leaders, 1918-37: A Biographical Dictionary* (Edinburgh: Mainstream, 1984), 114, 118.

36. Joanne Judd Brownsword, "Good Templars in Wisconsin, 1854-1880" (M.A. thesis, Univ. of Wisconsin, 1960), 9. Brownsword reports not the age of the delegates at the time that they attended a state convention but their age at the next census.

37. *Walter McElreath: An Autobiography,* ed. Albert E. Saye (Macon: Mercer Univ. Press, 1984), 45.

38. Forsyth, *Collected Writings,* 72.

39. In continental Europe drinkers remained important for IOGT recruitment. In 1880, when a Danish schoolteacher organized the second lodge in her country, she recruited many problem drinkers. Sidsel Eriksen, *Søster Silfverbergs Sorger* (Copenhagen: Spektrum, 1993), 320. In contrast, an English survey in the 1920s got 438 replies from members of the IOGT, of whom 391 described themselves as life abstainers. H. Weatherall, *Total Abstainers* (leaflet, 1924), place of publication and publisher unidentified, (London) United Kingdom Temperance Alliance library.

40. Joseph Malins in *GTW,* 18 April 1914, 190.

41. S.D. Hastings, "The Independent Order of Good Templars," in *One Hundred Years of Temperance* (New York: National Temperance Society and Publication House, 1886), 480.

42. Wagstaff, "Relationship of the I.O.G.T. to the Drunkard," 388. For a fictional account of the IOGT and problem drinkers, see Guy Hayler, *George Proctor, the Teetotaler* (London: S.W. Partridge, [1895]), chap. 35, "The Publican's Son."

43. GL of Illinois, *Proceedings* (1855), 22; (1856), [93]; (1857), 125; (1858), 150; (1859), 29; (1860), 41; (1861), [58]; (1862), 43; (1863), [59]; (1864), 65; (1865), [72]; (1867), 19; (1868), 32; (1869), 18. The *Proceedings* for 1866 do not provide figures for members or for violations; 1867 lists the number of members in 1866 but not the violations for that year (I owe this last information to Kenneth P. Scheffel, Bentley Historical Library, University of Michigan, Ann Arbor).

44. GL of England, *Proceedings* (1872), 40; (1875), 38.

45. Brownsword, "Good Templars in Wisconsin," 14, 15.

46. Good Templars, box 1, folder 2, State Historical Society of Wisconsin, Area Research Center, LaCrosse; Roy Rosenzweig, *Eight Hours for What We Will: Workers and Leisure in an Industrial City, 1870-1920* (Cambridge: Cambridge Univ. Press, 1983), 262-63 n. 60.

47. GL of Georgia, *Proceedings* (1877), "in memoriam" page; C.H.M., "Notes from the Field," in (Dayton) *Temperance Times,* 7 July 1870; Lawrence M. Lipin, *Producers, Proletarians, and Politicians: Workers and Party Politics in Evansville and New Albany, Indiana, 1850-87* (Urbana: Univ. of Illinois Press, 1994), 211, 216-17, 297; (London) *English Good Templar,* Aug. 1871, 78-79; Joseph Malins, *The Social Aspect of Good Templary* (Birmingham: Grand Lodge of England, n.d.), n.p.; *The Indian Templar Handbook,* 2d ed., (Calcutta: Grand Lodge of India, 1925), 256-59.

48. John Bramley, in *Quarterly Journal of Proceedings of the Northumberland District Lodge* (1878), 6; *Northumberland District Lodge . . . Report of the District Chief Templar* (1888), 3; Joseph Malins, "Our Duty to the Middle Classes," *GTW,* 20 Oct. 1906, 375.

49. GL of Illinois, *Proceedings* (1894), [97]; Silvanus P. Thompson, *A History of the Independent Order of Good Templars* (London: Curtice, 1873); Janet Smeal Thompson and Helen G. Thompson, *Silvanus Phillips Thompson, D.Sc., LL.D., F.R.S.: His Life and Letters* (London: T. Fisher Unwin, 1920), 13; Thomas F. Parker, *History of the Independent Order of Good Templars from the Origin of the Order to the Session of the Right Worthy Grand Lodge of 1887,* rev. ed. (1882; New York: Phillips & Hunt, 1887), 93.

50. *Recollections of William Arnold* (Northampton, Eng.: Privately printed, 1915), 45.

51. Although Templars belonged to pietist churches, they behaved in the IOGT as liturgicals, to adopt the language of Richard J. Jensen, *The Winning of the Midwest: Social and Political Conflict, 1888-1896* (Chicago: Univ. of Chicago Press, 1971), chap. 3, "Pietists and Liturgicals: The Religious Roots of Partisanship." In addition to their taste for lodge ritual, Templars exhibited other traits that Jensen associates with the liturgical mentality, notably a prickly sensitivity toward intellectual heresy and a generosity about forgiving the brother or sister who has sinned out of weakness.

52. Suffolk lodge, Cutchogue, Long Island, minutes, 12 Jan. 1880, fol. 54, New York Public Library Manuscript Division.

53. Norma Logan (later Denny), "Drink and Society: Scotland, 1870-1914" (PhD. diss., Glasgow Univ., 1983), 42. In 1884, of a membership of 14,311, Wisconsin had 181 ministers, according to GL of Wisconsin, *Proceedings* (1884), 1166, 1179.

54. Peirce, *History,* 36-37.

55. *IGT,* Jan. 1903, 22-23, 27.

56. Peirce, *History,* 76.

57. GL of Ohio, *Proceedings* (1856), 32; (1867), 12 (for 1866 and 1867); (1868), 16; (1874), 11.

58. Quoted in Peirce, *History,* 204.

59. See Louise Noun, "Amelia Bloomer, a Biography, Part I: The Lily of Seneca Falls," *Annals of Iowa* 47 (Winter 1985).

60. Peirce, *History,* 60; Amelia Bloomer's newspaper, *Lily,* apparently in 1853.

61. Peirce, *History,* 248, 260; GL of Massachusetts, *Proceedings* (1870), 593; GL of North Carolina, *Proceedings* (1876), 56.

62. *Hamilton Spectator,* 21 May 1921, quoted in *IGT,* July 1921, 43; John Robinson, "Historical Sketch of Enterprise Lodge, No. 356 [Guerneville, Calif.]," (Sacramento) *Weekly Rescue,* 5 July 1877, [1]; S.B. Chase, *Manual or Exposition of the Independent Order of Good Templars, Embracing Its History, Objects, and Workings,* rev. ed. (1864; N.p.: International Supreme Lodge, 1895), 29. In 1860 a lodge at Providence, R.I., lost influence because the Templars were accused of being a free-love society.

63. *GTW,* 1 Oct. 1874, 433.

64. Queen City lodge executive committee to Martha McClellan Brown, 8 Feb. 1873, box 8, folder 2; and William Kennedy Brown to Suzanne M.D. Fry, 28 April 1897 in box 8 folder 6, both in Martha McClellan Brown Papers, Wright State Univ., Dayton Ohio. In the same letter Brown's Methodist minister husband recounts that when a newspaper editor sneered at Brown and the other women of the Crusade of 1873-74, he "struck him to the pavement as a contemptible cur." As a consequence he had to pay a fine and justify his actions to his church conference.

65. *Iowa Temperance Magazine,* Oct. 1898, 16; GL of Illinois, *Proceedings* (1862), 11.

66. There are good biographical essays for Way (by Clifton J Phillips) and for Brown (by Francis Phelps Weisenburger) in Edward T. James, ed., *Notable American Women, 1607-1950: A Biographical Dictionary,* 3 vols. (Cambridge, Mass.: Harvard Univ. Press, 1971).

67. George W.E. Hill, *Hand Book of Good Templary: An Epitomized Good Templar History,* 2d ed. (Ames Iowa: Hodson Bros., 1897), 70; *Irish Templar,* May 1887, 52; Forsyth, *Collected Writings,* 124 n. 153.

68. Quoted in obituary, *Pacific Friend* 21 (March 1914): 14. According to Quaker scholars, the unpublished autobiography and Way's other papers were taken to Oregon, but they have not been traced.

69. Hill, *Some Good Templars,* 97; GL of Kansas, *Proceedings* (1892), 14; Robert Smith Bader, *Prohibition in Kansas: A History* (Lawrence: Univ. Press of Kansas, 1986), 51; Agnes Dubbs Hays, *The White Ribbon in the Sun-*

flower State: A Biography of Courageous Conviction, 1878-1953 (Topeka, Kans.: Woman's Christian Temperance Union, [1953]), 70-71.

70. GL of Ohio, *Proceedings* (1874), 8; *Independent Order of Good Templars,* leaflet n.d., box 9, folder 8, and "Good Templary," typescript, n.d., box 11 folder 11, in Martha McClellan Brown Papers.

71. *Proceedings of the Wisconsin Editorial Association* (1866), 28-29; GL of Wisconsin, *Proceedings* (1876), 300; (1889), 54-55. For Emma Brown, see the many scattered references in McBride, *On Wisconsin Women.*

72. Martha M. Pickrell of Elkhart, Ind., has generously provided material about Molloy.

73. *GTW,* 5 Feb 1874, 28; (London) *Temperance Star,* 18 Aug. 1871, 4.

74. Forsyth, *Collected Writings,* 116. A Scottish visitor to the Grand Lodge of England commented that "the sisters take a much more prominent part in the work of the G.L. than with us" (quoted in [Glasglow] *Good Templar,* May 1895, 261). The Grand Lodge of Scotland did not elect a woman as its secretary until 1972; see Robert McKechnie, *Good Templary in Scotland: Its Work and Workers, 1929-1979* ([Glasglow]: Grand Lodge of Scotland, International Order of Good Templars, 1980), 23.

75. Hill, *Some Good Templars,* 251; *GTW,* 17 April 1893, 181; George W.E. Hill in *Iowa Temperance Magazine,* June 1897, 18-19.

76. Forsyth, *Collected Writings,* 117-18.

77. Jan Noel, *Canada Dry: Temperance Crusades before Confederation* (Toronto: Univ. of Toronto Press, 1995), 59, 217; Ian R. Tyrrell, *Woman's World, Woman's Empire: The Woman's Christian Temperance Union in International Perspective, 1880-1930* (Chapel Hill: Univ. of North Carolina Press, 1991), 23-25.

78. Joseph Malins in (London) *Temperance Star,* 6 April 1871, 6. One of the nonwhite Templars in England at that time was A.M. Bose, a Bengali undergraduate at Christ's College, Cambridge. *GTW,* 28 March 1898, 145-46.

2. The Adversaries

1. Logan, "Drink and Society," 35, gives Scotland the implausible figure of 80,000 for 1872, without citing a source This membership total does not appear in RWGL records; Scotland failed to report its membership for the quarter ending 31 Jan. 1873. RWGL, *Proceedings* (1873), 27. In a historical retrospect the Grand Secretary reported that 52,800 were initiated in 1872 but did not list a total membership. GL of Scotland, *Proceedings* (1890), 18.

2. Another calculation puts 54 percent of the United States membership in the South by the early 1870s (Blocker, *American Temperance Movements,* 50). Whatever the percentage, it is safe to say that contemporaries believed the IOGT needed the white southerners.

3. J.G. Thrower in Henry Anselm Scomp, *King Alchohol in the Realm of King Cotton; or, A History of the Liquor Traffic and of the Temperance Movement in Georgia from 1733 to 1887* ([Chicago]: Blakeley, 1888), 623. The figure for Georgia seems suspiciously high. In 1887 Virginia had a much

larger membership than Georgia, but from its founding in 1869 through 1888 the Grand Lodge of Virginia recruited only about 61,000 members, a number including about 3,900 who were reinstated and apparently counted twice: GL of Virginia, *Proceedings* (1888), 27.

4. Local figures represent quarterly reporting dates different from those published by the RWGL, so Grand Lodge and RWGL statistics could differ for the same year. According to its official organ (Raleigh) *Spirit of the Age,* 3 July 1875, 4, the Grand Lodge of North Carolina had over 10,000 members in 1875.

5. Despite its name, the Grand Temple of Canada confined its jurisdiction to what became the province of Ontario. Until 1877 it kept the title Grand Temple, derived from a defunct constitution.

6. Prior to the Civil War the newly organized RWGL had met at Louisville. After the war but before the big growth in southern membership, it had met at two other border state cities, Baltimore and St. Louis.

7. For England, see Brian Harrison, *Drink and the Victorians: The Temperance Question in England, 1815-1872* (Pittsburgh, Pa.: Univ. of Pittsburgh Press, 1971; 2d ed., Keele, England: Keele Univ. Press, 1994); Lilian Lewis Shiman, *Crusade against Drink in Victorian England* (London: Macmillan, 1988). For Kentucky, see Thomas H. Appleton Jr., "'Like Banquo's Ghost': The Emergence of the Prohibition Issue in Kentucky Politics" (Ph.D. diss., Univ. of Kentucky, 1981).

8. GL of Kentucky, *Proceedings* (1871), 26-27.

9. RWGL, *Proceedings* (1875), 24. Jack Blocker Jr., *"Give to the Winds Thy Fears": The Women's Temperance Crusade, 1873-1874* (Westport, Conn.: Greenwood Press, 1985), table 1.2, counted eleven crusades in Kentucky, seven in West Virginia, and six in Tennessee.

10. For the Crusade at Louisville, see *Western Recorder,* 21 Feb. 1874, summarized in Olinda F. Wilson, "Temperance in Louisville, a Whiskey Distilling Capital, 1838-1882" (Southern Baptist Theological Seminary, 1985), 12-13. Anna Bain was a WCTU state president.

11. "Aunt Peggy," in (Louisville) *Temperance Advocate,* 28 Jan. 1874.

12. Capital lodge minutes and quarterly reports, 3 May 1871-29 January 1874, State Historical Society of North Dakota. Officials at the historical society have no records to explain why Kentucky materials ended at Bismarck.

13. Lilian Lewis Shiman, *Women and Leadership in Nineteenth-Century England* (New York: St Martin's Press, 1992), 151-70. A couple of wealthy aristocrats, Lady Henry Somerset and Lady Carlisle, used the British Women's Temperance Association as an institutional base to legitimize their claim to national influence. They owed much of their prominence to their titles and their money.

14. Hambleton Tapp and James C. Klotter, *Kentucky: Decades of Discord, 1865-1900* (Frankfort: Kentucky Historical Society, 1977), 299.

15. GL of West Virginia, *Proceedings* (1878), 14.

16. The figure for England omits traditionally Welsh Monmouthshire. See E.A. Wrigley and R.S. Schofield, *The Population History of England, 1541-1871* (Cambridge, Mass.: Harvard Univ. Press, 1981), 588.

17. The white population in the former slave states could not be comfortable with the controversy over prohibition until the black population was

disenfranchised and divisions among white voters became racially safe. See Richard F. Hamm, "The Killing of John R. Moffett and the Trial of J.T. Clark: Race, Prohibition, and Politics in Danville, 1887-1893," *Virginia Magazine of History and Biography* 101 (July 1993). The murdered man was a Templar.

18. GL of Kentucky, *Proceedings* (1866), 26.

19. GL of Kentucky, *Proceedings* (1867), 23.

20. Isaac Newton Peirce in *GTW,* 14 June 1876, 387.

21. GL of Kentucky, *Proceedings* (1871), 19-20.

22. Hickman in *The Negro Question and the I.O.G.T.: Report of Conference Held in London, October 19, 20, and 21, 1876* (London: J. Kempster; London: E. Curtice, 1876), 55-56.

23. For this paragraph I owe special thanks to Frank J. Merli.

24. Tapp and Klotter, *Kentucky,* 65.

25. GL of Kentucky, *Proceedings* (1871), 4-12.

26. George W. Bain, *Wit, Humor, Reason, Rhetoric, Prose, Poetry, and Story Woven into Eight Popular Lectures* (Louisville, Ky.: Pentecostal, 1915), 72.

27. As evidence for this subculture, GL of England, *Proceedings* (1873), 23, reported that 546 English lodges had bookstalls; 498, libraries; 39 bands; and 1,463, singing classes.

28. GL of England, *Proceedings* (1873), 67-68. Other evidence for denominational strength and weakness can be found in the meeting places for English lodges, only fifty of which owned their own halls. Nearly two-thirds of the lodges met at chapels and denominational schools: Wesleyan, 68 chapels, 216 schools; Primitive Methodist, 138 chapels, 135 schools; Independent or Congregational, 72 chapels and 72 schools; Baptist, 68 chapels, 55 schools; Church of England, 99 schools; United Methodist Free Church, 43 chapels, 49 schools; Methodist New Connexion, 33 chapels, 21 schools; Bible Christians, 31 chapels, 16 schools; Society of Friends, 23 meeting houses; 23 miscellaneous bethels; Presbyterians, 3 chapels, 19 schools; Unitarians, 11 schools; Calvinist Methodist, 10 chapels; Roman Catholic, 1 school.

29. Bain, *Wit,* 303.

30. *Journal of Proceedings of the Special Session of the Grand Lodge of England, Held at St George's Hall, Manchester . . . October 25th and 26th, 1876, Stephen Todd, G.W.S.* (Manchester: Grand Lodge of England, 1876), 21.

31. GL of Kentucky, *Proceedings* (1871), 15.

32. In the twentieth century Templars helped organize a Scottish Prohibition Party, which elected its parliamentary candidate at Dundee in 1922, defeating Winston Churchill.

33. It is difficult to see Malins as an ardent follower of Chamberlain, who in the 1870s proposed an experiment in municipal management of the retail drink trade. When a variant of this so-called Gothenburg Scheme gained popularity at the turn of the century, Malins was an outspoken opponent.

34. There is a brief account of the Templars in Shiman, *Crusade against Drink,* 178-82. Apparently there are no Grand Lodge archives or local lodge records in England. In her dissertation on the Scottish temperance movement, Norma Logan complains ("Drink and Society," 56 n. 70) that

"Good Templars misguidedly destroyed records each time a commissioned history appeared in Britain." In Scotland, records for the administration of Templar halls have survived.

35. Tim Needham in Parker, *History,* 157-63. This sketch of Hickman's life is supplemented in Ernest Hurst Cherrington, ed., *Standard Encyclopedia of the Alchohol Problem,* 6 vols. (Westerville, Ohio: American Issue, 1926-30); *IGT,* Nov. 1902, 340-41; International Supreme Lodge, *Proceedings* (1902), 220. There is no entry for Hickman in Mark Edward Lender, *Dictionary of American Temperance Biography* (Westport, Conn.: Greenwood Press, 1984).

36. *Vegetarian Messenger,* Nov. 1896, 367; Joseph Malins, "A Vegetarian Trip Round the World," (London) *United Temperance Gazette,* March 1901, 36-38.

37. GL of Kentucky, *Proceedings* (1871), 25.

38. GL of Kentucky, *Proceedings* (1871), 20.

39. GL of Kentucky, *Proceedings* (1871), 21.

40. GL of Wisconsin, *Proceedings* (1881), 977; Joseph Malins, in *GTW,* 25 July 1881, 469.

41. *The Cyclopedia of Temperance and Prohibition* (1891), 87-88, reproduced in Wilson, "Temperance in Louisville," app. D.

42. Southern conservatism should not be underestimated. To cite an example from Georgia, the temperance historian Henry Anselm Scomp lost his teaching appointment at Emory in 1894 because he encouraged female activism against drink and because he accepted the nomination of the Prohibitionists for state office. See Nancy A. Hardesty, "'The Best Temperance Organization in the Land': Southern Methodists and the W.C.T.U.," *Methodist History* 28 (1990): 194 n. 32.

43. For the Templars' "new lease on life" in Alabama, see James Benson Sellers, *The Prohibition Movement in Alabama, 1702 to 1943* (Chapel Hill: Univ. of North Carolina Press, 1943), 52; for North Carolina, Daniel Jay Whitener, *Prohibition in North Carolina, 1715-1945* (Chapel Hill: Univ. of North Carolina Press, 1945), [102]. In Virginia the Templars achieved their greatest membership on the eve of reunion. The IOGT benefited from the rise in temperance sentiment that produced a local option law in 1886; see Charles Chilton Pearson and J. Edwin Hendricks, *Liquor and Anti-Liquor in Virginia, 1619-1919* (Durham, N.C.: Duke Univ. Press, 1967), 174-77. In other southern states the IOGT retained the strength to organize new lodges: e.g., in Thomasville, Ga., in April 1884; see William Warren Rogers, *Thomas County, 1865-1900* (Tallahassee: Florida State Univ. Press, 1973), 430.

44. *GTW,* 23 April 1888, 214.

45. RWGL, *Proceedings* (1887), 343.

46. Missouri did not issue statewide death certificates in 1902.

47. Martha McClellan Brown, unpaginated leaflet reprinting her report as the IOGT's International Chancellor of Education in 1913, box 9, folder 6, Martha McClellan Brown Papers; Brown in (Alliance, Ohio) *Monitor,* 6 June 1872, clipping in S.D. Hastings Scrapbooks, The Prohibition Question, fol. 116, Historical Society of Wisconsin, Madison.

48. For Malins's early years and his private life I have relied on his second son's biography, Joseph Malins, *The Life of Joseph Malins: Patriarch Templar, Citizen, and Temperance Reformer* (Birmingham: Templar Press,

1932). It incorporates Malins's *Random Recollections,* published in the *Good Templar's Watchword* in 1923-25, together with his autobiographical farewell address in April 1914. I also cite letters by Malins in the Templar press. When sources disagree, I have favored the earliest published account.

49. Joseph Malins in *GTW,* 26 Sept. 1908, 459.

50. *GTW,* 26 Sept. 1908, 459. This newspaper article gives nine as the age at which he left school, but his son's biography says he left school at age ten.

51. Malins may have been influenced by two young teetotalers who shared his bedroom for two years when they boarded at his home. See Peter T. Winskill, *Temperance Standard Bearers of the Nineteenth Century,* 2 vols. (Liverpool: Published by the author, 1897-98), 1:106.

52. Clement Malins in (London) *Temperance Star,* 20 May 1870, 5.

53. The first quotation is from Patrick Joyce, *Visions of the People: Industrial England and the Question of Class, 1848-1914* (Cambridge: Cambridge Univ. Press, 1991, 178; the second is from Malins, *Life of Joseph Malins,* 23.

54. Malins in *GTW,* 20 April 1885, 249.

55. Clement Malins in (London) *Temperance Star,* 20 May 1870, 5.

56. About Portland, see (London) *Templar,* 28 Oct. 1873, 18.

57. For Malins's operating a furniture store, see *GTW,* 12 Sept. 1908, 439. By the late 1870s Malins's wife was an invalid.

58. Joseph Malins, "Two Trips to America—The Emigrants and the Embassy," (London) *Templar,* 16 Jan. 1873, 47. Malins had joined the Rechabites—the leading temperance insurance organization—before emigrating to the United States. See *GTW,* 20 April 1885, 249; *Independent Order of Rechabites (Salford Unity) Friendly Society . . . Jubilee Record* (1885), 74.

59. *GTW,* 2 May 1881, 279.

60. J. Hannum Jones to Solomon Ketchum, 22 May 1868, in T.S. [Thomas Scott], "Papers on 'Good Templarism'. No. 2—The Extension of the Order to Great Britain," (London) *Teetotal Star,* Dec. 1869, 79-80. See RWGL, *Proceedings* (1868), 56.

61. According to his friend John Stuart, in *GTW,* 9 May 1903, 224.

62. "Brother Malins in Liverpool," *Liverpool Leader,* 9 May 1874, 2. See also "Good Templarism," in *Liverpool Leader,* 4 Oct. 1873-9 May 1874, reprinted as a pamphlet in 1874, *Temperance Tracts* (microfilm), Guy Hayler Collection, Univ. of Wisconsin, Madison.

63. (Glasgow), *Good Templar,* Aug. 1872, 308; Forsyth *Collected Writings,* 76 n. 8; Joseph Malins, "Good Templary in the British Isles," in J.N. Stearns, ed., *Temperance in All Nations* (New York: National Temperance Society and Publication House, 1893), 1:239.

64. Malins in *GTW,* 22 Dec 1880, 625.

65. P.T. Winskill, *The Comprehensive History of the Rise and Progress of the Temperance Reformation* (Warrington Eng.: Published by the author, 1881), 469.

66. The Rechabites continued to grow after the Templars began their long decline and numbered several hundred thousand members between the world wars. For the English Rechabites, there are a couple of official histories and a short scholarly biography by a family member: Richarson Campbell, *Rechabite History* (Manchester: Board of Directors of the Order,

1911); Robert Highet, *Rechabite History* (Manchester: Board of Directors of the Order, 1936) Olive Checkland, *Sobriety and Thrift: John Philipson and His Family* (Newcastle upon Tyne: Philipson, 1989). For Scotland, see Norma Denny, "Self-Help, Abstinence, and the Voluntary Principle: The Independent Order of Rechabites, 1835-1912," *Scottish Labour History Society Journal* 24 (1989).

67. Malins to editor, *Birmingham Gazette,* reprinted in *GTW,* 16 April 1874, 151.

68. Samuel Wright, "Biographical Sketch No. 7–Bro. G.W. Keesey, P.G.W.C.T. of Midland Grand Lodge," *British Loyal Templar,* July 1884; Norman Longmate, *The Waterdrinkers* (London: Hamish Hamilton, 1968), 214-16.

69. (Glasgow) *Good Templar,* Aug 1872, 308; *GTW,* 10 May 1886, 292.

70. Jabez Walker, in (London) *Temperance Star,* 5 Aug. 1870, 5. Roberts had been Delaware's GWCT and later a Templar organizer in Pennsylvania; he died in Philadelphia in 1872. Winskill, *Temperance Standard Bearers* 2:380. For the early years of the IOGT in Scotland, see Tom Honeyman, *Good Templary in Scotland from Its Inception to Its Diamond Jubilee, 1869-1929* (Glasglow: Grand Lodge of Scotland, 1929), 14-21; Logan, "Drink and Society," 31-46, 56-66.

71. Thompson, *History,* 22; G.B. Clark in (Glasgow), *Good Templar,* July 1920, 146. Walker developed tuberculosis and as a result emigrated to Canada and then to California, where he was elected head of the Grand Lodge.

72. Logan, "Drink and Society" 32-33; Bernard Aspinwall, *Portable Utopia: Glasgow and the United States, 1820-1920* (Aberdeen: Aberdeen Univ. Press, 1984); GL of Scotland, *Proceedings* (1890), 18.

73. Wright, "Bro G.W. Keesey."

74. (London) *Temperance Star,* 20 May 1870, 5; Clement Malins to [editor], 6 July 1877, in (London) *Templar,* 11 July 1877, 22; Malins to Spencer, 8 May 1869, in RWGL, *Proceedings* (1869), 67-69; Thompson, *History,* 21; *GTW,* 27 Oct. 1884, 676.

75. "Joseph Malins, G.W.T.," in *IGT,* June 1888, 369; Malins "How Good Templary Came to England," *GTW,* 26 Sept. 1908, 459.

76. (London) *Temperance Star,* 19 Nov. 1869, 5.

77. (Glasgow) *Good Templar,* Aug 1872, 308.

78. Contemporary sources—e.g., (London) *Temperance Star,* 5 Aug. 1870, 5—identify the American consul who presided as J.B. Gould. This contradicts Templar histories, which put in the chair Elihu Burritt, a working-class autodictat and ardent teetotaler, who had been American consul from 1865 to 1869; see Malins, *Life of Joseph Malins,* 31.

79. *Scottish Temperance Annual,* ed. Tom Honeyman (Glasglow: Grand Lodge of Scotland, 1913), 26.

80. The figures are taken from *Templar Annual and Good Templars' Year Book* (London: Curtice, 1873), 23; Thompson, *History,* 30. The success of the Templars should be seen within the context of "the enormous growth of associational culture in late nineteenth-century Britain" (Harris, *Private Lives, Public Spirit,* 24).

81. The executive committee of the RWGL considered transferring the 1873 session to Montreal for reasons of time and expense: (London) *Temperance Star,* 10 Jan 1873, 6.

82. GL of England, *Proceedings* (1873), 67.
83. The youngest and last surviving son, Maurice, died in 1961: (London) *International Record*, Oct. 1961, 5.
84. (London) Somerset House probate records.
85. *GTW*, 4 Jan. 1892.
86. Long-serving Grand Lodge and international officers had no as-surance of reelection. For instance, B.F. Parker, first elected Grand Worthy Secretary of Wisconsin in 1873, was defeated in 1900. He also served as in-ternational secretary, beginning in 1885, and was defeated for reelection in 1908.
87. *May's British and Irish Press Guide* (1883), 29; Malins, "Good Templary in England," 32.
88. John B. Collings, "Good Templary in England," in *Good Templary in Scotland: Its Work and Workers, 1869-1894* ed. Tom Honeyman (Glasgow: Grand Lodge of Scotland, 1894), 250. The Guy Hayler Collection has a copy of this book with Hayler's biographical annotations, mostly dates of birth and death.
89. As a result of charges of irregularities, the old RWGL refused to seat Olov Bergström when he came to the annual session as representative of a new Grand Lodge of Sweden. Angrily, Bergström switched allegiance and invited Malins to Sweden: *IGT,* Oct.-Dec. 1880, 93-94; Alfred Kämpe, *Olov Bergström och Goodtemplarorden* (Stockholm: Oskar Eklunds Bokför-lag, 1929).
90. *GTW*, Nov 1925, 169. Other eccentricities included absent-mindedness; he was known to return home with two umbrellas (*GTW*, 29 April 1911, 201). See also Joseph Malins, "Misadventures with My Be-longings," *IGT*, March 1896, 94-97.
91. *GTW*, 1 May 1882; *GTW,* 18 April 1914, 190; Malins to editor, *New York Templar,* Oct. 1917, 8-9. See also Malins to A.M. Leffingwell, 14 March 1924, *New York Templar,* 15 April 1924, 9.
92. *Birmingham News*, 11 Oct 1924 (reprint); *Professor Alcoholico: A Temperance Poem* (Birmingham: Morris, 1876).
93. He sent the United Kingdom Alliance a daily letter, written, it was said, in "handwriting which was unique in its illegibility," and his friendship for the Alliance leader Leif Jones did not prevent Malins from sending him a stream of criticism. See George B. Wilson, *Leif Jones, Lord Rhayader, Tem-perance Reformer and Statesman 1862-1939* (N.p.: United Kingdom Alliance, [c. 1948]), 76.
94. *National Temperance Advocate*, July 1872, 107.
95. *GTW*, 25 April 1914, 202.
96. *Globe*, no. 3 (1994): 22-23.

3. The Road to Louisville

1. Harold V. B. Voorhis, *Our Colored Brethren: The Story of Alpha Lodge of New Jersey* (New York: Henry Emmerson, 1960); Alphonse Cerza, "Introductory Remarks," in Henry Wilson Coil Sr. and John MacDuffie Sher-man, with Harold Van Buren Voorhis, *A Documentary Account of Prince Hall and Other Black Fraternal Orders*, ed. Thomas C. Warden (N.p.: Missouri

Lodge of Research, 1982). For the *New England Freemason* quotation, see Joel Walker, "The Social Welfare Policies, Strategies, and Programs of Black Fraternal Organizations in the Northeast United States, 1896-1920" (diss., School of Social Work, Columbia Univ. 1985), 52. Smith represented Cambridge in the legislature, 1873-74. For black Freemasonry, see William A. Muraskin, *Middle-Class Blacks in a White Society: Prince Hall Freemasonry in America* (Berkeley: Univ. of California Press, 1975); Loretta J. Williams, *Black Freemasonry and Middle-Class Realities* (Columbia: Univ. of Missouri Press, 1980); Dennis H. Mihelich, "The Origin of the Prince Hall Masons Grand Lodge of Nebraska," *Nebraska History* 76 (Spring 1995).

2. Howard H. Turner, *Turner's History of the Independent Order of Good Samaritans and Daughters of Samaria,* comp. Wiley H. Jordan (Washington, D.C.: R.A. Waters, 1881).

3. *National Temperance Advocate*, Oct. 1871, 150.

4. W. E. H. Searcy, "The Negro Question—the Sons of Temperance and the Good Templars," (Griffin, Ga.) *Temperance Watchman*, 29 Sept. 1871, quoted in J. G. Thrower, *Circular to Members of the Order of Good Templars in Georgia* (broadside, 1872), Univ. of Georgia libraries.

5. *National Temperance Advocate*, Nov 1871, 170; Aug. 1872, 123. J.N. Stearns, editor of the *Advocate* and publication agent of the National Temperance Society, at one time or another headed both the National Division of the Sons of Temperance and the Supreme Council of the Templars of Honor and Temperance and also represented New York at many RWGL sessions. He helped segregated black temperance activities but opposed the racial integration of the white fraternal temperance societies. Stearns was a controversial personality, "a man of nervous composition, quick to compare, quick to act," "a living human electric battery, always ready to respond to the touch of the wire": obituary in International Supreme Lodge, *Proceedings* (1895), 97.

6. William Edward Farrison, *William Wells Brown, Author and Reformer* (Chicago: Univ. of Chicago Press, 1969), chap. 26. Unlike most of the elections in the Grand Division that year, the one that Brown contested took several ballots and ended in only a narrow victory.

7. Peirce, *History,* 90-91. Peirce supported the British in the great schism. For his services to the "underground railroad," see the obituary letter by his widow, in *IGT,* March 1908, 110.

8. Julius A. Spencer to editor 9 Dec. 1854, and Amelia Bloomer's editorial note, in *Lily,* 1 January 1855, 6-7; R.J.M. Blackett, *Beating against the Barriers: Biographical Essays in Nineteenth-Century Afro-American History* (Baton Rouge: Louisiana State Univ.,1986), 299-300. Spencer served as secretary and GWCT of the Grand Lodge of Ohio and secretary of the RWGL; in 1863 he was president of the Cleveland local of the National Typographical Union, according to *The Encyclopedia of Cleveland History,* ed. David D. Van Tassel and John J. Grabowski (Bloomington: Indiana Univ. Press, in association with Case Western Reserve Univ. 1987), 604.

9. Peirce, *History,* 164, 169, 291, 324; GL of Wisconsin, *Proceedings* (1866), 16. The Grand Temple of Canada rejected a color bar: "It is sufficient for us to know that [blacks] have a soul to save from the blighting effects of intemperance." See *A Digest of the Laws, Decisions, Rules, and Usages of the Independent Order of Good Templars,* comp. S.B. Chase, 6th ed. (Auburn, N.Y.: Wm. J. Moses, 1867), 89.

10. Earlier, two other fraternal orders in the United Kingdom acted with generosity toward African Americans, but without the risk that the English and Scottish Templars ran. The Masonic Grand Lodge of England recognized the legitimacy of the black Prince Hall Masons, and one of the Odd Fellow factions, the Grand United Order, accepted the authenticity of the black Odd Fellows The Freemasons and Odd Fellows lacked a centralized international organization. (Clawson, *Constructing Brotherhood*, 131-35).

11. Ezra Goodrich, *The Negro Imbroglio in the Milton Lodge of Good Templars* (Janesville, Wis.: Veeder & Devereux, 1865), 2.

12. Gl of Illinios, *Proceedings* (1866), 16, 32. There were five black lodges at four locations: Chicago, Galesburg, Knoxville, and Monmouth. In 1867 a Peoria city directory listed another black Templar lodge. See James Abajian, *Blacks in Selected Newspaper, Censuses, and Other Sources,* 3 vols., (Boston: G.K. Hall, 1977), 2:180. I am grateful to Chris Africa, Univ. of Iowa libraries for help with this citation.

13. W.E.H. Searcy, "To the Good Templars of the South," in (Griffin, Ga.) *Temperance Watchman* [late 1872?], fragment in S.D. Hastings Scrapbooks, The Prohibition Question, fols. 150, 152. Searcy based his account on a story in the (New York) *Temperance Oracle* for an unspecified date in 1872.

14. GL of Nova Scotia, *Proceedings* (1873), 12.

15. RWGL, *Proceedings* (1866), 8, 40-41.

16. Isaac Newton Peirce, quoted in *GTW,* 14 June 1876, 387.

17. RWGL, *Proceedings* (1867), 58, 77, 80. Some of the white southerners who joined the IOGT after the Civil War had been born outside the region. A Quaker who had moved from New York in the 1840s became the first GWCT of Virginia shortly after the Civil War; a recent English immigrant served as secretary of the Grand Lodge of North Carolina in the mid-1870s. For the Hawxhurst family, who settled in northern Virginia, see Susan Abramson, "The Independent Order of Good Templars: Fairfax County, Virginia," *Historical Society of Fairfax County, Virginia, Inc.* 16 (1980): 8 n. 11; and an obituary of Job Hawxhurst in *IGT,* March 1906, 103.

18. RWGL, *Proceedings* (1868), 16-17, 32; GL of Connecticut, *Proceedings* (1876), 21-22; William Wells Brown in *GTW,* 22 Aug. 1877, 563; *GTW,* 14 June 1876, 387.

19. Peirce, *History,* 460-61 (who provided the exclamation point); RWGL, *Proceedings* (1868), 88. Howard University was named in honor of General O.O. Howard.

20. GL of Maryland, *Proceedings* (1868), 8; (1873), 9-10.

21. GL of Missouri, *Proceedings* (1867), 17-18; GL of West Virginia, *Proceedings* (1868), 57; T.H.B., "History of Good Templary in West Virginia," discussing the ninth annual Grand Lodge session, 18 Nov. 1874, in (Garardstown) *West Virginia Good Templar,* 22 June 1882.

22. RWGL, *Proceedings* (1868), 41.

23. Peirce, *History,* 492.

24. RWGL, *Proceedings,* (1868), 79-82.

25. RWGL, *Proceedings,* (1868), 83.

26. RWGL, *Proceedings* (1868), 82-83; Peirce, quoted in *GTW,* 14 June 1876, 387. As early as 1867 whites had organized the Vanguard of Freedom as a temperance society for blacks.

27. Harriet N.K. Goff in *IGT,* Jan.-March 1879, 126-27.

28. W.E.H. Searcy in GL of Georgia, *Proceedings* (1872), 24-26.

29. There is no mention of the Templar controversy in the valuable books by Christine Bolt, *The Anti-Slavery Movement and Reconstruction: A Study in Anglo-American Co-Operation, 1833-77* (London: Oxford Univ. Press for the Institute of Race Relations, 1969); and *Victorian Attitudes to Race* (London: Routledge & Kegan Paul, 1971).

30. Malins, quoted in *The Negro Question and the I.O.G.T.*, 14, 33; Malins in GL of England, *Proceedings* (1872), app. F, 9-10; *GTW,* 4 April 1887, 209. William Wells Brown provided a different explanation, arguing that Malins introduced the proposal for a separate black organization after the white southerners had alleged that African Americans would not join the IOGT: *GTW,* 1 Nov. 1876, 724.

31. Joseph Malins, *The Unlawful Exclusion of the African Race: A Refutation of Mr. W. Hoyle's "Review of the Negro Question and the I.O.G.T."* (Birmingham: Grand Lodge Office; London: J. Kempster; Glasgow: Grand Lodge Office; Belfast: Grand Lodge Office; Wrexham: Grand Lodge Office, 1877), 11.

32. Hickman to Searcy, 3 June 1872, in (Griffin, Ga.) *Temperance Watchman*, 29 Sept 1872, quoted in Thrower, *Circular.*

33. W.E.H. Searcy, in (Griffin, Ga.) *Temperance Watchman,* "Answer to the Thrower Circular, Together with Other Thoughts Bearing upon the Negro Question," in S.D. Hastings Scrapbooks, The Prohibition Question, fol. 152.

34. Searcy, "To the Good Templars of the South"; *Keystone Good Templar,* 24 Aug. 1872. Accompanying Searcy's article is a caricature of a black man and a white man embracing. During the great schism the official seal of the RWGL of the World proudly portrayed a black man and a white man shaking hands.

35. *Keystone Good Templar*, 3 Aug 1872.

36. Malins, *Unlawful Exclusion*, 46. Hickman's Grand Lodge of Kentucky rejected "an invitation to join in a Southern Good Templar movement, on a 'white basis'" (*National Temperance Advocate*, Nov. 1872, 173). For the origins of the United Friends of Temperance, see the account based on information from Searcy and Col. C.P. Crawford in Scomp, *King Alcohol in the Realm of King Cotton*, 625-41; *Headlight of the United Friends of Temperance*, published in Tennessee in 1877, quoted in *GTW*, 15 Aug. 1877, 552.

37. (Raleigh) *Friend of Temperance,* 17 Sept. 1873, [2]; Scomp, *King Alcohol in the Realm of King Cotton,* 599; (Griffin, Ga.), *Temperance Watchman,* fragment c. 1872, in S.D. Hastings Scrapbooks, The Prohibition Question, fol. 152; *National Temperance Advocate,* Nov. 1872, 173; GL of Georgia, *Proceedings* (1873), 7-8, 26.

38. *National Temperance Advocate*, Nov. 1872, 173; GL of Georgia, *Proceedings* (1876), viii; O.P. Gordon to R.R. Hemphill, 21 June 1874, quoted in Joel Williamson, *After Slavery: The Negro in South Carolina during Reconstruction, 1861-1877* (Chapel Hill: Univ. of North Carolina Press, 1965), 293; GL of England, *Proceedings* (1877), 73.

39. In fact, as the *National Temperance Advocate* (Sept 1872) pointed out, the Templars of Honor and Temperance, a national society, restricted its membership to whites, as did a regional organization founded in Virginia, the Friends of Temperance.

40. Scomp, *King Alcohol in the Realm of King Cotton,* 628-29, 633. The United Friends also met at Chattanooga in July 1873 and at Nashville in May 1875. See *GTW,* 15 Aug. 1877, 552.

56. GL of Kentucky, *Proceedings* (1871), 36-37; William Wells Brown to editor, (Philadelphia) *Christian Recorder*, 21 Oct. 1880; *Ritual of the United Order of True Reformers for Subordinate Fountains, Prepared under the Authority of the Grand Lodge of Kentucky, I.O. of G.T.* (N.p., 1873); GL of Tennessee, *Proceedings* (1874), 38.

57. For a facsimile of the "mutilated" charter, granted 4 Dec 1873, and Joseph E. Lee to Malins, 14 Sept. 1876, see "The Negro and the I.O.G.T." a collection of pamphlets in the Boston Public Library; Hastings to Scomp, n.d., in Scomp, *King Alcohol in the Realm of King Cotton*, 613-14; Joseph Malins, "The 'Mutilated' Charter: A Narrative and an Apology," *GTW*, 26 Feb. 1879, 137.

58. (Louisville) *Riverside Weekly*, quoted in *The Negro Question and the I.O.G.T.*, 42.

59. Thomas Willet Casey, secretary of the Grand Temple of Canada, was co-editor or editor of the *Casket* from 1870 until it ceased publication in the mid-1880s. See Larry Turner in *Dictionary of Canadian Biography*, vol. 13, *1901-1910* (Toronto: Univ. of Toronto Press, 1994).

60. (Raleigh) *Spirit of the Age*, 3 July 1875, 4.

61. *GTW*, 26 Sept. 1881, 613.

62. Hastings in RWGL, *Proceedings* (1874), 1216-18; *The Negro Question and the I.O.G.T.*, 56; Thrower and Robinson to GL of North Carolina, 27 Sept. 1875, in GL of North Carolina, *Proceedings* (1875), 38. For the characterization of Thrower's speaking ability and personality, see *National Cyclopaedia of American Biography* 19 (New York: James T. White, 1926): 313-14. A printer named James K. Thrower, probably a cousin or nephew of James G. Thrower, served as Grand Worthy Treasurer. He was elected to Atlanta's city council on the Greenback-Labor ticket in 1878. See James Michael Russell, *Atlanta, 1847-1890* (Baton Rouge: Louisiana State Univ. Press, 1988), 207.

63. Searcy in GL of Georgia, *Proceedings* (1872), 26; GL of Alabama, *Proceedings* (1874), 21; manifesto quoted in William Patrick Burrell and D.E. Johnson Sr., *Twenty-Five Years History of the Grand Fountain of the United Order of True Reformers, 1881-1905* (1909; rpt. Westport, Conn.: Negro Universities Press, 1970), 17; GL of Alabama, *Proceedings* (1875), 16.

64. Scomp, *King Alcohol in the Realm of King Cotton*, 622-23. In September 1875 Georgia's Grand Fountain owed Georgia's Grand Lodge $243, according to GL of Georgia, *Proceedings* (1875), xvii. Before Browne joined the True Reformers, he tried unsuccessfully to join the Templars.

65. (Raleigh) *Spirit of the Age*, 9 Oct. 1875, 3.

66. *GTW*, 23 May 1877, 343; *The Negro Question and the I.O.G.T.*, 63-64; W.H.L. Combs [or Coombs], comp. *Degree Ritual of the Grand United Order of True Reformers* (Richmond: J.W. Ferguson, 1875); James D. Watkinson, "William Washington Browne and the True Reformers of Richmond, Virginia," *Virginia Magazine of History and Biography* 97 (July 1989); David M. Fahey, ed. *The Black Lodge in White America: "True Reformer" Browne and His Economic Strategy* (Dayton, Ohio: Wright State University Press, 1994), which provides an edition of Daniel Webster Davis's 1910 biography of W.W. Browne. Browne was the first Grand Worthy Secretary of the Grand Fountain of Alabama and later its Grand Worthy Master before moving to Virginia, where he headed that state's Grand Fountain.

41. GL of Kentucky, *Proceedings* (1868), 32-33, quoted in M
lawful Exclusion, 45.

42. *The Negro Question and the I.O.G.T.,* 65-67.

43. For Charles N. Hunter, see Robert L. Byrd, s.v. "Charle
Hunter," in William S. Powell, ed., *Dictionary of North Carolina B*
4 vols. (Chapel Hill: Univ. of North Carolina Press, 1979-91). In la
Hunter suffered from a drinking problem.

44. Osborne Hunter, quoted in John H. Haley, *Charles N. Hu*
Race Relations in North Carolina (Chapel Hill: Univ. of North Caroli
1987), 28; John L. Bell, s.v. "James W. Hood," in Powell, *Dictionary*
Carolina Biography; Paul Yandle, "Joseph Charles Price and His '
Work'", *North Carolina Historical Review* 70 (Jan. and April 1993);
Dancy (Dancy's son), *Sand against the Wind: The Memoirs of John (*
(Detroit; Mich.: Wayne State University, 1966), 61-64; Marvin Krie
"John C. Dancy" in Powell, *Dictionary of North Carolina Biography*.

45. Haley, *Charles N. Hunter,* 29. Although Haley says Hunte
ered this speech to the New Bern convention, a note (292) indicates
presented it to Queen of the South lodge. For Dudley, see Eric Fone
dom's Lawmakers: A Directory of Black Officeholders during Reconst
(New York: Oxford Univ. Press, 1993), 65-66. Dudley's daughter
Dudley Pettey married an A.M.E. Zion bishop.

46. GL of North Carolina, *Proceedings* (1874), 14, 31; (Raleigh
of the Age, 3 July 1875, 4; GL of North Carolina, *Proceedings* (1873),

47. Dudley to GL of North Carolina, in GL of North Carolina
ceedings (1873), 42; (1874), 6, 12.

48. Needham to Bain, 1 Aug. 1873, in (Raleigh) *Friend of Tempe*
17 Sept. 1873, [2], reprinted from (Griffin, Ga.), *Temperance Watchma*
also Elliott in GL of Alabama, *Proceedings* (1873), 11-12.

49. Quoted in (Raleigh) *Friend of Temperance,* 8 Oct. 1873, [2
also *National Temperance Advocate,* Nov. 1873, 173.

50. Scomp, *King Alcohol in the Realm of King Cotton,* 616; (Ral
Friend of Temperance, 8 Oct. 1873, [2]; GL of Georgia, *Proceedings* (1873
13, 23-24.

51. A Virginia newspaper described the Friends of Temperanc
"composed exclusively of white men" and affiliated "with no temper
organization, either in this or *in any other State,* that admits neg
to membership." The society "takes the Holy Bible as its only platfor
principles" and "teaches that the reformation of the drunkard can be
complished only by the aid of the Holy Ghost." See *National Tempera*
Advocate, June 1868, 94.

52. Quoted in *National Temperance Advocate,* March 1873, 3, and (
1873, 149.

53. GL of North Carolina, *Proceedings* (1874), 6-7; GL of South Ca
lina, *Proceedings* (1874), 7-8. South Carolina's Grand Lodge lacked e
thusiasm for this proposal.

54. Hastings to Dr J.O. Patton, GWCT of Alabama, 23 Sept. 1873,
Wisconsin Good Templar, 3 Oct. 1873, 2; *National Temperance Advoca*
Nov. 1873, 173; written answers by Hastings to questions posed by Hickma
and Hickman to Grand Lodge of Tennessee, in GL of Tennessee, *Proceeding*
(1873), 6-8.

55. *Wisconsin Good Templar,* 24 April 1874, 2, 7.

67. *The Negro Question and the I.O.G.T.*, 65-67.

68. Malins, *Unlawful Exclusion,* 25. Curiously, an English representative at the 1875 RWGL session claimed that Malins told him not to complain about the True Reformers and persuaded him to return to Britain early in order to ensure his silence: F.R. Lees in (Hickmanite) GL of England, *Proceedings* (1877), 7.

69. Allegedly, at the London session of the RWGL Malins had threatened to start a rival society in the United States if the IOGT adopted the proposal for multiple Grand Lodges. See *I.O.G.T., Proposed Declaration of the British Lodges Regarding the Boston Conference Proposals for Union* (Sunderland: J.D. Todd, 1886), 7.

70. James Black should be remembered too for building an outstanding temperance library, including much Templar material. He donated it to the National Temperance Society, which in turn presented it to the New York Public Library.

71. William Hoyle, *The Negro Exclusion: A Reply to Mr. Joseph Malins, Showing How Mr. Malins and the Leading Secessionists Aided the Exclusion and Hindered the Admission of the Negroes into the Order of Good Templars* (London: E. Curtice; Manchester: A. Ireland, 1877), 34.

72. James Black to F.R. Lees, 15 Nov. 1876, quoted in Hoyle, *Negro Exclusion,* 31. I have Americanized the spelling.

73. Thrower and Robinson to GL of North Carolina, 27 Sept. 1875, in GL of North Carolina, *Proceedings* (1875), 38; Elizabeth Oak Smith (or Oaksmith) in (New York) *Christian Witness,* cited in Malins, *Unlawful Exclusion,* 58. Ironically, Georgia eventually organized a Dual Grand Lodge, but North Carolina did not.

74. "The Hickman-Goosley Correspondence," *GTW,* 7 Aug. 1878, 518. See also Mood in GL of South Carolina, *Proceedings* (1874), 7-8.

75. Quoted in Malins, *Unlawful Exclusion,* 61; quoted in Thrower and Robinson, to GL of North Carolina, 27 Sept. 1875, in GL of North Carolina, *Proceedings* (1875), 38.

76. Thrower to Dudley, 17 Nov. 1874, and Dudley to [Malins?], 22 March 1876, in Malins, *Unlawful Exclusion,* 58, 57 (also in *GTW,* 28 June 1876, 429).

77. Dudley to Malins, 20 May 1876, in Malins, *Unlawful Exclusion,* 58.

78. *GTW,* 14 June 1876, 387; (London) *Temperance Star*, 4 Nov 1875, 4; *GTW,* 2 Dec. 1889, 565; Winskill, *Temperance Standard Bearers,* 1:226; *Good Templars and the Negro Question: A Full Report of Public Meeting in the Albion Hall, Glasgow, on Friday Evening, 12th January, 1877,* 3d ed. (Glasgow: H. Hamilton, n.d.), 23, 32; RWGL, *Proceedings* (1880), 95.

4. The Great Schism

1. *I.O.G.T.—Shall the Negro Be Excluded from the Order?* was reprinted in *GTW,* 7 June 1876, 372-74; GL of Ireland, *Proceedings* (1876), 46-55 (quotation, 53).

2. Gladstone in *Good Templars and The Negro Question,* 21; Malins quoted by F.R. Lees in (Hickmanite) GL of England, *Proceedings* (1877), 8.

3. Gladstone to Malins, 17 Dec. 1875, in *GTW,* 15 Nov. 1876, 769.

4. GL of England, *Proceedings* (1876), 48; *GTW,* 11 April 1877, 250.

5. GL of Wisconsin, *Proceedings* (1876), 369. See also GL of Iowa, *Proceedings* (1876), 7, 30.

6. Of the 139 ministers in the Scottish Grand Lodge, 37 belonged to this small Evangelical Union: (London) *Templar,* 29 July 1875, 49.

7. GL of Georgia, *Proceedings* (1877), v.

8. *GTW,* 1 Nov. 1876, 724.

9. GL of England, *Proceedings* (1877), 59-62, 73-74.

10. Oddly, the biographical sketch by Gayle M. Comeau-Vasilopoulos, recently published in the *Dictionary of Canadian Biography*, vol. 13, ignores Oronhyatekha's Templar activity. Instead, it focuses on his role in the Independent Order of Foresters, which he joined in 1878.

11. *GTW,* 15 Nov. 1876, 762; Malins, *Unlawful Exclusion,* 25-26. In turn, William Wells Brown sneered at Oronhyatekha as an incompetent "root doctor" and at Indians as "treacherous": *GTW,* 11 July 1877, 462.

12. The West Virginia delegate who voted against the Substitute lived at Wheeling, in the northern panhandle, where racial attitudes among whites likely were similar to those in adjacent Pennsylvania and Ohio.

13. GL of Minnesota, *Proceedings* (1876), 22.

14. *GTW,* 11 April 1877, 251.

15. John Harding to editor, 5 Sept. 1884, *British Loyal Templar,* Nov. 1884, 5. Harding alleged that Malins asked J.J. Talbott of Indiana, "What is to prevent our claiming to be the original Order, and that the Americans, having forsaken their principles, are no longer the Independent Order of Good Templars?" Briefly a supporter of Malins, the New Zealander claimed to have been present at the conversation.

16. GL of England, *Proceedings* (1877), 66; *GTW,* 11 April 1877, 253.

17. "Of the fourteen who seceded along with Mr. Malins, three were getting good salaries out of the membership [Kirton, Talbott, and perhaps Gladstone], one broke his pledge and died shortly after from the effects of drink [Talbott], another [who was elected] supreme head of the 'World' . . . has since *seceded from his country* for his country's good [Yeames], *two others finding out they had been deceived, returned to the fold they had left* [Simpson, Smythe], and some of the others have cut their connection entirely": *British Loyal Templar,* March 1885, 6, "Secession Seeking Compromise."

18. William B. Reed and E.D. Stacey to Gladstone, 17 May 1876, in *GTW,* 28 June 1876, 428.

19. Yeames in *GTW,* 21 June 1876, 402.

20. *GTW,* 15 Nov. 1876, 762-63; GL of England, *Proceedings* (1877), 71. The waiters did not pursue their application.

21. John J. Hickman, "The Late Secession and Mission to England," report in RWGL, *Proceedings* (1877), 158-76.

22. RWGL, *Proceedings* (1877), 159; Hickman to Grand Lodge of Pennsylvania, 12 June 1876, in *Which Are We to Believe?* (Grand Lodge of England leaflet, n.d.)

23. *GTW,* 11 April 1887, 233.

24. GL of Georgia, *Proceedings* (1877), ii.

25. Responding to Oronhyatekha's request of 12 July 1876, Kentucky's executive council and its secretary reported that the Grand Lodge

would remove the whites-only clause from its constitution but that to do so legally would require eighteen months. The Grand Lodge never had claimed jurisdiction over anybody other than the white population. See Needham to Oronhyatekha, 14 July 1876, in *The Negro Question and the I.O.G.T.*, 43.

26. Hastings to Thrower, 9 Nov. 1876; and Thrower to Hastings, 13 Nov. 1876, in *North and South: Exchange of Sentiments between the Two Sections,* broadside reprinted from *Sunny South,* (Dec. 1876?), University of Georgia libraries. For the reservations, see GL of Georgia, *Proceedings* (1876), x, [xvii] (errata).

27. Thrower to Hastings, 13 Nov. 1876, in *North and South;* GL of Georgia, *Proceedings* (1876), 25-27, viii-xiii.

28. GL of Georgia, *Proceedings* (1876), iii; Thrower in GL of Georgia, *Proceedings* (1877), iii-iv; *Will Southern Good Templars Do as They Agree? The Following Speaks for Itself, and Puts to Shame the Vile Slanders of the Seceders* (broadside 1876), University of Georgia libraries; *An Appeal from the Temperance Workers of Georgia to the Officers and Members of the Right Worthy Grand Lodge I.O.G.T. in Behalf of the Colored People of the South* (leaflet, 1882), New York Public Library.

29. For an account of the maneuvers in Maryland, see the American travel diary of Catherine Impey, *GTW*, 3 July 1878, 442-43. Earlier, a black Templar in Baltimore talked about organizing a Malinite Grand Lodge. See Samuel T. Fisher to [Malins], 18 Oct. 1876, in *GWT*, 27 Dec. 1876, 878: "May God bless the friends of my race; may they live long in this world and in the world to come have everlasting life."

30. GL of South Carolina, *Proceedings* (1878), 11-12.

31. J.W. Hood in *GTW*, 26 Sept. 1881, 613.

32. *The Negro Question and the I.O.G.T*, 73-75. There were differences between what Hickman quoted at the London meeting and what the Atlanta delegates had written, complained the Malinites (*GTW*, 11 April 1877, 233) after they read the text in the *Alabama Templar*, 8 Nov. 1876. The text of the Atlanta agreement also appears in the GL of South Carolina, *Proceedings* (1877), 10-12.

33. *The Negro Question and the I.O.G.T.*, 49.

34. A former RWGT, John Russell of Michigan, was appointed to the mission, but family illness kept him at home. Lorimer E. Harcus of South Australia served as secretary of the RWGL's English mission. He published a pamphlet called *A History of the Negro Question in the Right Worthy Grand Lodge* (Napanee, Ontario: *Canada Casket*, 1876). The Malinites despised Harcus because they had hired him to take minutes at Louisville before he changed sides. Harcus later moved to New South Wales.

35. RWGL, *Proceedings* (1877), 106-13 (with quotations from Hickman to Oronhyatekha, 13 Nov. 1876, and Oronhyatekha to Hickman, 6 Dec. 1876). See also Hickman's report and correspondence, RWGL, *Proceedings* (1877), 158-76.

36. RWGL, *Proceedings* (1877), 95.

37. GL of South Carolina, *Proceedings* (1877), 32.

38. The son of a farmer, Pyper was principal of the Belfast Mercantile Academy and then chief agent for the Irish Temperance League: *Irish Good Templar*, May 1873, 78; Jan. 1875, 32; March, April 1892, 31-32, 42-43 (by R. Semple). See also Elizabeth Malcolm, *"Ireland Sober, Ireland Free": Drink*

and Temperance in Nineteenth-Century Ireland (Syracuse, N.Y.: Syracuse Univ. Press, 1986), 278-79; and John Pyper et al., *Letters on Good Templarism and the Bible Wine Question* (Belfast: A. Ledlie, 1872).

39. (London) *Temperance Star*, 16 March 1876, 3. The newspaper added cryptically that Pyper's marriage was unpopular.

40. *I.O.G.T., The Grand Lodge of Ireland, and the Negro Question: Being the Journal of Proceedings of a Special Session, Held in the Clarence Place Hall, Belfast . . . 1877*, 2d ed. (Belfast: Grand Lodge Offices, 1877); (Malinite) GL of Ireland, *Proceedings* (1878), 6.

41. Scomp, *King Alcohol in the Realm of King Cotton*, 641.

42. William Hoyle, *The Negro Question and the I.O.G.T.: An Historical and Critical Disquisition* (London: E. Curtice; Manchester: A. Ireland, 1876); Malins, *Unlawful Exclusion;* Hoyle, *Negro Exclusion.*

43. R.H. Barker to editor, 11 Feb. 1884, in *British Loyal Templar*, March 1884, 3; Hoyle, *Negro Exclusion*, 48; Lees in (Hickmanite) *Journal of Proceedings of the Special Session of the Grand Lodge of England,* 10; (Hickmanite) GL of England, *Proceedings* (1877), 6.

44. (Hickmanite) GL of England, *Proceedings* (1877), 22-23; Garrett to Stephen Todd, 27 Sept. 1877, in *GTW,* 14 Nov. 1877, 760.

45. The article on Lees by David M. Fahey in *Biographical Dictionary of Modern British Radicals*, ed. Joseph O. Baylen and Norbert J. Gossman (Hemel Hempstead, Herefordshire, Eng.: Harvester Wheatsheaf, 1988), vol. 3, summarizes the biography by his grandson: [George] Frederic [William] Lees, *Dr. Frederic Lees, F.S.A. Edin., a Biography* (London: H.J. Osborn, 1904), to which F.R. Lees's son, Frederic Arnold Lees, contributed an introductory appreciation and bibliography. For Lees as an abolitionist, see C. Peter Ripley, *Black Abolitionist Papers*, vol. 1, *The British Isles, 1830-1865* (Chapel Hill: Univ. of North Carolina Press, 1985), 295. For Lees and another reform movement, see "A Chat with Dr. F.R. Lees, a Veteran Vegetarian," *Vegetarian,* Jan. 1896.

46. Malins, *Unlawful Exclusion*, 32.

47. Earlier, though, Malins had not demanded a commitment from Hoyle: "If you, my dear brother, will keep as you *have done hitherto*—quite neutral—it is all I want" (Malins to Hoyle, 9 Oct. 1876, in Hoyle, *Negro Exclusion*, 47).

48. Samuel Wright, "Biographical Sketch No. 4—Thomas Watson," *British Loyal Templar*, April 1884.

49. *GTW*, 15 May 1875, 328-29. The executive committee asked the *Alliance News* to keep "clear of the controversy" (London) United Kingdom Alliance minutes books, 15 May 1878, United Kingdom Temperance Alliance library. This was difficult when Alliance leaders like William Hoyle and F.R. Lees served as Hickmanite officers. J.H. Raper, formerly the Alliance's parliamentary agent, also supported the RWGL: *GTW,* 5 July 1876, 456-57; 22 May 1878, 345.

50. "Outline History of the Grand Lodge of England," *GTW,* 20 Oct. 1890, 500; Clement Malins to [editor], 6 July 1877, in (London) *Templar,* 11 July 1877, 22; (London) *Templar*, 27 June 1877, 308; *GTW*, 4 March 1877, 165.

51. (Hickmanite) Worthy Grand Lodge of Great Britain, *Proceedings* (1879), 15-16. The Grand Lodge of Yorkshire, so touchy over its prerogatives, had only 556 members: *GTW,* 25 July 1881, 469.

52. (London) *Templar*, 15 Nov. 1876, 546; *Journal of Proceedings of the Special Session of the Grand Lodge of England,* 10.

53. Quoted in F.R. Lees, "The Biography of William Hoyle," chap. 10, "The Rupture in the I.O.G.T.," app. to William Hoyle, *Wealth and Social Progress in Relation to Thrift, Temperance, and Trade* (Manchester: United Kingdom Alliance, 1887), 281; *GTW*, 9 Jan. 1882, 23, 25-26; GL of England, *Proceedings* (1882), 102-11.

54. *IGT*, July-Sept. 1881, 11.

55. Garrison to Brown, [c. 30 May 1878], in (Boston) *Daily Evening Traveller*, quoted in *GTW*, 19 June 1878, 406.

56. Phillips to Newman, n.d., in *GTW*, 23 Oct. 1878, 697; *GTW*, 19 June 1878, 406.

57. *GTW*, 3 July 1878, 442-43. W.M. Artrell, a Templar of multiracial descent, drew attention to the many blond-haired blacks in Alabama: Artrell to [Forsyth?], 30 Aug. 1886, in (Boston) *Temperance Brotherhood*, Oct. 1886, 5.

58. *Templar*, 12 Oct. 1876. After a British frigate liberated him from a slave ship on the high seas, Joseph May was educated in England, where he joined the Wesleyans and later the Templars. See his obituary, *GTW*, 13 April 1891, 172.

59. *GTW*, 11 April 1887, 232.

60. Malcolm R. Birnie to [?], n.d., in *GTW*, 16 Feb. 1880, 100.

61. See, for instance, S.H. Kearsey, "History of the Order in India," in (Poona) *Indian Good Templar* (1919), chap. 4, "The Split, 1878-9."

62. GL of New South Wales, *Proceedings* (1880), 33.

63. GL of Minnesota, *Proceedings* (1876), 8, 22-26, supp. [3]-16.

64. GL of Pennsylvania, *Proceedings* (1876), 43.

65. *GTW*, 11 July 1877, 453.

66. GL of Rhode Island, *Proceedings* (1876?), quoted in *Which Are We to Believe?*

67. GL of Maine, *Proceedings* (1877), 15.

68. *Halifax Chronicle*, quoted in *GWT*, 27 Dec. 1876, 878; Brown's speech in *GTW*, 1 Nov. 1876, 724-25 (see Appendix); Brown to Malins, 22 Sept. 1876, in *GTW*, 11 Oct. 1876, 675; GL of Massachusetts, *Proceedings* (1877), 194-207.

69. GL of Connecticut, *Proceedings* (1876), 24-25.

70. Talbott died in the home of Emma Barrett Molloy and her husband. Molloy told a friend that "nothing in all my work had so unnerved me" as the sad end of "our Jerry": Molloy to Hiatt, n.d., in James M. Hiatt, *The Ribbon Workers* (Chicago: Goodspeed, 1878), 301-2. I owe this reference to Martha M. Pickrell of Elkhart, Ind.

71. GL of England, *Proceedings* (1877), 71-72.

72. *To the Members of the R.W.G.L. Remarks of* [William B.] *Reed, of Minnesota, 30 May 1878* (broadside). As a result of Reed's complaints about censorship, the RWGL allowed him to publish his *Remarks,* but for Templars only.

73. *GTW*, 3 July 1878, 442.

74. Martha McClellan Brown to Catherine Impey, 31 Nov. 1879, in *GTW*, 31 Dec. 1879, 869.

75. Letter by Martha McClellan Brown, dated 4 May 1882, published as "Southern Temperance" in an unnamed newspaper, clipping in scrapbook,

Martha McClellan Brown Papers, box 11, folder 3. The southern reception of Stewart and Brown contrasted with that of Harriet N.K. Goff, who "received scarcely a lecturing engagement" when she toured the South during the winter of 1876-77. Although Goff had not yet joined the RWGL of the World, white southerners assumed that she traveled as its agent: *IGT*, Oct.-Dec. 1879, 194. By the 1880s the white southern Templars no longer feared the RWGL of the World.

76. Finch grew up in New York state and during his years as RWGT made Evanston, Ill. his home, but since he first became prominent in Nebraska he was regarded as a westerner.

77. (Philadelphia) *Christian Recorder,* 29 June 1882, 1. Goff's letter also appeared in the (New York) *Globe,* 17 June 1882, reprinted in *British Loyal Templar,* [c. Oct. 1882]. Since 1870 Goff had traveled as a temperance lecturer, but she may be best known for her antiracist novel set in South Carolina, *Other Fools and Their Doings; or, Life among the Freedmen* (1880; rpt. Freeport, N.Y.: Black Heritage Library Collection, Books for Libraries Press, 1972).

78. Malins to H.N.K. Goff, 17 July 1882, in (Philadelphia) *Christian Recorder,* 3 Aug. 1882, 2.

5. The Black Templars

1. For recent research on black temperance reformers, see Donald Yacovone, "The Transformation of the Black Temperance Movement, 1827-54," *Journal of the Early Republic* 8 (Fall 1988); Denise Herd, "The Paradox of Temperance: Blacks and the Alcohol Question in Nineteenth-Century America," in *Drinking: Behavior and Belief in Modern History*, ed. Susanna Barrows and Robin Room (Berkeley: Univ. of California Press, 1991); Patricia A. Schechter, "Temperance Work in the Nineteenth Century," in *Black Women in America*, ed. Darlene Clark Hine (Brooklyn: Carlson, 1993). See also Kenneth Christmon, "Historical Overview of Alcohol in the African American Community," *Journal of Black Studies* 25 (Jan. 1995).

2. Donald W. Beaton, "Washingtonianism in Maine: A Phase of the Temperance Movement in the 1840s" (M.A. thesis, Univ. of Maine, 1951), 66; *Columbia Missouri Statesman,* 12 July 1867, cited in Laura Louise Martin, "The Temperance Movement in Missouri, 1846-1869" (M.A. thesis, Washington Univ., 1935); 97-98; Edward H. Moseley in (Boston) *Temperance Brotherhood,* July 1886, 2.

3. The elder was Florida's Thomas Darley. W.M. Artrell to editor, 6 Sept. 1878, in (Philadelphia) *Christian Recorder,* 10 Oct. 1878.

4. Catherine Impey, "Diary of the Voyage," 24 May 1878, in *GTW,* 19 June 1878, 409. The A.M.E. Church had over 200,000 members in 1876. See John Hope Franklin and Alfred A. Moss Jr., *From Slavery to Freedom: A History of Negro Americans,* 6th ed. (New York: Knopf, 1988), 211.

5. (Philadelphia) *Christian Recorder,* 20 June 1878, 2. Soon Fraternity lodge was renamed in honor of Octavius V. Catto, a school principal murdered in 1871: *GTW,* 22 Jan. 1879, 60.

6. *GTW*, 3 Aug. 1881, 499; GL of England, *Proceedings* (1882), 75. See also *IGT*, Oct.-Dec. 1881, 10-14; (Philadelphia) *Christian Recorder*, 27 Oct. 1881, 1; 3 Nov. 1881, 1; *GTW*, 19 Sept. 1881, 593-94.

7. For William H. Hillery, see Sue Bailey Thurman, *Pioneers of Negro Origin in California* (San Francisco: Acme, 1952), 31; (Petersburg, Va.) *Star of Zion*, 10 Oct. 1884.

8. Forsyth, *Collected Writings*, 93 n 16. Eliza Ann Gardner died in 1922, past the age of ninety. See Sarah L. Fleming in Hallie Q. Brown, *Homespun Heroines and Other Women of Distinction* (1926; New York: Oxford Univ. Press, 1988), 117-18; (Salisbury, N.C.) *Star of Zion*, 28 April 1887; Eliza A. Gardner, "Historical Sketch of A.M.E. Zion Church, Boston, Mass., U.S.A.," and "Glimpses in Zion's Hall of Fame—1838-1918," in Jacob W. Powell, *Bird's Eye View of the General Conference of the African Methodist Episcopal Zion Church* (Boston: Lavelle Press, 1918), 21-41.

9. Artrell to editor, 6 Sept. 1878, in (Philadelphia) *Christian Recorder*, 10 Oct. 1878.

10. William P. Hastings to Catherine Impey, 11 Jan. 1883, in *GTW*, 5 March 1888, 146; Artrell to editor, 6 Sept. 1878, in (Philadelphia) *Christian Recorder*, 10 Oct. 1878.

11. Betty M. Kuyck, "The African Derivation of Black Fraternal Orders in the United States," *Comparative Studies in Society and History* 25 (1983).

12. H.S. Smothers to Malins, 6 Jan. 1885, in *GTW*, 23 March 1885, 187. Smothers, an A.M.E. pastor, was president of the Colored Farmers' Association in Texas.

13. Hastings to Impey, 21 Feb. 1883, in *GTW*, 14 May 1883, 315; Caleb A. Stevens, "Diary of a Good Templar's Visit to the Old Slave States" (abridged), in *GTW*, 31 Aug. 1885, 562. The leader of the black Templars in Washington, a man named Turner, organized a benefit insurance scheme for his three lodges.

14. Lee in *GTW*, 29 Oct. 1879, 713; Dancy to Right Worthy Grand Secretary, n.d., in *IGT*, Jan.-March 1883, 10; John C. Shelton, "Circular Letter from the Grand Worthy Secretary of the Dual Grand Lodge Independent Order of Good Templars of Georgia," c. 1 Feb. 1877, Univ. of Georgia libraries.

15. S.C. Gooseley to editor, 21 July 1878, in (Philadelphia) *Christian Recorder*, 8 Aug. 1878, 3; Stevens, "Diary of a Good Templar's Visit to the Old Slave States," in *GTW*, 14 Sept. 1885, 603; Brown to Impey, 10 March 1879, in *GTW*, 16 April 1879, 251; Brown to Impey, 16 Feb. 1880, in *GTW*, 8 March 1880, 147; J.T. White to Impey, 30 Sept. 1879, in *GTW*, 29 Oct. 1879, 713 (about regalia); W.S. Wilson to [Impey], 27 Feb. 1883, in *GTW*, 23 April 1883, 268; Charles P. Wellman to [Impey], 4 January 1881, in *GTW*, 31 January 1881, 67; Henry Hammond to Impey, 7 June 1880, in *GTW*, 19 July 1880, 455.

16. *GTW*, 23 March 1885, 187.

17. For the case of a Brother Anderson in East Camden, N.J., see Stevens, "Diary of a Good Templar's Visit to the Old Slave States," *GTW*, 31 August 1885, 562; William Wells Brown to James Clark, 10 March 1879, in *GTW*, 16 April 1879, 251.

18. Henry Parsons to [?], 9 Dec. 1876, in *GTW*, 3 Jan. 1877, 5; F.N. Boney, Richard L. Hume, and Rafia Zafar, *God Made Man, Man Made the*

Slave: The Autobiography of George Teamoh (Macon, Ga.: Mercer University Press, 1990), 157, 158; and for Lee, Foner, *Freedom's Lawmakers*, 130; (Jacksonville) *Times-Union*, 26 March 1970 [fiftieth anniversary of Lee's death], clipping provided by Black Archives, Florida A&M University; Hank Drane, "Joseph E. Lee Was a Power in Republican Politics," *Florida Times-Union*, 22 Feb. 1982, clipping provided by C.H. Harris, Florida Collection, Jacksonville Public Libraries.

19. Parsons to [?], 9 Dec. 1876, in *GTW,* 3 Jan. 1877, 5; Artrell to editor, 5 May 1879, in *GTW,* 25 June 1879, 421; Parsons in (Philadelphia) *Christian Recorder*, [15 April 1877]; *GTW,* 13 Dec. 1876, 835; A.G. Marment to [Impey], n.d., in *GTW,* 30 Aug. 1880, 556; *GTW,* 18 Feb. 1889, 75; *IGT,* April 1889, 250; Wellman to Impey, Jan. 1882, in *GTW,* 21 Aug. 1882, 538.

20. RWGL, *Proceedings* (1877), 185; J.H. Whiteley in RWGL, *Official Circular*, quoted in *IGT*, April-June 1884, 12.

21. T.W. Casey to Williams, 10 April 1877, in RWGL, *Proceedings* (1877), 38-39; John Prichard at charter suit hearings, in *GTW,* 27 June 1881, 410; *British Loyal Templar,* May 1884, 6; GL of New York, *Official Organ,* Jan. 1884, 23.

22. William A. Pledger, in (New York) *Witness,* 5 July 1877; Harriet N.K. Goff, in (New York) *Witness,* 11 June 1877, quoted in *GTW,* 25 July 1877, 502. According to Goff, a Georgia representative admitted during the heat of an RWGL debate that the Grand Lodge had threatened the Grand Fountain of True Reformers with the revocation of their charter, "to break them up entirely," unless they agreed to reorganize as a Dual Grand Lodge. For a bland account, see *Minutes of the Dual Grand Lodge of the Independent Order of Good Templars Held in Atlanta, Ga., Dec. 5 and 6, 1876* (Atlanta: Dual Grand Lodge, 1876).

23. Pledger to editor, n.d., in (Philadelphia) *Christian Recorder,* 3 Oct. 1878, 3; RWGL of the World, *Proceedings* (1879), 19. Bess Beatty contributed an entry for Pledger to *Dictionary of Georgia Biography,* ed. Kenneth Coleman and Charles Stephen Gurr, 2 vols. (Athens: Univ. of Georgia Press, 1983).

24. W.W. Turnbull in RWGL of the World, *Proceedings* (1887), 266.

25. GL of West Virginia, *Proceedings* (1878), 19-20; GL of South Carolina, *Proceedings* (1878), 11-12; (Boston) *Temperance Brotherhood,* July 1886, 5.

26. J.C. Owens to editor, n.d., in (Philadelphia) *Christian Recorder,* 17 Oct. 1878, 3, complained that blacks had "lost hundreds of dollars fooling with other worthless societies, that are doing more to curse our people than to educate them."

27. (Sacramento) *Weekly Rescue,* 7 June 1877, 8; *GTW,* 25 June 1881, 469; A. Barry of Kentucky, in RWGL, *Official Quarterly*, quoted in *IGT*, April-June 1884, 12.

28. Forsyth, *Collected Writings,* 90, 364.

29. Grand Master of True Reformers to [Malins?], 17 Dec. 1876, in Malins, *Unlawful Exclusion,* 61. Two years later Malins cherished similar hopes for Alabama, where William Washington Browne headed the True Reformers: "As a consequence of my sending our address to the Editor of the *Christian Recorder,* W.W. Brown[e], G.W. Master of the True Reformers of the State [of Alabama], has written our Bro. W.W. Brown, as to the terms

under which his 62 fountains of 6,000 members can join us" (*GTW,* 6 June 1878, 422). Browne never became a Templar, however.

30. James A. Ball to Brown, 6 Oct. 1877, in *GTW,* 14 Nov. 1877, 764.

31. *National Temperance Advocate,* March 1873, 43. During Parsons's brief foray into Virginia, the Englishman conferred with Coombs.

32. *GTW,* 10 Dec. 1877, 840; (Richmond) *Virginian Star,* 17 Nov. 1877, cited in *GTW,* 2 Jan. 1878, 12.

33. Summaries of Brown's letters in *GTW,* 19 Dec. 1877, 840; Brown to the editor, 14 March 1881, in *National Temperance Advocate,* April 1881, 62-63.

34. Brown to editor, (Philadelphia) *Christian Recorder,* 21 Oct. 1880, [2?].

35. *GTW,* 26 June 1878, 427. During most of the great schism the Mission Committee was called the Negro Mission Committee.

36. Impey to readers of *GTW,* 4 April 1879; and Brown to [Impey?], 6 March 1878, both in *GTW,* 16 April 1879, 251.

37. Brown to Impey, 10 March 1879, in *GTW,* 16 April 1879, 251. A few white visitors, apparently British sailors, attended the black lodges in Norfolk: W.H. Brooke to Brown, Dec. 1879, in *GTW,* 16 Feb. 1880, 19.

38. Brown to Impey, 3 and 15 April 1879, and Brown to [Impey?], 21 April 1879, in *GTW,* 7 May 1879, 311; Catherine Impey, "Our Work in the Southern States of the American Union," *IGT,* July-Sept. 1879, 167-69.

39. Stearns to W.S. Williams, 5 March 1880, in RWGL, *Proceedings* (1880), 58-60; W.H.L. Coombs to S.D. Hastings, n.d., in *National Temperance Advocate,* March 1881, 36; Brown to editor, 14 March 1881, in *National Temperance Advocate,* April 1881, 62-63.

40. Brown to Impey, 15 April 1879, in *GTW,* 7 May 1879, 311; Brown to Impey, 23 May 1879, in *GTW,* 18 June 1879, 405; Brown to [Impey?], 21 April 1879, in *GTW,* 7 May 1879, 309; Brown to Impey, 23 April 1879 and Brown to [Impey?], n.d. and 10 May 1879, in *GTW,* 4 June 1879, 378.

41. Impey, "Our Work in the Southern States," 167-69; Brown to Impey, 23 April 1879, in *GTW,* 4 June 1879, 378; Brown to Impey, 9 Aug. 1879, in *GTW,* 17 Sept. 1879, 613; Brown to [Impey?], 16 Dec. 1879, in *GTW,* 16 Feb. 1880, 19; circular signed by Rev. B. Frierson and other Dual GL officers, dated 17 Dec. 1879, in *GTW,* 16 Feb. 1880, 103; RWGL of the World, *Proceedings* (1880), 21; Hastings to Impey, 9 Sept. 1882, in *GTW,* 2 Oct. 1882, 631.

42. Brown to Impey, 16 Feb. 1880, in *GTW,* 5 March 1880, 4.

43. [George Phillips?] to Impey, n.d., in *GTW,* 16 Aug. 1880; Forsyth, *Collected Writings,* 323-24; (Boston) *Temperance Brotherhood,* Dec. 1883, quoted in *IGT,* April-June 1884, 11; (Boston) *Temperance Brotherhood,* reprinted in *GTW,* 5 Nov. 1883, 706.

44. *GTW,* 8 Nov. 1876, 739; James Yeames, circular, "The Mission to the South," in *GTW,* 15 Nov. 1876, 765. Fea spoke at a meeting of three Poughkeepsie, N.Y., lodges (two white and one black) commemorating the thirtieth anniversary of the IOGT, 23 June 1882: (Philadelphia) *Christian Recorder,* 6 July 1882, 2; reprinted from *Poughkeepsie Daily News,* in (Philadelphia) *Christian Recorder,* 3 Aug. 1882, 1. For Fea's engagement for May-October 1882 and $770.28 in pay and expenses, see RWGL of the World, *Proceedings* (1883), Report of the Mission Committee, 37, 41.

45. Hastings to Impey, 9 Nov. 1882, in *GTW,* 1 Jan. 1883, 3.

46. Letters from Impey and Hastings in *GTW,* 2 Oct. 1882, 631.

47. The phrase, "spontaneous growth," the Mission Committee's, is quoted in GL of Florida, *Proceedings* (1884), 23.

48. (Halifax, Nova Scotia) *Morning Chronicle*, 25 July 1877.

49. Goosley to GWCT of Nova Scotia, Sept. 1876, in GL of Nova Scotia, *Proceedings* (1877), 13. Stephen Goosley's brother William was Grand Worthy Chaplain of Nova Scotia.

50. RWGL of the World, *Proceedings* (1887), 310. Blacks assumed that the white members of the RWGL of the World were racists too. Rev. H.J. Boyd reported that at the 1883 session of the RWGL of the World at Halifax, Nova Scotia, a black sister asked him to change places with her when the members rose to shake hands, so that a white sister would not have to suffer the indignity of shaking hands with a black woman: *GTW,* 28 April 1884, 258.

51. Artrell to Thrower, 15 Oct. 1876, in *GTW,* 27 Dec. 1876, 876; Artrell in GL of Florida, *Proceedings* (1882), quoted in *GTW,* 25 Sept. 1882, 612; Artrell in GL of Florida, *Proceedings* (1879), quoted in *GTW,* 29 Oct. 1879, 713.

52. Artrell to editor, 16 Sept. 1878, in (Philadelphia) *Christian Recorder,* 10 Oct. 1878. I owe this reference to Canter Brown Jr.

53. *GTW,* 5 Sept. 1887, 571.

54. Letter from S.C. Goosley and other details in GL of Nova Scotia, *Proceedings* (1877), 12-13.

55. *The Good Templars and the Coloured People of America* (N.p.: RWGL of the World, 1885), 6, South Caroliniana Library, University of South Carolina.

56. Thomas Hardy to *Birmingham Daily Post,* 9 Sept. 1879, and Malins to *Birmingham Daily Post,* 11 Sept. 1879, reprinted in *GTW,* 17 Sept. 1879, 618.

57. *New York Freeman,* 31 July 1886, 2. I owe this reference to Canter Brown Jr.

58. There is a sketch in David M. Fahey, "The Good Templars and the African American Temperance Movement: W.M. Artrell of Florida," *Social History of Alcohol Review,* no. 28/29 (Fall 1993-Spring 1993). See also *GTW,* 12 March 1877, 161-62 (includes Artrell's letter to Malins, 8 July 1876), 12 Oct. 1885, 667; (Boston) *Temperance Brotherhood,* Nov. 1885, 6. Artrell was one of the few Episcopalians among the black Templars.

59. (Boston) *Temperance Brotherhood,* Nov. 1885, 6; Frank N. Wicker (collector of customs at Key West since 1873) to George A. Lamphere, 19 March 1880, in National Archives, General Records of the Department of the Treasury, Records Relating to Customs Service Appointments, Key West, RG 56, entry 246, box 068. I owe this reference to Canter Brown Jr.

60. *GTW,* 29 Sept. 1890, 457; successive Key West city directories, Maloney's (1900), 62; R.L. Polk & Co.'s (1906-7), 83. I owe these references to Tom Hambright, Local and State History Department, Monroe County May Hill Russell Library, Key West. Sharon Wells, *Forgotten Legacy: Blacks in Nineteenth Century Key West* (Key West, Fla.: Historic Key West Preservation Board, 1982), 36, describes Artrell as deputy collector of internal revenue but does not give any dates. *Webb's Jacksonville and Consolidated*

Directory (1886), 69, identifies Artrell as principal, Stanton Grammar School; the 1891 and 1893 volumes (70, 72) list Artrell as principal of Jacksonville Graded School No. 50. For a brief tribute by a former student, see *Along This Way: The Autobiography of James Weldon Johnson* (New York: Viking Press, 1963), 61-62, 122.

61. Hickman to Artrell, 4 Nov. 1874, in Malins, *Unlawful Exclusion,* 61; *GTW,* 27 Dec. 1876, 878.

62. *GTW,* 29 Sept. 1890, 457; RWGL, *Proceedings* (1889), 368.

63. Jerrell H. Shofner, "Florida," in *The Black Press in the South, 1865-1979,* ed. H. Lewis Suggs (Westport, Conn.: Greenwood Press, 1983), 101.

64. Rodolphus Bowden to [Forsyth?], in *GTW,* 27 Oct 1884, 676; Forsyth, *Collected Writings,* 91; (Boston) *Temperance Brotherhood,* June 1886, 2; RWGL of the World, *Proceedings* (1887), 15.

65. Parsons to [?], 9 Dec. 1876, in *GTW,* 3 Jan. 1877, 103.

66. Wooden to Forsyth, 12 June 1884, in *GTW,* 27 Oct. 1884, 676; (Boston) *Temperance Brotherhood,* April 1886, 2; (Boston) *Temperance Brotherhood,* Nov. 1886, 4. Later, Wooden became secretary of her Grand Lodge: *IGT,* Sept. 1890, 531-32.

67. Denise Herd, "Prohibition, Race, and Class Politics in the Post-Reconstruction South," *Journal of Drug Issues* 13 (1983).

68. (Boston) *Temperance Brotherhood,* March 1886, 6.

69. Artrell to editor, 5 May 1879, in *GTW,* 25 June 1879, 421; George Phillips to Impey, 17 Sept. 1879, in *GTW,* 8 Oct. 1879, 665; *IGT,* Jan.-March 1884, 11.

70. In these years the Malinites were stronger in the British islands off the southeastern United States. For instance, in 1877 the GWCT of Bermuda said that in the previous two years, 2,000 people (of a total population of 12,000) had joined the Order: *GTW,* 4 July 1877, 438.

71. RWGL of the World, *Proceedings* (1887), 308-13.

72. RWGL, *Proceedings* (1886), 41.

6. The Reunion

1. *GTW,* 4 April 1887, 210.

2. Forsyth, *Collected Writings,* 130. See Finch to Malins, 30 Dec. 1884, and a friendlier second letter, 18 March 1885, in W.W. Turnbull, "John B. Finch—The Good Templar," *IGT,* May 1889, 258-59.

3. *GTW,* 4 April 1887, 210.

4. *GTW,* 14 June 1876, 388.

5. Malins to Keens, March 1886, in *GTW,* 5 Sept. 1887, 571.

6. Finch to Malins, 6 April 1886, in Frances E. Finch and Frank J. Sibley, *John B. Finch: His Life and Work* (New York: Funk & Wagnalls, 1888), 220-24; RWGL of the World, *Proceedings* (1887), 304; *GTW,* 20 June 1887, 385.

7. *Good Templar,* Aug. 1886 (published by the RWGL), quoted in RWGL of the World, *Proceedings* (1887), 266.

8. Finch to Malins, 6 April, 3 June, 6 July, 11 Aug. 1886, in Finch and Sibley, *John B. Finch,* 215-18; RWGL, *Proceedings* (1887), 17-19. Lane was

an English-born Methodist minister who came to Canada after living in India and New Zealand, another instance of the geographical mobility of many Templars. See *IGT*, May 1896, 161.

9. *Australian Temperance World*, Dec 1926, 4; Jan. 1927, 5-6.

10. Forsyth, *Collected Writings*, 131-33.

11. For the text of the Boston resolutions, see RWGL, *Proceedings* (1887), 19-26. See also Forsyth, *Collected Writings*, 130-34.

12. GL of Tasmania, *Proceedings* (1878), 3. In contrast, the two Grand Lodges in New Zealand at first maintained "the utmost cordiality," although N.Z. North supported the RWGL of the World and N.Z. South the old RWGL: GL of New Zealand South, *Proceedings* (1877), 10. This cordiality soon broke down: As the change in Grand Lodge name suggests, each organization soon claimed jurisdiction over all of New Zealand. GL of New Zealand, *Proceedings* (1878), 7-8.

13. With almost 38,000 adult members at the end of the great schism, the Grand Lodge of Scotland had enrolled a much larger percentage of the general population than had the Grand Lodge of England.

14. RWGL of the World, *Proceedings* (1887), 266-67 (different printings have different pagination). Turnbull's article in the (Glasgow) *Good Templar*, June 1886, supposedly convinced Finch that at least outside England the RWGL of the World was ready for reunion.

15. (Boston) *Temperance Brotherhood*, July 1886, 5; *GTW*, 4 April 1887, 210.

16. Finch to Turnbull, 15 Feb. 1887, in Turnbull, "John B. Finch—The Good Templar," 260. In the 1880s J.N. Stearns's National Temperance Society hired black teetalers to organize African Americans on behalf of temperance.

17. The National Division of the Sons of Temperance included members in both the United States and Canada, but the Sons of Temperance in Britain were entirely independent.

18. Finch and Sibley, *John B. Finch*, 215.

19. At the turn of the century Malins dramatized Templar internationalism by undertaking an IOGT around-the-world voyage.

20. *GTW*, 20 June 1887, 388. He had fallen ill after the Grand Lodge of England session: *GTW*, 2 May 1887, 281.

21. *GTW*, 25 April 1887, 263. A combination of the burden of old debts, the expense of the charter suit, the shrinkage of the Grand Lodge membership, and the stingy indifference of most members prevented Malins's Grand Lodge from spending much of its own money in support of the Mission Committee.

22. RWGL of the World, *Proceedings* (1887), 262. A year later he unconvincingly denied that he had called the years of schism a failure—"The disruption was a fair success, so far as negro enrolment was concerned, but in its secondary purpose of promoting the fraternization of both races in the South it failed"—or that the decline in membership in many jurisdictions could be blamed on the great schism: "The idea that the Order lost heavily in any country through the disruption is erroneous." See Malins to editor, 20 Feb. 1888, in (New York) *Official Organ*, May 1888, 427.

23. RWGL of the World, *Proceedings* (1887), 313.

24. Charles Smith, an English Hickmanite, complained that this passage had not been published in the report of Malins's speech to the Grand Lodge: *GTW*, 2 May 1887, 281.

25. In 1887 the Grand Lodge of Virginia received as guests two black Templars, Prof. D.N. Vassar of the Richmond Institute, who headed a black Grand Lodge in the state, and Rev. A. Truatt: *IGT*, Jan. 1888, 63. For Georgia, see *GTW*, 4 April 1887, 211. Dennis H. Bourbon represented the Dual Grand Lodge of Virginia at the RWGL session at Richmond: RWGL, *Proceedings* (1886), 7.

26. RWGL of the World, *Proceedings* (1887), 266-67.

27. Forsyth, *Collected Writings*, 135.

28. *GTW*, 20 June 1887, 385.

29. RWGL of the World, *Proceedings* (1887), 303-4; *GTW*, 4 July 1887, 421. The account in the old RWGL's *Proceedings* is silent on much of the controversy.

30. *GTW*, 20 June 1887, 385; Forsyth, *Collected Writings*, 139 n. 41.

31. *GTW*, 2 May 1887, 281; Turnbull's circular, *GTW*, 9 May 1887, 298.

32. RWGL, *Proceedings* (1887), 27.

33. RWGL, *Proceedings* (1887), 142-43; *GTW*, 4 July 1887, 620; GL of England, *Proceedings* (1888), 52, 54.

34. *GTW*, 4 July 1887, 420-21.

35. *IGT*, Jan. 1888, 59-60; Finch to Turnbull, 26 April 1887, in *IGT*, April 1889, 284, 286; GL of Virginia, *Proceedings* (1888), 15.

36. *IO.G.T., Proposed Declaration of the British Lodges Regarding the Boston Conference Proposals for Union; GTW*, 21 March 1887, 184-85.

37. *Irish Templar*, April 1887, 38-39.

38. *GTW*, 19 March 1888, 138-39; 23 April 1888, 206; 22 April 1889, 181-83; 8 July 1889, 315. At the time of the reunion there were three Grand Lodges in Scotland, two in Ireland, and seven in England. Although the Irish and Scottish ones united in 1887, union in England was "as yet only partial" (*GTW*, 5 Nov. 1888, 540); it was not complete until 1896. Malins also was irritated when reprinted Hickmanite histories of the IOGT presented a version of the past that he believed a reunited IOGT could not support: *GTW*, 22 April 1889, 184.

39. *Standard Encyclopedia of the Drink Problem*; E. Adair Impey, *About the Impeys* (Worcester, Eng.: Ebenezer Baylis, 1963), 63-64; *Anti-Caste*, March 1895, [1]; *GTW*, 10 Jan. 1887, 19. On Impey as a vegetarian beginning in 1879, see *GTW*, 2 May 1887, 277.

40. RWGL of the World, *Proceedings* (1887), 292-98.

41. "Debate on Reunion in R.W.G. Lodge of the World, Saratoga, New York, May 25, 1887," in *GTW*, 27 June 1887, 402-4; "The Reunion Debate in the R.W.G.L. of the World: Another Account," in *GTW*, 4 July 1887, 418-21; Catherine Impey, "Supplementary Report," in GL of England, *Proceedings* (1888), 61-62; *New York Freeman*, 30 April 1887, 2. Tanner had edited the (Philadelphia) *Christian Recorder* when it was the RWGL of the World's official organ.

42. RWGL of the World, *Proceedings* (1887), 243. Ordinarily only Templars with an RWGL degree, both delegates and ex-delegates, could participate in a RWGL session. Tanner forfeited his RWGL degree when his

membership lapsed. The RWGL of the World compromised by holding the debates in a subordinate lodge degree format.

43. Forsyth, *Collected Writings*, 363-65.

44. *GTW*, 16 April 1888, 193. Apparently the quoted words had appeared in a letter from Tanner to Catherine Impey.

45. Artrell to editor, 11 June 1887, in *New York Freeman*, 2 July 1887, 1.

46. Impey in *GTW*, 16 April 1888, 193.

47. Forsyth, *Collected Writings*, 365-70.

48. *GTW,* 16 April 1888, 193; Artrell to editor, nd., in *New York Freeman*, 11 May 1887, 1.

49. *IGT*, Aug 1888, 490-91.

50. For Kempster's explanation of his change in position, see *GTW*, 25 April 1887, 262.

51. Malins, "The Reunion Controversy: A Fraternal Reply to Friendly Critics," *GTW*, 11 April 1887, 233.

52. George Dodds to [editor?], 4 April 1887, in *GTW*, 11 April 1887, 234.

53. *GTW*, 4 July 1887, 418-19.

54. *GTW*, 4 July 1887, 419.

55. *GTW*, 25 April 1887, 259.

56. *GTW*, 2 May 1887, 273.

57. Malins to Kempster, 2 May 1887, and Kempster to Malins, 4 May 1887, in *GTW*, 9 May 1887, 298.

58. *GTW*, 4 July 1887, 419-20.

59. Impey, "Supplementary Report," 62.

60. *GTW*, 25 July 1887, 468.

61. Malins to editor, *Birmingham Daily Times,* reprinted in *GTW* 5 Nov. 1888, 540.

62. *GTW*, 20 June 1887, 389.

63. *GTW*, 16 April 1888, 191-92.

64. In formulating her position, Impey consulted leading African Americans such as Frederick Douglass.

65. *GTW*, 16 April 1888, 197.

66. *GTW*, 13 May 1889, 219.

67. *GTW*, 27 May 1889, 247; see also Impey in *GTW*, 27 May 1889, 241-42.

68. *Anti-Caste* was published March 1888-July 1895, with an interruption in 1893-94. See the footnote at Catherine Impey to Booker T. Washington, 5 March 1890, in *The Booker T. Washington Papers*, ed. Louis R. Harlan (Urbana: Univ. of Ilinois Press, 1974), 3:34. Frederick Douglass was a lifetime subscriber to *Anti-Caste*. The best-known Templar subscriber was John Kempster. See *Anti-Caste*, March 1895, 8.

69. W. Evans Darry, editor of *Bond of Brotherhood,* to H.C. Smith, editor of *Cleveland Gazette,* 4 Dec. 1894, in *Cleveland Gazette,* 5 January 1895, 1.

70. GTW, 21 April 1890, 190.

71. *GTW*, 30 Nov. 1891, 570-71. After its first eighty-four weeks of publication in Birmingham at the Grand Lodge offices, Kempster had moved the periodical to London, where he edited and published it at his own expense.

72. For Turnbull, see James Yeames, "W.W. Turnbull, R.W.G.T.," *Irish Templar*, Dec. 1887, 133. Turnbull made his livelihood out of paid administrative work for temperance organizations. After retiring as RWGT, he became secretary of the West of England Temperance League.

73. *GTW*, 13 Aug. 1888, 401. Oronhyatekha's Foresters had broken away from the English organization in 1874, two years before the Templars' great schism occurred. For the role of Malins the elder and of his son Joseph in Oronhyatekha's organization, see Oronhyatekha, *History of the Independent Order of Foresters* (Toronto: Hunter, Rose, 1894), 767-70.

74. *GTW*, 11 June 1894, 279; 16 July 1894, 347; *IGT*, June 1901, 14. In 1908 A.R. Williams, a black Baptist minister from Florida, was appointed to a minor international Templar office: *GTW*, 29 Feb. 1909, 91.

75. *GTW*, 20 Feb. 1909, 91.

76. *IGT*, Aug. 1910, 158.

77. H.L. Spindler to William J. Jessup, 18 July 1876, in (London) *Templar*, 1 Nov. 1876, 525; GL of South Africa, *Proceedings* (1875), 13; Theo. Schreiner in *IGT*, Dec. 1896, 397-99. The South African Templars received a copy of the ritual for the American organization of True Reformers. Some Templars in the Cape Colony threatened to join a schismatic Templar faction, the United Temperance Order, if the Grand Lodge of South Africa did not eliminate its color bar and make other concessions: (London) *Temperance Star*, 27 May 1875, 3. See also Wallace Mills, "The Roots of African Nationalism in the Cape Colony: Temperance, 1866-1898," *International Journal of African Historical Studies* 13 (1980): 205-9.

78. GL of South Africa, *Proceedings* (1877), xx-xxiii; RWGL of the World, *Proceedings* (1885), 12.

79. *GTW*, 23 Jan. 1909, 43; *IGT*, Feb. 1909, 30.

80. Theo. L. Schreiner, circular, 15 May 1909; Theo. L. Schreiner and others, *Reply of the Executive of the Right Worthy True Temple of the Independent Order of True Templars to the Circular of the Executive of the International Supreme Lodge I.O.G.T.* (N.p.: IOTT, 1911), George F. Cotterill papers, University of Washington. For the other side of the dispute, see "Native Lodges in South Africa," *IGT*, Feb.-March 1910. Schreiner belonged to an accomplished family. His brother W.P. Schreiner was prominent in politics (for a time prime minister of the Cape Colony); his sister Olive Schreiner wrote *The Story of an African Farm.*

81. *IGT*, Oct 1969, 64; *Globe*, Dec. 1985, 11.

82. Lars Lars-Ledet, *Good Templary through [a] Hundred Years* (Aarhus, Denmark: International Supreme Lodge, 1951), 16. For those like me unable to read Scandinavian languages, there are bits and pieces about the Swedish Templars in Madeleine Hurd, "Liberals, Socialists, and Sobriety: The Rhetoric of Citizenship in Turn-of-the-Century Sweden," *International Labor and Working-Class History*, no. 45 (Spring 1994). See also Sven Lundkvist, "The Popular Movements in Swedish Society, 1850-1920," *Scandinavian Journal of History* 5 (1980).

83. A few African American members remained, such as Samuel Osborne, janitor at Colby College, who represented the Grand Lodge of Maine at the international session at Stockholm in 1902. See *IGT*, April 1904, 320; Frederick Morgan Padelford, *Samuel Osborne: Janitor* (Boston: LeRoy Phillips, 1913).

84. See History Committee, Northwest Grand Lodge, *1857-1957: In Commemoration of the One Hundred Anniversary of the Northwest Grand Lodge, IO.G.T. (Minnesota Sen.) (Minnesota Jr.), June 27, 28, 29 and 30th, 1957*, ed. Carl E. Carlson ([N.p.] Northwest Grand Lodge, [1957]).

Appendix

1. *GTW*, 1 Nov. 1876, 724-25; see also Brown to Malins, 22 Sept. 1876, in *GTW*, 11 Oct. 1876, 675. The English newspaper anglicized Brown's spelling. I thank Curtis W. Ellison, School of Interdisciplinary Studies, Miami University, for his advice about interpreting Brown's speech.

2. Malins, *Unlawful Exclusion*, 25-26.

3. At the annual session of the Grand Lodge in Boston the Massachusetts Templars criticized the RWGL but remained loyal to it. William Wells Brown was elected the RWGL of the World's Counsellor, the second highest office, at Glasgow, Scotland, in 1877. At the end of that year he instituted a small, breakaway Grand Lodge of Massachusetts.

Bibliography

This is my second book about the Templars; the earlier one focuses on an overlapping period, from the early 1870s until shortly after the First World War. My edition of *The Collected Writings of Jessie Forsyth, 1847-1937: The Good Templars and Temperance Reform on Three Continents* (Lewiston, N.Y.: Edwin Mellen Press, 1988) includes a lengthy introduction, "One Woman's World," and Forsyth's memoirs. An English-born resident of Massachusetts, she supported Malins in the great schism and edited *Temperance Brotherhood.* Eventually she emigrated to Western Australia.

Besides the two books and my forthcoming article "Blacks, Good Templars, and Universal Membership" (in *The Changing Face of Drink: Substance, Imagery, Behaviour,* edited by Jack S. Blocker Jr. and Cheryl Krasnick Warsh, to be published by the University of Toronto Press for *Histoire sociale),* the only academic work that focuses on the Templars in English-speaking countries is Joanne Judd Brownsword, "Good Templars in Wisconsin, 1854-1880" (M.A. thesis, University of Wisconsin, 1960).

Members of the IOGT often have written its history. The pioneering work by Isaac Newton Peirce, *The History of the Independent Order of Good Templars* (Philadelphia: Daughaday & Becker, 1869), made a careful examination of documents for the origins of the Order and preserved what would otherwise have been lost material from the 1850s and 1860s. Unfortunately, this unindexed, chronologically organized book is awkward to use. In 1873 Silvanus Phillips Thompson wrote a pamphlet, *A History of the Independent Order of Good Templars* (London: Curtice, 1873). He also was responsible for an "English Edition" of Peirce's book, described as "Edited, Revised, and Rewritten" by Thompson (Birmingham: Grand Lodge of England, 1873). Thomas F. Parker, *History of the Independent Order of Good Templars from the Origin of the Order to the Session of the Right Worthy Grand Lodge of 1887* (rev. ed., 1882; New York: Phillips & Hunt, 1887), is important for the excerpts Parker borrowed from Templar periodicals that have not survived. Less detailed historical accounts appear in William W. Turnbull, *The Good Templars,* ed. James Yeames (N.p.: IOGT, 1901); and Lars Larsen-Ledet, *Good Templary through [a] Hundred Years* (Aarhus, Denmark: International Supreme Lodge, 1951).

There are several histories for Britain. For England there is a pamphlet by Joseph Malins, *A Brief History of Good Templary in England,* 3d ed. (Birmingham: Grand Lodge Offices; London: R.J. James, [1922]); and E.H. Welcome, *The World Our Field: A History of the Good Templar Order* (Birmingham: Templar Press, [1954]). The Grand Lodge of Scotland published Tom Honeyman, ed., *Good Templary in Scotland: Its Work and Workers, 1869-1894* (Glasgow, 1894), updated by Honeyman as *Good Templary in Scotland: Diamond Jubilee, 1869-1929* (Glasgow, 1929); and Robert McKechnie, *Good Templary in Scotland: Its Work and Workers, 1929-1979* (Glasgow, 1980).

For biography, the indispensable titles are Joseph Malins (second son), *The Life of Joseph Malins: Patriarch Templar, Citizen, and Temperance Reformer* (Birmingham: Templar Press, 1932); Frances E. Finch and Frank J. Sibley, *John B. Finch: His Life and Work* (New York: Funk & Wagnalls, 1888); George W.E. Hill, *Some Good Templars I Have Known: Brief Biographies of Our Most Eminent Workers* (Grand Valley, Mich.: Valley City, 1893).

There are many books in Scandinavian languages and a few in German, among them Arne Svensson, *De visade vägen: IOGT-NTO 100 år— en krönika* (Stockholm: Sober, 1979); Hilding Johansson, *Den svenska godtemplarrörelsen och samhallet* (Stockholm: Oscar Eklunds, 1947), based on extensive research; Per Fuglam, *Kampen om Alkoholen i Norge, 1816-1904* (Oslo: Universitetsforlaget, 1972); *Der Guttempler-Order in Deutschland* (Hamburg: Neiland-Verlagsgellschaft, 1979-81), the first volume (for 1889-1945) by Theo Gläss and Wilhelm Biel and the second (for 1945-80) by Theo Gläss and Martin Klewitz. A retired railroad worker, Alfred Koss, compiled a kind of scrapbook of useful information, *Zur Geschichte der Internationalen Organisation der Guttempler* (Oslo: International Organization of Good Templars, 1985). Alas! I know no Scandinavian languages and have forgotten most of my German.

The major primary sources are the *Proceedings* of Grand Lodge and international sessions and the various publications of the Templar press. The *Proceedings* for the Right Worthy Grand Lodge and the continuation for the International Supreme Lodge and for the rival Right Worthy Grand Lodge of the World have survived, as have those of the Grand Lodge of England. Virtually complete for the nineteenth century are the *Proceedings* of the Grand Lodges of Wisconsin, New York, and, to a lesser extent, Illinois. For North America there is nothing comparable to the Templar press in Britain: for England, complete runs of the *Templar* and the *Good Templars' Watchword* and of brief-lived serials such as the *English Good Templar,* as well as most of the *British Loyal Templar,* and, for Scotland, nearly all the *Good Templar. Temperance Brotherhood* has survived for the years after its merger with the RWGL of the World's *International Good Templar* 1885-87. The RWGL's magazine, also called the *International Good Templar,* began publication in 1888. General temperance serials such as the *National Temperance Advocate* provide bits and pieces of Templar news.

Fortunately, lost or hard-to-locate sources are quoted at length in other places, such as *The Negro Question and the I.O.G.T.: Report of Conference Held in London, October 19, 20, and 21, 1876* (London: J. Kempster; London: E. Curtice, 1876); William Hoyle, *The Negro Question and the I.O.G.T.: An Historical and Critical Disquisition* (London: E. Curtice; Manchester: A. Ireland, 1876); Joseph Malins, *The Unlawful Exclusion of the African Race: A Refutation of Mr. W. Hoyle's "Review of the Negro Question and the I.O.G.T."* (Birmingham: Grand Lodge Office; London: J. Kempster; Glasgow: Grand Lodge Office; Belfast: Grand Lodge Office; Wrexham: Grand Lodge Office,

1877); William Hoyle, *The Negro Exclusion: A Reply to Mr. Joseph Malins Showing How Mr. Malins and the Leading Secessionists Aided the Exclusion and Hindered the Admission of the Negroes into the Order of Good Templars* (London: E. Curtice; Manchester: A. Ireland, 1877).

A good starting point for research is the printed *Dictionary Catalog* of the New York Public Library. Much of the Templar material listed there has been microfilmed recently. There are hundreds of Good Templar entries in electronic catalogs such as WorldCat, but much material at cooperating libraries is not listed, and private libraries such as London's United Kingdom Temperance Alliance do not participate.

Some Templar sources turn up at places where researchers might not look for them. For instance, a manuscript magazine produced in 1879 by Carter lodge, Thorn Grove, Tennessee, was published by Grace Leab and Charles Z. Roettger as "A Good Templar 'Journal,'" *East Tennessee Historical Society's Publications* 31 (1959). The minutes and quarterly reports of Capital lodge, Frankfort, Kentucky, 3 May 1871-29 January 1874, can be found at the State Historical Society of North Dakota in Bismarck. Presumably a Kentuckian who moved to North Dakota took the records there. *Temperance Brotherhood,* published at Boston, Massachusetts, survives for 1885-87 courtesy of its editor's own copy at the State Library Service of Western Australia, Perth.

Index